TWAYNE'S WORLD LEADERS SERIES

David Hume

TWLS 48

David Hume

David Hume
The Newtonian Philosopher

By NICHOLAS CAPALDI

Queens College of the City University of New York

TWAYNE PUBLISHERS
A DIVISION OF G.K. HALL & CO., BOSTON

Library of Congress Cataloging in Publication Data

Capaldi, Nicholas.
David Hume.

(Twayne's world leaders series)
Bibliography: pp. 227-35.
Includes index.
1. Hume, David, 1711-1776.
B1497.C3 192 74-20931
ISBN 0-8057-3685-9

MANUFACTURED IN THE UNITED STATES OF AMERICA

For
Antony Flew

Contents

About the Author

An internationally known Hume scholar and a founder of the Hume Society, Nicholas Capaldi is professor of Philosophy at Queens College, where he has taught since 1967. He has also held teaching positions at State University of New York at Potsdam, Hunter College of C.U.N.Y. and Columbia University. He received the B.A. degree from the University of Pennsylvania (1960) and the Ph.D. from Columbia University (1965). In the summer of 1967 he was the recipient of a National Endowment for the Humanities.

Dr. Capaldi is General Editor of the Pegasus (Bobbs-Merrill) *Traditions in Philosophy* series. His articles have appeared in *Journal of Philosophy, Ethics, Philosophical Journal, Journal of Critical Analysis* and *Philosophy Forum.*

Dr. Capaldi's published works include: *The Enlightenment, The Proper Study of Mankind* (G. P. Putnam's Sons, 1967); *Human Knowledge* (Bobbs-Merrill, 1969); *Clear and Present Danger, The Free Speech Controversy* (Bobbs-Merrill, 1969); and *The Art of Deception* (Prometheus Press, 1971). He co-edited with Boruch Brody *Science: Men, Methods, Goals* (W. A. Benjamin, 1968).

Preface

In 1952, T. E. Jessop made us realize that the "assumption that the exegesis of Hume was in effect finished needs to be challenged. The exegesis has become rigidified in the text-books of the history of philosophy." Since the early 1960s Hume's writings have undergone a renaissance wherein philosophers have come increasingly to recognize the hidden subtlety of Hume's thought. Antony Flew was able to devote a whole book just to the study of the first *Enquiry*. Páll Ardál reminded us of the treasure buried in Hume's discussion of the passions. Robert Anderson showed what rewards awaited the patient scholar who shunned the usual paths. In fact, during the 1960s there emerged a new generation of Hume scholars, both here and abroad. In retrospect, that period saw the production of a remarkable number of high-quality dissertations and articles on Hume, and it can be asserted that we are still in a period of revitalization in Hume scholarship. I have tried to convey some sense of this new scholarship.

One of the things which has always impressed me is the complexity of the *Treatise*. Behind the façade of his easygoing and teasing style, Hume's first work has an ingenious structure, a structure which has convinced me that the *Treatise* is on a par with Immanuel Kant's *Critique of Pure Reason*. I am consistently surprised with what additional things I discover by way of issues posed, problems resolved, and the interlocking nature of Hume's arguments whenever I delve into the *Treatise*. The more I work on Hume, the more I have become convinced that the exegesis of Hume is not a job for one person but for generations of serious students of the history of philosophy. To that end, what I have offered is a kind of topological survey of the *Treatise*, an analysis of those features which seem to remain constant even under the transformation of the continuous development of Hume's ideas. This task has proved more complex than I originally imagined, so that even my discussion of the later works is intended primarily to throw more light on the *Treatise* rather than to do justice to these works themselves. Here and there I have plumbed some issues such as causation, the self, and the moral "ought," by way of indicating both what lies under the surface and how that material might be profitably explored and developed by reference to the surface structure.

There are of course innumerable ways of getting into Hume and his *Treatise*, but one path which I have found particularly useful is the influence of Newton upon Hume. Other writers have duly noted this influence, as far back as Ernst Cassirer and most recently and notably James Noxon. But I have tried to indicate in a detailed way the specific use to which Hume put Newtonian ideas about the nature of the universe and the proper way of studying the universe. I have been encouraged to pursue this direction by the recognition in recent years that the history of science is of more than just academic interest. If I may lay claim to any novelty, it will be in showing how many of Hume's ideas and their implications can be explained with reference to Newton.

Finally, I should say something about the originality and importance of Hume himself. Like all modern figures Hume owes a great deal to his predecessors so that his genius will be more readily seen in the way in which he combines thoughts, rejects earlier ones, and develops the implications of others. Thus, many others had criticized the Aristotelian position on causation, but Hume was the first to do so from the Newtonian point of view. To a contemporary reader this is very important especially when Hume develops from this new conception of physical science a remarkable view on the nature of the social sciences and a new kind of ethical theory. It will also be clear to the reader that I am rather enthusiastic about Hume, hence I have avoided making the obvious criticisms and dwelling on the more bizarre aspects of his thought. I have tried, rather, to set the stage for a more informed and sympathetic reading of a very great philosopher.

Acknowledgments

My earliest studies of Hume were done as a graduate student at Columbia University. There I was encouraged and aided by Abraham Edel, Robert Cumming, David Sidorsky, Richard Taylor, Arthur Danto, Martin Golding, and Peter Gay. Along the way I had the good fortune to profit from meetings with Vere Chappell, Lewis White Beck, Ronald Glossop, Angelo Juffras, Peter Jones, and Donald Gotterbarn. I owe special thanks to James King for a vote of confidence which came at a time when I had almost decided to abandon my studies of Hume. All Hume scholars are indebted to both James King and Donald Livingston for their creation of the Hume conference. My debts to the well-known Hume scholars are obvious.

Special thanks are due to Willard Hutcheon, Wade Robison, David F. Norton, and Robert Anderson for reading earlier versions of this manuscript and making corrections and suggestions which in many, but not all cases, I had the wisdom to follow.

I am grateful to the *Journal of Philosophy, Ethics*, and the *International Journal for Philosophy of Religion* for allowing me to use material previously published. Thomas Knight and Arthur Brown, the editors of this series, have been unusually generous with their time. Finally, in dedicating this book to Tony Flew, I am acknowledging a variety of debts, which I could not express in words.

Chronology

1710 Leibniz publishes *Essays on Theodicy*; Berkeley publishes *A Treatise concerning the Principles of Human Knowledge.*

1711 David Hume born on April 26, at Edinburgh.

1712 Birth of Jean Jacques Rousseau.

1713 Newton publishes second edition of *Mathematical Principles of Natural Philosophy* (original appeared in 1687). This edition was edited by Roger Cotes and includes the General Scholium in which Newton presents his view of God. Berkeley publishes *Three Dialogues*.

1715 Death of Malebranche.

1717 Samuel Clarke publishes the Leibniz-Clarke correspondence of 1715–16.

1721 Berkeley publishes *On Motion*.

1723 Birth of Adam Smith.

1724 Birth of Immanuel Kant.
William Wollaston publishes *The Religion of Nature Delineated.*

1725 Hutcheson publishes *Inquiry into the Original of our Ideas of Beauty and Virtue*.

1727 Death of Newton.

1728 Hutcheson publishes *Essay on the Nature and Conduct of the Passions, with Illustrations upon the Moral Sense*.

1731 Posthumous publication of Ralph Cudworth's *A Treatise concerning Eternal and Immutable Morality*.

1732 Berkeley publishes *Alciphron*.

1734 Hume writes letter to Dr. Arbuthnot on "new scene of thought."

1734–1737 Hume writes the *Treatise* at La Flèche, France.
1735 Birth of James Beattie.
1736 Butler publishes *Analogy of Religion, Natural and Revealed, to the Constitution and Course of Nature.*
1737 Hume writes letter to Lord Kames on Butler and the omission of the section on miracles. Hume writes letter to Michael Ramsay (August 26) recommending the reading of Descartes' *Meditations*, Berkeley's *Treatise concerning the Principles of Human Knowledge*, and Malebranche's *De la recherche de la vérité.*
1739 Hume publishes *A Treatise of Human Nature* (first two books appear in January).
February 13, Hume writes letter to Henry Home in which it is claimed that the *Treatise* contains a "total alteration in philosophy." September 17, Hume writes a letter to Hutcheson in which he claims that "virtue can never be the sole motive to any action."
1740 March, distribution of the *Abstract.* November, Book III of the *Treatise* is published.
1741 Hume publishes first volume of *Essays, Moral and Political.*
1742 Second volume of *Essays, Moral and Political.*
1743 January 10, 1743, Hume writes to Hutcheson and denies the special moral authority of "ought."
1744 Berkeley publishes *Siris.*
1744–1745 Hume an unsuccessful candidate for philosophy chair at the University of Edinburgh.
1745 *A Letter from a Gentleman to his Friend in Edinburgh* is published.
1746 Death of Francis Hutcheson.
1747 David Hartley publishes *Enquiry into the origin of the human appetites and affections.*
1747–1772 Diderot edits the *Encyclopédie.*
1748 Hume publishes *Three Essays Moral and Political; Philosophical Essays concerning Human Understanding; Account of Stewart.*
1749 Hartley publishes *Observations on Man.*
1751 March 10, Hume writes letter to Sir Gilbert Elliot crit-

icizing the *Treatise* and praising the *Enquiries*, and he asks Gilbert to suggest arguments for Cleanthes. Hume publishes *Enquiry Concerning the Principles of Morals* in December.

1751–1755 Hume writes the *Dialogues* (posthumously published).

1752 Death of Bishop Butler.

1752 Hume publishes *Political Discourses* in February.

1753 Death of Bishop Berkeley.

1753–1756 Hume publishes *Essays and Treatise on Several Subjects* (an edition of his work excluding the *Treatise*).

1754 Hume writes a letter to John Stewart claiming that he "never asserted that any thing might arise without a Cause." Hume publishes *The History of Great Britain* (1603–49).

1756 Hume publishes *The History of Great Britain* (1649–89).

1757 Hume publishes *Four Dissertations* (Of the Passions, Tragedy, Standard of Taste, and Natural History of Religion).

1758 Richard Price publishes *A Review of the Principal Questions and Difficulties in Morals*.

1758 Hume retitles the Philosophical Essays as the *Enquiry concerning Human Understanding.*

1759 Hume publishes *The History of England* (1485–1603).

1759 Adam Smith publishes *A Theory of Moral Sentiments*.

1762 Hume's works placed on the *Index Librorum Prohibitorum*.

1762 Rousseau publishes *Social Contract* and *Emile*.

1762 Hume publishes *The History of England* (55 B.C.–1485).

1763 Hume corresponds with Reid on the latter's *Inquiry*.

1764 Kant publishes *An Inquiry into the Distinctness of the Fundamental Principles of Natural Theology and Morals*.

1764 Thomas Reid (1710–96) publishes *An Inquiry into the Human Mind on the Principles of Common Sense*.

1766 Hume quarrels with Rousseau and publishes *A Concise and Genuine Account of the Dispute between Mr. Hume and Mr. Rousseau*.

1766–1768 Hume serves as undersecretary of State for ecclesiastical patronage in Scotland!
1770 Kant publishes *Dissertation on the Form and Principles of the Sensible and Intelligible World*. Beattie publishes *Essay on Truth*. Holbach publishes *System of Nature*.
1770 Hume adds Advertisement to the *Enquiry*.
1775 Hume writes letter on Oct. 26 claiming that the *Enquiry* is a "complete answer to Dr. Reid."
1776 Hume writes letter to Strahan on the *Dialogues*. Hume dies at Edinburgh on August 25.
1776 Adam Smith publishes *Wealth of Nations*.
1777 Posthumous edition of *Autobiography*.
1779 *Dialogues concerning Natural Religion* published posthumously.

CHAPTER 1

The Life of David Hume

DAVID Hume was born on April 26, 1711, in Edinburgh. He was to be the youngest son of the laird of Ninewells in Berwickshire, who died when David was still a baby. Thereafter, David Hume was raised by his mother who devoted herself to raising and educating her children. Hume's relationship with his mother was never wholly satisfactory for either of them, and no doubt much can be and has been made of this fact. Despite his later preeminence in some circles, his mother is credited with saying of his childhood that David was a poor creature without much intelligence.

Hume entered the University of Edinburgh sometime around 1723. This makes Hume a university student at about the age of twelve. This fact may seem rather remarkable except that in itself it is not significant, for that was the age when most students entered the last phase of their schooling during the eighteenth century. Education was then restricted to a few, even in liberal Scotland, which had the first system of free public education; and it was more intensive. Generally speaking, most men including scholars completed their major work rather early and could not expect to be productive beyond the age of fifty. Although few details are known about David's actual academic program, the typical program in the arts at that time consisted of Greek, logic, metaphysics, and Newtonian natural philosophy. It was also possible to take electives in ethics and history. We do know that in time Hume acquired a knowledge of Greek, Latin, Italian, and French.

Given the importance of Newton's influence on Hume, it is worthwhile to reconstruct how Hume acquired that information. Outside Cambridge where Newton himself was established, the University of Edinburgh was the first institution of higher learning to teach Newton's natural philosophy. Robert Stewart, originally a Cartesian, was the outstanding exponent of Newton's principles at Edinburgh during the time that Hume attended the University. Moreover, Robert Wallace, later to become Hume's close friend and defender, was then lecturing in the mathematics department and advocating the Newtonian position. It is very likely that Hume acquired his first knowledge of Newton from these men. Hume was certainly familiar with Newton's *Opticks*, at the close of which Newton said: "If natural philosophy in all its parts by pursuing the inductive method, shall at length be perfected, the bounds of moral philosophy will also be enlarged." This theme, namely, that moral philosophy can be enlarged by adopting the method of natural philosophy, became the keynote of Hume's philosophy as a whole and especially of the *Treatise of Human Nature*.

Hume claimed that he had obtained the idea for the *Treatise* and projected it at about the time he was twelve or thirteen. That would correspond exactly with the time he was at the University of Edinburgh being exposed to Newtonian philosophy. Not only does his claim that he obtained the idea for the *Treatise* at so early a date now seem plausible, but my contention that Newtonianism is the key to Hume's *Treatise* seems even more plausible. I might also add that Alexander Pope wrote the *Essay on Man* between 1732 and 1734, and in that poem Pope not only praised Newton in the now familiar fashion, but added the expression "account for moral, as for natural things." It was in 1734 that Hume wrote his letter to Dr. Arbuthnot describing something called the "new scene of thought."

But we are here getting ahead of the story. After leaving the University of Edinburgh, Hume had an unsuccessful business venture and an unsuccessful period of studying the law. Although he learned a great deal about the law, he secretly confided that he spent most of his time reading literature from classical authors such as Virgil, Cicero, and Longinus. This may have inspired his lifelong ambition to be a successful man of letters. It is difficult for the modern reader to understand what it means to be a man of letters. We live in a highly specialized world of professionals in philosophy, science, history, etc., and, while we recognize the value of newspaper reporters, we would hardly consider journalists to be men of letters. In the eighteenth century it was still possible to combine learning, wisdom, and a writing style.

In 1729 Hume suffered what we would call a nervous breakdown, a period of despondency. When he wrote to his physician about it, the physician called it the disease of the learned. In the eighteenth century men were classified according to the four temperaments, and intellectuals were assumed to be subject to the mood of melancholy. Hume was no exception. His symptoms persisted for about five years, then suddenly vanished when he left for France. Throughout his life, France was to be a tonic for Hume's spirits. He went at first to Reims and then settled at La Flèche.

The reasons for going to France were various. Certainly, this permitted Hume to live more frugally and to be independent of his family. The latter was always a sore point with him. It also permitted him some anonymity, a factor not to be overlooked in a sensitive young man who yearns for a reputation but is still insecure. La Flèche is in the beautiful province of Anjou. It was also the site of the Jesuit college where Descartes had originally studied. Hume obviously knew about this.

One might well ask what sort of impression Hume made upon people. Three things stood out. First, he was fat, very fat. Second, he had a kind of vacant stare with which he would presumably look right through people. Third, he had a very noticeable Scotch accent. None of these characteristics would seem to be very helpful to someone who wished to impress people.

During his stay at La Flèche he wrote the *Treatise.* We have already discussed Newton's profound influence upon Hume, but what about other writers? It has of course been the custom for historians of philosophy to insist upon seeing Hume as the last member of the trilogy of Locke-Berkeley-Hume. In fact, in the collected works edited by Green and Grose, Grose said that the "*Treatise* was the work of a solitary Scotsman, who has devoted himself to the critical study of Locke and Berkeley." We now know that this was an extreme distortion. Surely someone who spent so much time in France would be influenced by French writers, especially if he knew the language. Hume was definitely influenced by the French in his writing of the *Treatise.* Hume was greatly influenced by Pierre Bayle's *Dictionary* of philosophy, a widely read compendium of the time. In fact, it is believed that Hume's knowledge of Spinoza is derived mainly from this source and that the discussion of time found in the *Treatise* is derived from the entry in Bayle on Zeno the Eleatic. There is also reason to believe that Claude Buffier influenced Hume's discussion of the similarity of errors in both the ancients and moderns, and the notion that continuous change in the world requires that identity of resemblance take precedence over identity of substance. It is also obvious that Hume read the famous *Port Royal Logic.* Port Royal was a monastery and school in Paris which served as the center of Jansenism. Jansenists were members of the Catholic Church who sought a return to the doctrines of St. Augustine, stressing predestination and austerity. Not only did Hume condemn these views but he certainly did not share the view expressed in the *Port Royal Logic* that animals were automata, which did not feel. One might argue that the *Port Royal Logic* served in many ways as a foil for Hume.

Although Hume did not cite references, and in this he was following the common practice of his time, he does on a few occasions mention other writers. For example, in his letter to Michael Ramsay (August 26, 1737), he suggests that Ramsay read Descartes and Malebranche to understand better what the *Treatise* is about. Descartes and Malebranche and the Cartesians are mentioned in both the *Treatise* and *Enquiry.* The famous example of the billiard balls is borrowed from Malebranche though Hume uses it somewhat differently.

There is no doubt that Hume read Locke, for so much of the *Treatise* is an attack on Locke specifically cited by name. Locke and Berkeley, by the way, are also cited in the above mentioned letter to Ramsay. The reference to Berkeley is to the *Treatise on the Principles of Human Knowledge* published in 1710, a year prior to Hume's birth. While the major tradition has it that Hume read only Locke and Berkeley, one modern commentator, Richard Popkin, once suggested that Hume never read Berkeley, although admittedly Hume knew about

Berkeley's philosophy. There has been much controversy on this point, but I think the letter to Ramsay indicates that Hume had read Berkeley. For me the most memorable part of the controversy over whether Hume had actually read Berkeley was the suggestion made by one scholar that both Hume and Berkeley had the same dentist in London at the same time and so they must have met in the waiting room at the very least.

The other British writer who most clearly influenced Hume was Thomas Hobbes, whose theory of the social contract Hume rejects but from whom Hume borrowed the notion that the imagination has the power to unite ideas in new combinations. In fact, the example Hume used in the *Treatise* of the golden mountain comes right out of Hobbes. Two other writers whom Hume attacks are Ralph Cudworth and Samuel Clarke, the latter the most famous metaphysician of Hume's day.

Despite the esteem in which it is now held, the *Treatise* according to Hume "fell dead-born from the press, without reaching such distinction, as even to excite a murmur among the zealots." There was one long but negative review by someone who failed to understand him. Later an anonymous *Abstract* of the first two books of the *Treatise* was published in which the *Treatise* was praised. While this was for a long time attributed to Adam Smith, the great economist and friend of Hume, we now know that Hume was the author of a review of his own work. But even the *Abstract* failed to generate interest. Throughout his life, Hume regretted the haste with which he had published the *Treatise*, not because of the content but because of the style. In this he may have been right; for, as I shall show, many readers have come away from reading the *Treatise* with the wrong impression. B. M. Laing in his book on Hume speculated that Hume may have published the *Treatise* in a great hurry in order to save face with his family by justifying his period of residence in France. I tend to believe that there is some truth in this.

Some good things did come out of it. Hume later met a man he admired and read with great profit, Francis Hutcheson, who held the chair of moral philosophy at Glasgow University. Hutcheson even offered to have his own publisher bring out Book III of the *Treatise*, "Of Morals." Moreover, Hutcheson introduced his student Adam Smith to the *Treatise* and eventually to Hume himself. Hume and Smith became the closest of friends for life. It is difficult to imagine a more impressive combination than David Hume and Adam Smith, since both men were largely responsible for founding the social sciences in the eighteenth century, Hume by the *Treatise* and Smith by the *Wealth of Nations.*

In 1741 and 1742 Hume finally achieved a notable public success as a man of letters with the publication of the *Essays, Moral and Political.* Hume was encouraged by this success to seek in 1744–45 an academic position, namely, the chair of philosophy at the University of Edinburgh. The series of events surrounding this incident are truly remarkable. Hume was encouraged by one of the two factions at the university including high officials to seek the position, and there was some expectation that he might actually get it. There was a long factional struggle involving political considerations both local and national, but the final decision went against Hume largely for religious reasons. During the controversy, the chair was actually offered to Francis Hutcheson but he turned it down. However, among other things he wrote a letter saying that David Hume was not fit for such an office since among his duties he would have to lecture every Monday on the truth of the Christian religion. Hume was perturbed by this information, but he could not deny the specific reasons given.

Hume was so anxious at one point to obtain the position that he wrote *A Letter from a Gentleman to his Friend in Edinburgh* in response to accusations both written and verbal that he was an atheist and a skeptic. This letter in essay form is really an excellent and valuable commentary by Hume himself on a number of issues raised in the *Treatise.* It goes a long way to dispelling popular misconception about his alleged atheism and skepticism, but it nowhere proves that Hume could claim to be a consistent Christian. He was not the right kind of believer.

Eventually the chair was given to William Cleghorn (1718–1754), who was one of those brilliant young men, seven years younger than Hume, who had not written a thing up until then and who died nine years later without having published a single work. The academic world has not changed very much in this respect from Hume's time. Academia's loss was the world's gain.

After this event, Hume served as a tutor to the young Marquis of Annandale, where he came into conflict with the rather sinister individual Captain Vincent. It was here that Hume learned about human character, the difference between men of good will and evil men. Following this unhappy experience, General St. Clair invited Hume to act as his secretary on a military expedition originally planned for Québec but finally diverted to Brittany. Later, in 1748, Hume attended St. Clair as his aide in the embassies of Turin and Vienna. In the meantime, Hume published the *Philosophical Essays concerning Human Understanding*, later known as the first *Enquiry*.

In 1749, Hume returned to live at Ninewells in Scotland, but he left again in 1751 with his sister to settle in Edinburgh after the marriage of his brother. In 1751, Hume published his second *Enquiry*, the *Enquiry Concerning the Principles of Morals*, a work he considered to be his best. In fact, in 1751 he wrote to his friend Gilbert Elliot that he now considered the *Treatise* a mistake and wanted the *Enquiries* to be taken as his philosophic position. The relationship in content and structure between the *Treatise* and the *Enquiries* is discussed in a separate chapter.

In 1752 he obtained the position of Keeper of the Advocates Library and Clerk to the faculty of Edinburgh. At last Hume was to have access directly to a great library, and he took this opportunity to begin writing his monumental history of Great Britain. This work was to achieve for him in his lifetime his greatest fame. However, it was over the opposition of the president and dean of the faculty that he obtained his position, and gradually pressure mounted until Hume was forced to clear his choice of books with the curators. He resigned the position in 1757.

It was also during this period that Hume wrote to his friend Balfour a letter in which he said, "I have endeavored to refute the skeptic with all the force of which I am master; and my refutation must be allowed sincere because drawn from the capital principles of my system." This is an important comment because it reinforces my claim that Hume's basic principles have been consistently misunderstood because of their novelty. It is against the pretensions of rationalism that Hume plays off the skeptic, but it is against both that he presents his own interpretation of the principles of human reason and behavior. It was also during this period that Hume began writing his *Dialogues*. In the meantime Hume continued to publish on a variety of topics.

In 1763 Hume made one of his rewarding trips to France, this time as acting secretary to the British Embassy. Much to his sincere surprise Hume found that the French considered him to be a genius. They lionized him, again mostly for his work in history. Here Hume found the success and encouragement he desperately needed. He was most fortunate in meeting the *Philosophes*, his Enlightenment counterparts in France. Specifically he met Helvetius, Buffon, Diderot, Holbach, and his favorite, d'Alembert.

At the house on the Rue Royale of the wealthy Baron d'Holbach, an avowed atheist and materialist, the philosophes met for their symposia. At one of these meetings and dinner parties, Hume made the remark so typical of those who really knew and understood him that he personally had never met a real atheist. The reply of his host, Holbach, was, "sir, you are looking at twelve of them." In time, and though he respected them greatly, Hume came to feel that the philosophes were too narrow in their general views, too limited by the physiocrat views on economics, which Adam Smith was later to attack, and too optimistic about the future.

Not only was Hume a favorite of the intellectuals, but he was also a favorite of the ladies at the court. There is one story, whose authenticity I cannot vouch for, in which allegedly on his knees, he proposed to one young lady while her lover hid behind a curtain. Not only was he rebuffed, but it is said that Hume could not afterward get up from the floor without help, mostly because of his weight.

More certainty surrounds Hume's relationship with the Comtesse de Bouffers. When they met (Hume was fifty-two), she was thirty-eight and married, but her husband was always away. She was also the mistress of another member of the nobility. Eventually, they became lovers, confidants, and great friends. Hume never married and had no children that we know of. The beauty and stimulation and recognition he received in France made Hume seriously consider living there on a permanent basis, and he did maintain a residence there for some time.

Another acquaintance made by Hume while in Paris was Jean Jacques Rousseau. While Rousseau is generally lumped together with the other philosophes, especially because of his having written some of the articles in Diderot's *Encyclopedia*, his basic philosophy and temperament were antithetical to that of the other philosophes, especially Voltaire. In addition, Rousseau had a personality which could only be described in part as being paranoid. He quarreled with everyone including those who most loved and respected him. While the other philosophes warned Hume about Rousseau, the former's kindly nature was so sympathetic to Rousseau that an invitation was extended to accompany Hume on his return to England. After some time, Rousseau accepted. Both men went to London in 1766, where Hume had another official position and some influence with the court. Despite all of Hume's best efforts, including obtaining for Rousseau a pension from King George, Rousseau's nature got the better of him. True to the worst Gallic tradition he refused to learn English. In addition, he felt that he was not getting as much recognition as he should, and when some letters critical of him began to appear in the newspapers, he even blamed Hume as one of the sources of this malicious gossip. Inevitably their friendship crumbled, and both men printed public attacks on the other, although Hume did so after much hesitation and only at the urging of d'Alembert.

In a lighter vein, I should note that Hume's official position from 1766–68 was that of undersecretary of State for ecclesiastical patronage in Scotland. Considering Hume's reputation among the Scotch clergy, this has to be the greatest irony of his career.

In view of Hume's relation to the court and the official bureaucracy, it is interesting to raise the question about his personal political views. It has been said by John Herman Randall, Jr. that Hume wrote a Tory history of the Stuarts because the Whigs were in power. It is implied that Hume's only interest was in notoriety. There are even some remarks to substantiate the claim that Hume wanted to be a conservative

Tory or be taken for one. But the weight of opinion is against this interpretation. It would be more accurate to describe Hume as neither Whig nor Tory, for no label or political organization could embody a position to fit the subtlety of Hume's outlook. Hume in an important sense had a Whig theory of government, for he truly believed in checks and balances; but he also had a Tory view of men, for men are sometimes evil. Moreover, Hume sincerely detested what he took to be the Whig theory of history, which was largely an apologetic for a revolution. As history, he considered it was distortion. Finally, Hume was a supporter of the American revolution, and among his friends he numbered Benjamin Franklin. The reason is important. Like Burke, Hume believed that what the American colonists were defending were the traditional rights of Englishmen. It should be remembered that long before 1776, the colonists repeatedly sought representation in the British parliament, and turned to revolution as a very unpopular last resort. There were a number of policies of the then British government which Hume rejected. As he said in a letter in 1768 to Gilbert Elliot, "O! how I long to see America and the East Indies revolted, totally and finally—the revenue reduced to half—public credit fully discredited by bankruptcy—the third of London in ruins, and the rascally populace subdued!"

In 1769, Hume retired to Edinburgh, where he sold his old house to James Boswell, the famous biographer of Johnson. Hume then built a new house on what he called St. David's Street. Aside from the controversies with Reid and Beattie, these were happy days for Hume. Thomas Reid had been an earlier admirer of Hume, or so he said in correspondence. But after the publication of Reid's *Inquiry into the Human Mind on the Principles of Common Sense* (1764), it became increasingly clear that Reid not only disagreed with Hume but had taken liberties in the representation of Hume's views. This rivalry grew into a personal dislike especially as people read Reid but continued to ignore Hume's philosophic works. Another opponent who insisted upon presenting Hume's views in a poor if not distorted light was James Beattie. Hume went out of his way to insist that these men had misunderstood the *Treatise*, perhaps deliberately, and that anyone who read the *Enquiries* would see that Hume was not guilty of the charges leveled against him.

As an interesting sidelight, it should be noted that when Beattie was not misinterpreting Hume, Beattie was himself an extremely moral and sensitive man who championed in his sermons the rights of the downtrodden. He was especially concerned with the plight of blacks in the colonies. Hume, on the other hand, had made derogatory remarks both about the Irish and, it seems, about blacks. It has been argued by David Norton that despite his other admirable qualities Hume was perhaps a racist or, at least, insensitive.

Around 1773 Hume contracted a fatal disease, probably cancer of the rectum. Nevertheless, he lived to the end in a jovial mood, jesting with his friends and exchanging lewd stories. Boswell was amazed that Hume had no fear of death or concern for the afterlife. As Hume put it, since he never wondered about where he was before he was born he could not be expected to wonder about what was going to happen after he died. Moreover, Hume did not welcome the prospect of seeing again some of the people he had known in this life. Hume remained humorous to the end, and in this respect he caused the last great scandal of his life.

The suspicions of Hume's real religious beliefs began in the reading of the *Treatise*. Those suspicions were to a large extent responsible for his not having obtained the chair at Edinburgh. The real attacks on Hume came during the 1750s after the publication of the *Enquiry Concerning Human Understanding*, especially with the addition of the chapter on miracles. Hume had not been the first to attack the concept of miracles; in fact many clergymen of his time had done likewise. But of course it was the manner in which Hume had done it and the fact that he showed so clearly that miracles and Newton do not go together. The attacks grew in number, and Hume resigned himself to the situation. In fact, he planned and wrote with great secrecy the *Dialogues* which he arranged to have published after his death. It was not God and religion that Hume objected to, only orthodox clergymen and most religious practices. This is a distinction that has escaped many.

After his death, and in fact for twenty-five years at least, clergymen continued to write on, and attack the manner of

Hume's death. Not only had Hume been unrepentant but he had the gall to laugh. When John Locke had died in 1704, it was while Lady Masham, the daughter of Ralph Cudworth, read the Psalms to him. When Bishop Berkeley died it was while his wife was reading to him the passage in St. Paul's first letter to the Corinthians on Christ's victory over death. True to himself, and certainly untrue to the tradition in which so many try to cramp him, Hume refused to follow suit.

Hume was buried on Calton Hill. He left instructions in his will that his headstone should be in the form of a Roman temple with only the words "David Hume" on it.

Hume died on August 25, 1776. On November 9 of the same year, Adam Smith wrote to the publisher William Strahan:

> Thus died our most excellent, and never to be forgotten friend; concerning whose philosophical opinions men will, no doubt, judge variously, every one approving, or condemning them, according as they happen to coincide or disagree with his own; but concerning whose character and conduct there can scarce be a difference of opinion. His temper, indeed, seemed to be more happily balanced, if I may be allowed such an expression, than that perhaps of any other man I have ever known. Even in the lowest state of his fortune, his great and necessary frugality never hindered him from exercising, upon proper occasions, acts both of charity and generosity. It was a frugality founded, not upon avarice, but upon the love of independency. The extreme gentleness of his nature never weakened either the firmness of his mind, or the steadiness of his resolutions. His constant pleasantry was the genuine effusion of good-nature and good-humor, tempered with delicacy and modesty, and without even the slightest tincture of malignity, so frequently the disagreeable source of what is called wit in other men. It never was the meaning of his raillery to mortify; and therefore, far from offending, it seldom failed to please and delight, even those who were the objects of it. To his friends, who were frequently the objects of it, there was not perhaps any one of all his great and amiable qualities, which contributed more to endear his conversation. And that gaiety of temper, so agreeable in society, but which is so often accompanied with frivolous and superficial qualities, was in him certainly attended with the most severe application, the most extensive learning, the greatest depth of thought, and a capacity in every respect the most comprehensive. Upon the whole, I have always considered him, both in his lifetime and since his death, as approaching as nearly to the idea of a perfectly wise and virtuous man, as perhaps the nature of human frailty will permit.

CHAPTER 2

Hume's Conception of Philosophy

I *Introduction*

IN order to do justice to Hume's philosophy we must begin with his understanding of his task as a philosopher. We might find that we disagree with his conception of philosophy, but such a criticism is better made after we have attempted to state his case fairly. Even if we do not agree with his conception, we may still want to criticize some of his philosophical positions as being inconsistent with his basic aim, but this cannot be done unless we have first stated this aim. Finally, a clear statement of Hume's conception of philosophy will not only allow us to understand Hume but may even enable us to agree with his viewpoint once it is clearly understood.

My exposition of Hume's conception of philosophy will be given in four parts. First, I shall present in his own words Hume's common sense view of philosophy. This will immediately shock a number of readers, especially those with preconceptions about Hume's views, but it is precisely this kind of shock which must be got over quickly as a kind of scholarly therapy and because it reinforces my point that there are too many incorrect preconceptions about Hume. This is also why I shall rely so heavily on Hume's own statements. It is against the background of the very special way in which Hume is a common sense philosopher that we shall understand so much of what he is to say later. Second, it is often easier to understand a philosopher if we know what he is against, what doctrines and which previous thinkers he considers to be so wrong that he is impelled to present his own alternative view. There is a kind of rationalist philosophy which Hume considers to be absurd and which in a strange way is allied with certain socially pernicious tendencies in the religion of his day. The rationalist philosophy, as we shall see, violates common sense. At the same time, by claiming that certain religious tendencies are dangerous, Hume is indirectly asserting a positive view of his own, a perspective from which he feels entitled to make judgments of this kind.

This brings us to the third part, Hume's positive doctrines. The negative aspects of Hume, which are real enough, have been overemphasized to the point of obscuring his positive side. This positive side is to be understood in terms of the Enlightenment program of constructing a science of man. I shall argue that this notion of philosophy as a science of man is the most revolutionary and significant part of Hume. Failure to appreciate the full significance of this positive doctrine has led not only to misunderstandings about Hume's philosophical positions but to certain serious criticisms of Hume's conception of philosophy. These criticisms, which are primarily contemporary, involve the charge that Hume confuses logic with psychology and that it is this confusion that plays havoc with so much of what Hume has to say. In the fourth part, I shall consider these criticisms of Hume, defend him against the charges, and show that he has been misunderstood because his view of philosophy is so different from, and alien to, what so many philosophers of our day believe. This point, as we shall see, applies even to many of those who are sympathetic with Hume's philosophy. One does not have to agree with Hume in order to understand him, but it just may be that we shall come to agree with him after we have understood him.

II *Common Sense*

There are several senses in which Hume may be said to be a common sense philosopher. First, he believes in a public world which is also social, a world populated by physical objects as well as other people. Second, he takes for granted our common sense beliefs about the world, and in fact consistently argues that no philosopher who argues against these beliefs can be taken seriously. Third, and most important, Hume employs common sense both as a starting point for his own analysis and as a touchstone in terms of which he judges the adequacy of the formulation of a philosophical issue and the answers to it.

At the same time it should be stressed that Hume is not an uncritical adherent of common sense, because common sense is made up of a number of beliefs not all of which are on the same footing and some of which conflict with one another. Where common sense conflicts with itself, it will be necessary to resolve the dispute, but the resolution will always be carried out within the common sense framework. Hume's clearest statement of this conception of philosophy is the following: "philosophical decisions are nothing but the reflections of common life, methodized and corrected" (EHU, 162). Hume thus seeks to render common sense consistent with itself by presenting it in a coherent and sophisticated fashion.

It is worth pointing out that British philosophers have had a long history of defending common sense although not all of them view it in quite the same manner. Even the prevalence of what is vaguely called empiricism among British philosophers frequently amounts to no more than the insistence that philosophical doctrines be consistent with common sense beliefs about the world. Ironically, there is a movement called the Scottish philosophy of common sense founded by one of Hume's contemporaries, Thomas Reid, which is supposed to owe its origin to a critique of Hume's philosophy. I say ironic because Hume was the first to criticize some of the doctrines of these common sense philosophers as being alien to common sense. It took someone more sympathetic to see that Hume was unfairly attacked by the so-called common sense school, and that was Kant: "It is positively painful to see how utterly his opponents, Reid, Oswald, Beattie, and lastly Priestly, missed the point of the problem; for while they were ever taking for granted that which he doubted, and demonstrating with zeal and often impudence that which he never thought of doubting, they so misconstrued his valuable suggestion that everything remained in its old condition. . . . I should think that Hume might fairly have laid as much claim to common sense as Beattie and, in addition, to a critical reason (such as the latter did not possess). . . . "[1] Hume never challenged certain common sense beliefs, but he did challenge certain philosophical accounts or explanations of these beliefs.

In his first work, *A Treatise of Human Nature*, Hume insisted that "true philosophy approaches nearer to the sentiments of the vulgar" (T, 222–23), meaning the common man, than to the explanations of so-called philosophers. In this same work where he describes his own philosophical ambitions he tries to limit his speculations to the sphere of "common life" (T, 271). In the *Abstract*, when speaking about difficulties with the concepts of space and time, Hume expresses the wish that there were some way to "reconcile philosophy and common sense."[2] In *An Enquiry Concerning Human Understanding*, Hume claims that a philosopher will always be safe if he realizes that an "appeal to common sense, and the natural sentiments of the mind, returns into the right path, and secures himself from any dangerous illusions" (EHU, 7). Finally, in *An Enquiry Concerning the Principles of Morals*, Hume begins his analysis of morals by an appeal to "common life," to the way in which we routinely praise and blame (EPM, 173). At the same time Hume reminds us that we must still offer a consistent account of common sense beliefs, that while "the very nature of language guides us almost infallibly" we must still "discover the circumstances" which are "common to these qualities" we praise and blame (EPM, 174).

The key point to keep in mind about Hume's common sense philosophy is that whereas common sense is the starting point of his analysis and the touchstone of the correctness of his analysis, Hume is himself offering an explanation of common sense beliefs.

III *Critique of Rationalist Philosophy*

There is a view of human nature to which Hume is opposed; for lack of a better expression, I shall call it the rationalist philosophy. It is not to be confused with the term "rationalism" as in the expression "continental rationalism" which is usually taken to refer to the philosophies of Descartes, Spinoza, and Leibniz among others. There is of course a sense in which these philosophers are guilty of advocating a form of rationalism to which Hume is opposed, but Hume's opposition is much broader and includes ancient philosophers as well as moderns and is probably directed against certain currents of thought in England of the seventeenth and eighteenth centuries.

The view to which Hume is opposed may be characterized as follows. There are those who view human existence in terms of a conflict between reason and passion or between human reason and human desire. In addition, these philosophers tend to have a rather narrow view of reason wherein they think of mathematics or the structure of mathematics as the model for how all of human reason operates. It is in this sense that the term "rationalist" is an appropriate description of the view. Finally, these philosophers, thinkers, and theologians advocate that as human beings we should join the conflict of reason and passion on the side of reason. Such a view is not only alien to Hume's personal experience, but he believes that it leads to both absurd and dangerous social consequences. It is impossible to understand Hume's philosophy and the biting edge of his criticism unless we keep in mind this standing opposition to the rationalist model of human nature.

This being the case, it is necessary for Hume to do the following: first, he must show that there can be no ultimate conflict between reason and passion; second, he must argue against the rather narrow view of reason by showing the true manner in which we think; and finally, he must offer his own theory of human motivation and action. This Hume does in the *Treatise*. It is important to mention here that Hume is not advocating a form of irrationalism, and that it is not Hume but his opponents who espouse a narrow conception of human reason and understanding.

In seventeenth-century England the best examples of the rationalist philosophy were probably the Cambridge Platonists, such as Ralph Cudworth and Henry More, men who advocated that ethics rested on certain absolute and self-evident truths akin to the axioms of geometry. An eighteenth-century figure whom Hume takes to task for a similar view is William Wollaston.

Hume offers a kind of standing refutation of the rationalist model which takes the following form:

1. If reason operated solely in terms of the rationalist model (mathematical-deductive), and
2. If men were guided solely by reason, then
3. Men would not act.
4. Therefore this is equivalent to the truth of extreme skepticism.

5. But men do act.
6. Therefore extreme skepticism is false.
7. Therefore either reason does not operate solely in terms of the rationalist model
8. Or men are not guided solely by reason.

With regard to (7) Hume will argue that reason does not operate solely in terms of the rationalist model, so we have to have a broader conception of reason. And he will also argue that men are not guided solely by reason but by the passions as well.

It could be argued, and was by some, that while reason does operate solely in terms of the rationalist model, it is just not the case that men are guided by reason alone in their behavior. That is, one can maintain the truth of (1) and admit the falsity of (2). This seems to be Descartes' position when he argues that the doubts of the first meditation and the proper mode of reasoning have no effect on the practical aspects of life. Descartes, of course, does not explain why this is so.

It is at this point that we must take into consideration another of Hume's interests, namely, morality. Descartes never wrote an ethical treatise, but some later philosophers who shared his conception of reason as operating solely in terms of the rationalist model did try to argue that men could be guided and ought to be guided by this kind of reason. It is against these later moral philosophers that Hume's conclusion (7) will prove to be so devastating.

In Hume's time the rationalist model became associated with religion in a number of ways. One of the Cambridge Platonists, More, had influenced Newton, and Newton's own theological beliefs as well as his scientific discoveries were somehow associated as indications both of God's providence and the divine origin of reason. It was then but a short step to the conclusion that God wants us to join the side of reason in the conflict with passion. While Hume was prepared to dismiss the philosophers who advocated the rationalist model because their recommendations had to be and in fact were ignored, he was not so generous with his theological foes. Like Kant after him, Hume believed that organized religion in his time was socially disruptive. That is why he could say that "the errors in religion are dangerous; those in philosophy only ridiculous" (T, 272). The clearest statement of Hume's opposition to the rationalist model is the following:

> Nothing is more usual in philosophy, and even in common life, than to talk of the combat of passion and reason, to give the preference to reason, and to assert that men are only so far virtuous as they conform themselves to its dictates. Every rational creature, it is said, is obliged to regulate his actions by reason; and if any other motive or principle challenge the direction of his conduct, he ought to oppose it, until it be entirely subdued, or at least brought to a conformity with that superior principle. On this method of thinking the greatest part of moral philosophy, ancient and modern, seems to be founded; nor is there an ampler field, as well for metaphysical arguments, as popular declamations, than this supposed pre-eminence of reason above passion.

Next, Hume reminds us of how this view has some theological overtones: "The eternity, invariableness, and divine origin of the former have been displayed to the best advantage: The blindness, unconstancy and deceitfulness of the latter have been as strongly insisted upon." Hume then announces that it is his purpose "to show the fallacy of all this philosophy" (T, 413).

IV *The Enlightenment Science of Man*

Since the time of the ancient Greeks Western philosophy has been dominated by the notion that there was a cosmos or totality of existence and that this cosmos was intelligible. In short, the belief arose that there was a rationale for everything and that this rationale was within human grasp. This is one of the origins of Western philosophy. Even during the medieval period when we know that the best minds were preoccupied with religious issues, it was assumed by the most outstanding of these men that religion itself was part of the rationale.

During the sixteenth and seventeenth centuries, the scientific revolution occurred in Western thought. Even though there is still some controversy about the nature of this revolution, it is nevertheless true that a new attitude emerged. It was assumed that the science of the time was to become in large part the model of what constituted the ultimate rationale. Some thinkers came to regard that science as a key to understanding the ultimate rationale. Moreover, most of these men did not think that using that science as a key would in any way conflict with religious beliefs. On a number of issues the proponents of science may have disagreed, but they all somehow assumed physical science was crucial to our understanding of the world.

The next obvious question concerns how they understood this new scientific model. Many such as Galileo and Descartes were impressed with the mathematical nature of the new developments in science. Some later historians and philosophers of science have overemphasized this mathematical aspect, and by that I mean they fail to see that there has been a tradition of mathematical science in Western thought going all the way back to the Pythagoreans.[3] In any case, such philosophers as Descartes, Spinoza, and Leibniz among others were impressed with the fact that mathematics seemed to be the key to physical science, that mathematics had a demonstrative character, that is, one can prove things by demonstrating how conclusions follow from the first principles or axioms. This, of course, is very Platonic; and it also allowed these philosophers free play with respect to the basic principles or axioms.

Yet an important scientific development forever altered the early optimism about this model. The Copernican theory of planetary motion considerably complicated the simple faith in mathematics. Briefly, we must recall that Copernicus challenged the prevailing Ptolemaic theory in which it was assumed that the earth was both stationary and the center around which the other heavenly bodies revolved. Copernicus postulated a sun-centered universe wherein the earth revolved around the sun. Copernicus published his views in 1543, but it was not until the eighteenth and nineteenth centuries that his view was completely accepted. This fact is difficult for the contemporary reader to appreciate, for the history of science is usually told as a tale of successes without consideration of actual controversy. For several hundred years both the Copernican and the Ptolemaic theories accounted for *all* of the facts, and both of them were presented in a sophisticated mathematical format. Frequently, the controversy turned on purely metaphysical issues. The crucial importance of the fact that *two* mathematically and factually compatible theories could exist at the same time is that it underscored the necessity for a more sophisticated conception of the scientific model.

The man most responsible for this new and sophisticated model was Isaac Newton. Like his predecessors and contemporaries, Newton was both a mathematical and a theoretical genius at inventing conceptual schemes. But unlike his predecessors and his contemporary Leibniz (who invented the calculus at the same time as, but independently of, Newton), Newton was a genius at experimental design. Newton realized that in the presence of the possibility of alternative theories, all of which were mathematical and accounted for the facts as then known, some test for determining which theory or theories were really correct was needed. Hence he suggested that theories had to be tested in order to determine which were correct. But Newton was not content with merely making a methodological point, part of his genius lay in devising such experiments. Even to this day most people remain unaware of the creative thinking which is required to devise experiments. Most philosophers are not aware that among physicists there is a division of labor between theoretical physicists and those who invent experimental tests. Newton's greatness lay in the fact that he could do it all. So important was the new methodological point of experimentally testing a theory that Newton never tired of reiterating his rejection of all hypotheses which could not be tested.[4] Many of his contemporaries failed to grasp his meaning.

During the eighteenth century in Western Europe, a period known as the Enlightenment, other thinkers extended the conception of the scientific model to include the idea that even human beings could be the object of scientific knowledge. In this sense, we may say that the social sciences emerged as serious disciplines during the Enlightenment.[5]

It is now time to ask where Hume fits into all of this. To begin with, Hume subscribes to the assumption that there is a rationale for the totality of existence. There is no such thing as chance in Hume's universe, for "what the vulgar call chance is nothing but a secret and concealed cause" (T, 130). The same point is made in the first *Enquiry* where Hume affirms that "there be no such thing as *Chance* in the world," rather this is a mere negative word signifying our "ignorance of the real cause of any event" (EHU, 56). Not only is there an explanation for everything which happens, but these explanations are when properly understood capable of forming a "complete system of the sciences" (T, xx). The same rationale applies to human beings.[6]

It is also Hume's primary intention to develop a science of man, that is, to extend the scientific method to the study of human nature. That is why his book is entitled *A Treatise of Human Nature*, and why it has the subtitle, "Being an Attempt to introduce the experimental Method of Reasoning into Moral Subjects." Hume is thus an early practitioner of the social sciences, and here it is important to recall that he was a historian as well as a psychologist. In Hume's time it was customary to distinguish between natural philosophy, which was the study of nature independent of human nature, and moral philosophy, which was taken in the broad sense of meaning the study of all aspects of human nature. Hume adheres to this distinction, and when he speaks of moral philosophy he means anything which concerns the activities of men. The fact that both branches of study were referred to as philosophy, either natural or moral, is indicative of the fact that thinkers still operated within the assumption that all knowledge was somehow part of one system. To this day, some academic chairs in physics departments are still referred to as chairs of natural philosophy.

Hume was quite self-conscious about this participation in the construction of the social sciences or moral philosophy. As he says in the introduction to the *Treatise*, "it is no astonishing reflection to consider, that the application of experimental philosophy to moral subjects should come after that to natural at the distance of above a century; since we find in fact, that there was about the same interval betwixt the origins of these sciences; and that reckoning from Thales to Socrates, the space of time is nearly equal to that betwixt my Lord Bacon and some late philosophers in *England*, who have begun to put the science of man on a new footing" (T, xx-xxi). By the latter he specifically means Locke, Shaftesbury, Mandeville, Hutcheson, and Butler. Moreover, Hume takes his cue from Newton.

In listing the rules for experimental philosophy he gives in the *Treatise (ibid.)* Newton's famous four rules. In the first *Enquiry* he makes the same point with an even more direct reference to Newton:

> But may we not hope, that philosophy, if cultivated with care, . . . may carry its researches still farther, and discover, at least in some degree, the secret springs and principles, by which the human mind is actuated in its operations? Astronomers had long contented themselves with proving, from the phenomena, the true motions, order, and magnitude of the heavenly bodies: Till a philosopher, at last, arose, who seems, from the happiest reasoning, to have also determined the laws and forces, by which the revolutions of the planets are governed and directed. The like has been performed with regard to other parts of nature. And there is no reason to despair of equal success in our enquiries. (EHU, 14)

Someone will say that this is really psychology and not philosophy. The logic of that argument I shall examine in the next section, but something about this belief is worth noting here. Hume would probably argue that the belief that philosophy constitutes a different kind of knowledge from scientific knowledge is a violation of the assumption of the unity of all knowledge. If all knowledge is one, then the assertions of philosophers must be like the assertions we make elsewhere. In fact, Hume's belief that we can give an empirically scientific explanation of philosophy itself is not only a novel claim but, I contend, the most brilliant suggestion in all of modern philosophy. Hume himself is aware of the novelty: "In pretending therefore to explain the principles of human nature, we in effect propose a complete system of the sciences, built on a foundation almost entirely new, and the only one upon which they can stand with any security" (T, xx).

It could be persuasively argued that both Descartes and Locke thought they were giving a scientific explanation of philosophy itself. If this is true, then Hume is not unique or even novel. But it is worth pointing out that Descartes and even Locke had a notion of science as demonstration from first principles. It is precisely this notion of science as demonstration from self-evident principles which Newton had in large part abandoned and which Hume completely abandons. Just as it was obvious that there were any number of alternative systems with self-evident principles in science, such as the Ptolemaic and Copernican theories, so there could be any number of alternatives, and sometimes bizarre alternatives, in philosophy. Just as Newton rejected this view of science in favor of something that could be empirically confirmed by experimentation, so Hume will suggest a view of philosophy which is empirically scientific in the sense of being confirmable by experimentation and which does not appeal to self-evident first principles. In this sense, then, Hume had a different and novel view of science which, although shared by some others, he alone applies to philosophy itself.

As I indicated in the previous section on Hume's critique of the rationalist philosophy, it is part of Hume's program to show that reason does not operate solely in terms of the rationalist model. That is why he must offer a broader or at least a different view of reason. Hume does this by rejecting the rationalist notion of a demonstrative or purely deductive conception of science, and in its place he defends a more empirical and experimental notion of what constitutes science and scientific knowledge. Thus Hume's critique of the rationalist moral system necessitated an entire rethinking of the notion of what constitutes scientific reason.

Hume is as aware as anyone else of the traditional philosophical distinction between reasoning about the world, which seems to be the province of scientists, and reasoning about human reason, which seems to be the province of philosophers. "We ourselves are not only the beings, that reason, but also one of the objects, concerning which we reason" (T, xix). But to Hume it is essential that these two bodies of knowledge be the same. If someone asserts, as many philosophers have for a variety of reasons, that philosophical claims are somehow different from scientific claims, then what results is a situation in which there is no basis upon which one can resolve philosophical disputes. Hume found this state of affairs intolerable:

It is easy for one of judgment and learning, to perceive the weak foundation even of those systems, which have obtained the greatest credit, and have carried their pretensions highest to accurate and profound reasoning. Principles taken upon trust, consequences lamely deduced from them, want of coherence in the parts, and of evidence in the whole, these are everywhere to be met with in the systems of the most eminent philosophers, and seem to have drawn disgrace upon philosophy itself. . . . The most trivial question escapes not our controversy, and in the most momentous we are not able to give any certain decision. . . . Amidst all this bustle it is not reason, which carries the prize, but eloquence; and no man needs ever despair of gaining proselytes to the most extravagant hypothesis, who has art enough to represent it in any favorable colors. (T, xvii-xviii)

For Hume, the only way out is to argue that philosophy is the science of human nature. That is why we can say that the "true philosophy" shows us "the original qualities of human nature" (T, 562).

Some philosophers will demand some special sort of philosophical or metaphysical justification for what we discover as "the original qualities of human nature." Descartes would have been one, and in fact the whole rationalist orientation in philosophy would demand this. Now it is one of Hume's unique claims that this very demand is part of the pathology of human reasoning, and that what the science of man can do is to explain its pathological origins and therefore explain away the necessity for having to meet that demand! "We are no sooner acquainted with the impossibility of satisfying any desire, than the desire itself vanishes" (T, xxii).

In this very crucial respect, Hume's conception of philosophy is antithetical to that of Kant, and the contrast is nowhere more evident than in comparing the previous quotation from Hume with the opening statement of the preface to Kant's first *Critique*: "Human reason has this peculiar fate that in one species of its knowledge it is burdened by questions which, as prescribed by the very nature of reason itself, it is not able to ignore, but which, as transcending all its powers, it is also not able to answer." Hume not only thought we could ignore these questions, but he also thought we would stop taking them seriously. Hume's science of man thus becomes a devastating critical weapon by which he seeks to "undermine the foundations of an abstruse philosophy, which seems to have hitherto served only as a shelter to superstition, and a cover to absurdity and error!" (EHU, 16).

The only time one has to justify the principles upon which he operates is when they are in actual or potential conflict with other principles. But, as Hume argues, once we understand the original qualities of human nature we shall see that there is only one set of principles on which men can operate. Therefore there can be no conflict. Hence there is no need to justify the principles on which we ultimately operate. That is why animals, children, the ordinary person, and even the professional philosopher in his saner moments, have no difficulty dealing with reality in total opposition to what we might expect if we took most philosophy seriously. "When we see, that we have arrived at the utmost extent of human reason," he argues, "we sit down contented; although we be perfectly satisfied in the main of our ignorance, and perceive that we can give no reason for our most general and most refined principles, beside our experience of their reality; which is the reason of the mere vulgar, and what it required no study at first to have discovered for the most particular and most extraordinary phenomenon" (T, xxii). In short, Hume's appeal to common sense and his critique of the rationalist model converge in, and are explained by, the science of man.

Lest we think that there is any possible conflict between the dictates of common sense and the rules of scientific procedure or the findings of science, Hume asserts that the rules of scientific procedure are the same as our natural mode of thought when the latter is done self-consciously and consistently in order to avoid the carelessness of the imagination. He adds, "We must correct this propensity by a reflection on the nature of those circumstances" which mislead the imagination (T, 148). It is precisely in this sense that the science of man and a corrected and methodized common sense are identical.

Another way of making this point is to challenge outright the rationalist preconception about what constitutes explanation. Within the rationalist model, all explanation proceeds from basic and self-evident first principles. The challenger will argue that in an important sense there can be no logic which is totally independent of the facts. Put more strongly, it can be urged that what we think are our logical principles are really abstracted from the world of common experience.

The serious problem for those who insist on the factual foundation of logic is how one is to interpret the notion of abstraction. Is logic the structure already embodied in the facts, or is logic the activity of the mind applied to the facts? Starting with Ockham, there were those who argued the latter point. Logic was to be construed as the activity of the knowing mind, and since it was universally present in all men, common sense reasoning was already the depository of this structure. One could by the analysis of common sense find some, if not all, of the elements of that structure. In this sense Ockham was the founder of the continuing "common sense" tradition in British philosophy, a tradition stretching through Hume right up to contemporary linguistic analysis.

Although labels will be the undoing of us all, they are inescapable. With this warning, we may for the sake of convenience follow J. H. Randall, Jr.[7] and also designate the rationalist tradition Augustinean or Neoplatonic in origin, and it is certainly the case that Cartesianism is a revival of it as is the rest of the rationalist tradition. Hume clearly rejects the Neoplatonic, or rationalist, or Augustinean, or Cartesian tradition. The existence of alternative mathematical systems is its undoing. The second major tradition to be distinguished is Aristotelianism of the Thomistic variety, a tradition which believed in the capacity of the mind to grasp the inherent and essential structure of the world. When I speak later of Hume's opposition to Aristotelianism, I shall not mean a hostility to Aristotle himself but to a specific philosophical tradition which believes in the ability of man to grasp this permanent and essential structure. This is what Hume meant when he said, "The Schoolmen supposed also a real power in matter" (L, 28). The third tradition, the *via moderna* of Ockham, is also a version of Aristotle, but a second version which continually chides the first version for attributing to reality what is really a property of mind, or of the knower. Hume is definitely a philosopher within the Ockhamistic tradition in this epistemological sense. Thus, a true science must take into account the knower as well as the thing known. It should be noted that even the Cartesian rationalists attack the first version of Aristotelianism, but, whereas the rationalist proposes a mathematical scheme for the knowing mind, Hume will propose a different one, one which is more akin to reason as discovered in its common sense operations.

The foregoing distinctions will now enable us to understand the difference between Reid's notion of common sense and Hume's notion of common sense. Reid, who is an Aristotelian, believes in the mind's direct ability to abstract the permanent and objective structure in the things themselves. This is what Hume sometimes calls the vulgar view, the notion that we have an immediate awareness of things. As we shall see, Hume advocates the correction of the vulgar view on the grounds that it fails to take into account the activities of the mind. Thus for Hume common sense consists of the common qualities or structures of the mind. The mind, so to speak, is a kind of repository of common sense. Hume then suggests the novel view of explaining the activities of the mind by means of the Newtonian model.

V *Logic and Psychology*

One of the most persistent charges made against Hume's philosophy is that it is based upon a confusion of psychology with logic.[8] Those who make this charge have a variety of things in mind, and we shall be returning to this criticism from time to time throughout the book. Some answer to this charge and some crucial distinctions are, however, in order here, because I want both to defend Hume against the charge and to indicate that Hume's position is far more profound than both his detractors and his admirers realize. If the charge of confusing logic and psychology is supposed to mean that Hume failed to make certain distinctions, then, as I shall repeatedly show, Hume not only made those distinctions, but he was among the first, if not the first, to insist that the distinctions had to be made and to criticize others for failing to make them. Second, if the charge of confusing logic and psychology is supposed to mean that psychological facts are irrelevant to logical considerations, then it would be Hume's reply that those who make this assertion are operating with the misconceived rationalist model of explanation. Finally, it would be Hume's major contention that one cannot be a philosopher unless he subscribes to the thesis that at some level all knowledge is one and that there can be no ultimate difference in status between the various knowledge claims we make.

To make these assertions at least initially plausible, we can distinguish among the following questions:

1. Is X following the rules of reasoning?
2. What are the rules of reasoning?
3. What constitutes an adequate explanation of our rules?

Question 1, "Is X following the rules of reasoning?" is a factual question to be determined by discovering what the rules are and then seeing whether X is using them in the proper context. That is, the answer to question 1 is easy once we have the answer to question 2. The most critical function of philosophers is to point out that people are not following the rules of reasoning. Hume himself was a master of this, especially in the theological and moral sphere, and most philosophers continue to respect Hume for his excellent work in dissecting the violations of the rules of reasoning in others. Some philosophers think that this is all that Hume was good for, and they have stressed therefore the negative or skeptical aspect of his thinking. I shall claim later that those who stress Hume's skepticism still misconstrue Hume's philosophy, because they fail to recognize that Hume also dealt with the remaining questions.

Question 2, "What are the rules of reasoning?" is also one with which Hume dealt, and his answers are still widely respected. Hume's discussion of the rules is given in terms of what he calls "philosophical relations" of ideas, as well as rules of scientific procedure, rules for causal reasoning, and a discussion in the *Treatise* of probability theory. The most famous distinction among the rules of reasoning which Hume employs is that between what philosophers now call analytic and synthetic statements. Hume was not the first to make the distinction, and there is reason to believe that he discovered this distinction in Leibniz. But Hume was the first to use the distinction so devastatingly in answering question 1 above. The logical positivists in the twentieth century have lavished much praise on Hume for his explication and use of this distinction, but this adulation has had the unfortunate effect of reinforcing Hume's reputation as a negative thinker. Even more interesting, Hume's serious discussion of probability, which has been appreciated by some thinkers, like the economist Keynes, is confined almost exclusively to the *Treatise*, and the same is true for Hume's rather brilliant exposition of the rules of causal reasoning. Too many readers are familiar only with the first *Enquiry*, and thus they miss altogether much of what is important and positive in Hume's philosophical writings.

The third question, "What constitutes an adequate explanation of our rules?" is the most controversial, because it is precisely this question which Hume is supposed to have ignored. On the contrary, this third question is one which Hume did not ignore; rather, he spent a great deal of time on it. Hume's opponents were either within the Platonic tradition or within the Aristotelian tradition. Either way, they argued that the basic first principles or the basic rules, from which all others were derived, were intuitively grasped as self-evident. By this they meant that the contradictory of these basic principles was inconceivable and hence these basic principles were incontestable. In short, their conception of an adequate explanation was the model of deduction. To explain was to justify by deduction. Time after time, Hume argued that one could always conceive or imagine the opposite of the alleged basic principle; hence the alleged basic principles were contestable on the very grounds offered by those who proposed them. It is not that Hume wished to deny all of these principles but only that he wished to show they could not be explained if to explain meant to justify and to justify meant deducing them from some incontestable metaphysical framework: "As an agent, I am quite satisfied in the point; but as a philosopher, who has some share of curiosity, I will not say scepticism, I want to learn the foundation of this inference. No reading, no enquiry has yet been able to remove my difficulty, or give me satisfaction in a matter of such importance" (EHU, 38). Having recognized the question, and having dealt with it honestly on the terms proposed by those who raised the question, Hume next proceeds to show that their notion of how the question is to be answered was wrong.

Before moving to Hume's own analysis of the question, we should note the relationship of the third question to moral theory. Just as they argued that general principles of reasoning had to be derived from incontestable first principles which were self-evident, so Hume's opponents argued that there must be moral first principles which were self-evident and of course immune to revision. In fact, one could speculate that it was the desire to defend an ethical theory of this type which frequently motivated the whole theory of metaphysical first principles. If Hume can successfully challenge the need for metaphysical first principles in philosophy as a whole, then he could challenge such a need in the more narrow field of moral theory. Hume's continuing and unrelenting attack on "reason" is frequently to be viewed as an attack on the notion that we either need or can have self-certifying first principles.

What Hume does is to accuse his opponents of having the wrong model of explanation, that is, the deductive model. This misconception about what constitutes the proper method of explaining rules, he claims, is part of their misconception of what it means to give a scientific explanation. For Hume, the only proper method of explanation is an empirical description. Thus the proper type of answer to question three is an empirically descriptive enterprise. Again we can draw a parallel to Hume's moral and political theory wherein he criticizes the notion of a social contract as both an historical fiction and an inadequate notion of what constitutes the basis of social and political life. One cannot understand the foundations of society by trying to deduce them from a mythical act.

The third question can now be answered, and the answer is provided by the science of man. "If the mind be not engaged by argument to make this step, it must be induced by some other principle of equal weight and authority; and that principle will preserve its influence as long as human nature remains the same" (EHU, 41–42). The answer which he gives in the *Treatise*, the *Abstract*, and in the first *Enquiry* is custom,[9] and custom is defined as "a species of natural instincts, which no reasoning or process of the thought and understanding is able either to produce or to prevent" (EHU, 46–47).

Hume does understand the logical demands being made in the third question, but it is his contention that such demands are misconceived. Moreover, he proves that these demands are misconceived not by an appeal to psychology but by examining the kinds of arguments which have been offered in support of question three. It is only after he has shown on logical grounds that his opponents' answer to question three is misconceived that he offers his own. It is also clear at this point that the answer to question three can only be a psychological (biological-sociological) answer, that is, an answer about human nature.

It is important to notice that Hume has added the qualification that his description of the human thinking process holds only as long as "human nature remains the same." There is always the possibility that the human reasoning process might change or undergo a development as the result of new forces. Two comments can be made about this possibility. First, the possibility of its existence makes Hume's theory compatible with developmental theories of human reasoning. Even the distinction between what Hume thinks are the more stable and the less stable rules of reasoning makes this possible. Second, this possibility makes our anchor to reality a tenuous one. Since many of Hume's opponents were frightened by this prospect, it is no wonder they wanted a guaranteed system. But here it is appropriate to point out that it is not Hume but his opponents who are making irrelevant psychological demands on the facts.

A fluid notion of the reasoning process is also compatible with, and in fact necessitates, Hume's notion of philosophy as common sense methodized and corrected. In attacking the deductive model of explanation Hume again shows himself to be within the *via moderna* tradition whose strength has always been to distinguish between the activities of the mind and the activities of the world of nature, between the properties so to speak of our conceptual systems and the properties of the world. What is peculiar to Hume, what constitutes his genius, is the suggestion that after making the distinction we can still offer at another level a univocal account of both the mind and the world of nature. This he proposed to do by an extension of Newtonian science.[10]

CHAPTER 3

Hume's Newtonian Program

I *Introduction*

IT is generally accepted that Hume's philosophical program was greatly influenced by Newton.[1] Some indication of this influence has already been given in chapter 2 in the discussion of the science of man. Nevertheless, what has never been made clear is the exact manner in which that influence is translated into Hume's specific philosophical statements. An understanding of the exact nature of Newton's influence on Hume can serve as the key to understanding Hume's philosophy as a whole, and it can explain why Hume structures the *Treatise* as he does. Finally, it can serve as the basis for correcting a number of misconceptions about Hume's philosophy.

Before launching into our discussion, it is worthwhile to add a few qualifications by making some distinctions. We may distinguish (a) what Newton said officially in his published works, (b) what he said or implied unofficially in his correspondence, (c) what implications he personally drew from his theories, (d) what implications others thought could be drawn from his theories, and (e) the conflicting interpretations of Newton made by others both in his time and subsequently. With regard to (c), it should be noted that Newton subscribed to theological doctrines which he thought were compatible with his scientific work but which are not implied by, or derivable from, his physical theories. With regard to (d) it is noteworthy that both Leibniz and Berkeley recognized some of the nontheistic implications of Newton's theories, implications which others might have derived even if Newton chose not to do so. For metaphysical reasons, they, too, chose not to draw those implications or to develop them. With regard to (e), we note that a great deal of controversy surrounded various conflicting interpretations of Newton, and Hume himself participates in, and makes reference to, the controversy. We are, therefore, less concerned with Newton's intentions and more with how Hume read Newton.

Hume was the first philosopher to understand fully, to appreciate, and to articulate the philosophical implications of Newtonian physics. When I speak of philosophical implications, I mean how changes in our conception of the world or some part of it lead us to reexamine our conception of some other part of the world including man. This is what is unique about Hume's analysis of causation and why it cannot be understood by trying to derive our understanding of Hume's analysis of causation from some misbegotten notion of Hume's phenomenalism or his positivism or what not. In articulating the implications of Newton's analysis, Hume was doing something which can only be described as philosophical and which in no way depended upon a previous conception of human psychology. In fact, Hume's psychology is derivative from the Newtonian analysis. This approach also explains the difference between Hume and those previous philosophers who foreshadowed some of the elements of Hume's analysis of causation. There are some elements of the analysis which are peculiar to Hume because he derived them from Newton, and Hume alone drew all of the implications.

Historically the importance of Hume's analysis is that he carefully articulates what happens when we substitute Newtonian physics for Aristotelian physics. Again, it is not true that Hume was the first to criticize the Aristotelian framework; rather, he was the first to criticize it from a purely Newtonian point of view. The persistence, in the minds of those who fail to grasp Newton, of the Aristotelian framework and the asking of questions and the expectation of answers that only make sense within that framework accounts for the sense of novelty, if not outrageous surprise, which Hume's analysis continues to provoke. The point is not to decide on whether Newton's views are ultimately correct but rather what it would mean if his views were correct. Hume's analysis is an attempt to spell out precisely what the consequences would be.

II *Aristotle's View of Causation*

The fundamental, most persistent, and most primitive notion of causality is anthropomorphic.[2] Causes have always been construed on the model of human activity or purposive behavior. In mythopoeic thought, which is the most primitive form of thought with which we are acquainted, every description attributes humanlike purposes even to inanimate objects. That is why trees and bodies of water, for example, are thought to be inhabited by godlike creatures who must be propitiated. This anthropomorphic view has survived within the Judeo-Christian tradition of monotheism as God's will, is subsumed within the classical tradition as the efficient cause, was revived by the occasionalists, and even appears in the philosophy of John Locke.

The classical tradition as represented in ancient Greek thought advanced beyond mythopoeic thought and anthropomorphism by distinguishing between the objective and subjective, between the nonhuman and the human element within experience. It also added a number of elements to our understanding of the concept of cause and of causal explanation. These elements were finally formalized by Aristotle as the traditional four causes. It is no accident that Aristotle is the philosopher who provides the definitive analysis for both his own time and the later medieval period. Aristotle's *Physics*, and the view of the world which it embodies, dominated the Western intellectual tradition down to the time of Newton. It provided the model of what a rational account of events must be like, what sorts of questions could be asked, and what kinds of answers could be expected.

The traditional four causes are (1) material cause, (2) efficient cause, (3) final cause, and (4) formal cause. The relative importance of these four causes is determined by the Aristotelian assumptions about motion. It is assumed by Aristotle that the "natural," or ideal state, of a body is rest. Hence, what needs to be explained is how motion begins or starts and, of course, the return of something to its final resting place.

The aim of rational inquiry is to discover the causes of a phenomenon. The material cause is that of which a thing is made; the efficient cause is that by which it comes into being;

the formal cause is its essence or essential nature; and the final cause is that end for which it exists. In the case of natural objects, as opposed to the products of human art, the last three causes coincide. That is, the efficient, formal, and final causes are the same.

What does this statement mean? Let us distinguish between the products of human art like a statue or a house and a natural object like an acorn. We are concerned with natural objects. To explain an acorn we might describe the organic material of which it is made, but this is relatively unimportant for the Aristotelian. What is important are the other three causes. Where does an acorn come from? It comes from an oak tree. What happens to an acorn? It grows into an oak tree. Why does this all happen? It happens because the essence or form of an acorn is just that, namely, to become an oak tree. If we really understood or grasped the nature of the acorn we could see that it must have come from an oak tree and that it is destined itself to become an oak tree. This biological fact is generalized by Aristotle into a full-blown theory about how the universe works.

In Aristotelian language, the end or final cause of an object in nature is to realize its essence or formal cause. It also means that this formal cause or essence is embodied in another individual which possesses an identical form or essence and serves as the efficient cause of its production. It is this coincidence of formal and efficient causes which permits us to infer unerringly what a cause must *necessarily* be from mere acquaintance with the effect. The formal cause becomes in practice the basic explanatory principle since what a thing is essentially is built into it.

Locomotion, or change of place, which for Aristotle is presupposed by all kinds of change, cannot be explained by impact alone. The motion of primary bodies depends upon the fact that each has a natural place in which it finally comes to rest. Since rest is natural, every movement requires the existence of a mover. Moreover, if the world has a rationale, there cannot be an infinite series, or chain, of causes or movers. Hence, there must be a self-sufficient, self-explanatory, unmoved (uncaused in the efficient sense) mover. In short, there must be a first mover. Finally, since motion is eternal, the first mover or movers must be eternal.

While Aristotle in some places asserts the existence of more than one first mover, the medieval philosophers who adopted his physics opted for a single first mover. It did not require much imagination to conceive of God as *the* first cause or creator.[3]

It is obvious that Aristotle was not a Christian. But the body of Aristotle's philosophical and scientific work underwent a metamorphosis in the hands of later Arabic, Jewish, and Christian philosophers. The term "Aristotelian" applies to these later philosophers who were inspired by Aristotle but chose to develop his thoughts and suggestions in their own peculiar manner and in the light of other intellectual concerns. The medieval "Schoolmen," as they were called, were the most prominent of the Aristotelians, but it is by no means the case that all of them were. Hereafter, when I speak of Aristotelians I shall mean the philosophical tradition that was inspired by Aristotle but which was more properly developed during the medieval period and continued thereafter.

The cosmological proof of God's existence is the most popular, the most convincing, and the most powerful of arguments in the light of the Aristotelian framework. If rest is natural, and if motion is what has to be explained, and if a belief in rationality requires the elimination of the notion of an infinite regress, then there must be a first cause. Hence, within this framework we absolutely must posit the existence of God. The argument seems rather unconvincing to a contemporary reader, but that is because we operate within a different framework. Even without religious considerations, any intellectual familiar with Aristotle's *Physics* during the medieval period could not resist the cosmological argument. Not only Christian but Jewish philosophers (e.g., Maimonides) and Arab philosophers as well accepted this argument. Within the Aristotelian framework, one could always stun his opponents by asking what came first, the chicken or the egg.

The identity of the final, formal, and efficient causes leads to another important consequence, the grouping of the ontological, cosmological, and teleological proofs of God's existence. Not only do we need a first cause but God is by definition (ontological proof) the only being self-sufficient enough to be considered the first cause. It follows from our definition of God that he is benevolent, so that what he causes to happen (teleological proof) must ultimately be good. One has only to observe his bounty to see the proof of his existence. If we recall those philosophers who support the cosmological argument, men like Aquinas, Descartes, Spinoza, Leibniz, Locke, and Berkeley, we shall immediately recognize that these same philosophers couple the cosmological argument with either or both of the other arguments. This is not shoring up one argument with another but working out the inner logic of Aristotelian physics. It was Kant who later remarked that all three arguments depend upon the ontological argument.

In this sense it is easy to see that even after giving up some of the preconceptions of the rationalists, both Locke and Berkeley feel that it is necessary to argue for a first cause or origin. Berkeley argued that an "idea" must have some special kind of cause, a mind, "an incorporeal, active substance or spirit." Other empiricists may have read and profited some from Newton, but they did not understand him fully. That is one reason why it is a serious error to interpret Hume simply as part of the Locke-Berkeley tradition and to think that his conception of causation is a mere by-product of the theory of ideas. I might even add in this context that Newton himself did not fully comprehend the revolution he had wrought. Thus there is a sense in which Hume is more consistent than Newton.

III *Newton on Motion*

This brings us to the crucial question of what revolution was introduced by Newton's physics. Newton's first law of motion states that: "Every body continues in its state of rest or of uniform motion in a right line unless it is compelled to change that state by forces impressed upon it." The revolutionary idea is that uniform motion in a straight line is as natural a state as rest. If uniform rectilinear motion is a natural state, then it is no longer either necessary or meaningful to ask for the original cause of motion. It is not motion but a change in motion that has to be explained. Moreover, a change in motion results from the action of a force, for example, another independent body which collides with the body whose change of motion is to be explained. In short, change of motion can be explained in the Newtonian system by impact alone (or by gravity in the case of a falling object). The relation between the two colliding bodies can only be discovered empirically and can never be discovered by the mere examination of just one of the bodies. In conclusion, there is no reason to believe that anything is built-in.

If a philosopher understood this new Newtonian framework, then he would derive five philosophical consequences.

1. There is no need for a first cause or for a cause of why something exists or begins to exist.
2. Since change of motion is produced by an external body, no examination can reveal a potential to be moved. There is no built-in necessity or essence. In short, there are no formal causes.
3. Since change of motion is produced by an external body, no examination of an isolated individual object can reveal its potential to be a mover or to move another object or its power to be a mover. In short, efficient causes can only be discovered empirically and after the fact.
4. If (3) is true, then there is no ground for the assumption that an efficient cause must embody the same essence as the effect. In other words, no observation of the effect alone can justify any assertion about the nature of the cause.
5. If rest is not universally natural, then there is no end to be realized. In short, there is no final cause.

IV *Hume's Newtonianism*

Like all educated people of his day, Hume was generally familiar with Newton's work. But Hume specifically developed the points which I have mentioned above. To begin with, Hume was aware of the crucial Newtonian assumption that motion is natural. In the *Dialogues,* there is a passage in which Philo asserts as a matter of uncontested fact that matter is perpetually in motion: "Matter is and always has been in continual agitation, as far as human experience or tradition reaches. There is not probably, at present, in the whole universe, one particle of matter at absolute rest" (D, 183). More to the point, Hume refers to the first law as follows: "a body at rest or in motion continues for ever in its present state, till put from it by some new cause" (EHU, 73n).

An examination of the *Treatise*, Hume's first work, reveals that the philosophical consequences of the Newtonian framework are precisely the conclusions which Hume drew.

1. Hume specifically refutes the arguments of Hobbes, Clarke, and Locke which were intended to show that "*whatever begins to exist, must have a cause*" (T, 78). Hume argues that all of these arguments are question-begging in that they could only convince someone who does not understand that motion is as natural as rest. "The necessity of a cause to every beginning of existence is not founded on any arguments either demonstrative or intuitive" (T, 172). Later in the *Dialogues* he will challenge his opponents with the question: "Why may not motion have been propogated by impulse through all eternity"? (D, 183).

2. The existence of a formal cause which Hume specifically denies is extended into a full-scale attack on the concept of necessary connection. If there is no formal cause, then the close connection between formal-final-efficient cause is undermined. This is perhaps the most important and the most misunderstood part of Hume's analysis. He writes:

> We must distinctly and particularly conceive the connection between the cause and effect, and be able to pronounce, from a simple view of the one, that it must be followed or preceded by the other. This is the true manner of conceiving a particular power in a particular body. . . . Now nothing is more evident, than that the human mind cannot form such an idea of two objects, as to conceive any connection between them, or comprehend distinctly that power or efficacy, by which they are united. Such a connection would amount to a demonstration, and would imply the absolute impossibility for the one object not to follow, or to be conceived not to follow upon the other. (T, 161–62)

If we cannot see the connection between an object and what precedes it, then we cannot see the efficient cause by an examination of the alleged form or essence of an object. At the same time, if we cannot by the observation of what we take to be the form or essence of an object predict what will follow from it, then we cannot infer the final cause from the examination of the alleged formal cause.

If objects lack formal causes or essences, then science can only be conceived of as the discovery of facts and generalizations of a purely empirical kind. Without essences there can be no such thing as a scientific law in the traditional sense, since every relation between objects is subject to further influence from other objects, influences which can only be discovered empirically. That is why every generalization might have appended to it the rider "as far as we know." Without laws in the traditional sense of an inviolable regularity, science cannot be construed as a demonstrative enterprise wherein from the basic laws we are led to deduce particular events. This explains both Newton's aversion to a priori hypotheses and Hume's rejection of the rationalist model of science and scientific explanation. Finally, nothing can be explained by deriving it from something else; or in contemporary technical language explanation is not an entailment relationship. This we saw in chapter 2. Explanation can only be empirical description. We shall return to this important consequence in the chapter on causation.

It should now be clear that Hume's claim that we cannot see a cause is not intended as a denial of the fact that we observe causation in nature. What Hume is denying is that we can observe formal causes or essences.[4]

3. Hume attacks the Lockean argument that we have an idea of power or can by examination discover such a power either in ourselves or in external bodies.

> In this research we meet with very little encouragement from that prodigious diversity, which is to be found in the opinions of those philosophers, who have pretended to explain the secret force and energy of causes. There are some, who maintain, that bodies operate by their substantial form; others, by their accidents or qualities; several, by their matter and form; some, by their form and accidents.... Upon the whole, we may conclude that it is impossible in any one instance to show the principle in which the force and agency of a cause is placed.... If any one think proper to refute this assertion, he need not put himself to the trouble of inventing any long reasonings; but may at once show us an instance of a cause, where we discover the power or operating principle. This defiance we are obliged frequently to make use of, as being almost the only means of proving a negative in philosophy. (T, 158–59)

4. Hume asserts that we cannot infer the existence of any one object of which we cannot form an idea, and that no examination of an effect can lead to an inference about the cause unless we have also experienced the cause.

We can never have reason to believe that any object exists, of which we cannot form an idea. For as all reasonings concerning existence are derived from causation, and as all our reasonings concerning causation are derived from the experienced conjunction of objects, not from any reasoning or reflection, the same experience must give us a notion of these objects, and must remove all mystery from our conclusions. (T, 172)

5. In his general summary of his analysis, Hume notes that there are no final causes. This conclusion and the preceding one have theological consequences, but Hume does not draw the theological consequences in the *Treatise.*[5]

It will only be proper, before we leave this subject, to draw some corrollaries from it, by which we may remove several prejudices and popular errors, that have very much prevailed in philosophy. First, We may learn from the foregoing doctrine, that all causes are of the same kind, and that in particular there is no foundation for the distinction, which we sometimes make between efficient causes, and causes *sine qua non*; or between efficient causes, and formal, and material and exemplary, and final causes. (T, 170–71)

The foregoing analysis of Hume's Newtonian conception of causation has been given without reference to Hume's theory of the mind or of perception. It is an analysis of the real external world. It is Hume's understanding of what was going on in the physics of his day. It is important to make this point because so many readers obtain the impression that Hume's analysis of causation is a subjective one which depends upon his theory of perception. In no way does Hume's analysis of causation depend upon his theory of perception: it is rather an explanation of the transition from an Aristotelian to a Newtonian physics.

It is the Newtonian analysis of causation as applied to the external world which forms the basis of Hume's analysis of the internal world of our mind. It is not Hume's analysis of the mind which is extended to the external world but Hume's analysis of the external world which is extended to the mind. This reverses the traditional order for the presentation of Hume's philosophy.[6] It can be seen by consulting the introduction to the *Treatise* that Hume intended his analysis to be understood in this order. Hume argued that we can learn from our examination of external bodies something which is applicable to our examination of internal states. As he put it, "For to me it seems evident, that the essence of mind being equally unknown to us with that of external bodies, it must be equally impossible to form any notion of its powers and qualities otherwise than from careful and exact experiments . . . Nor ought we to think that this latter improvement in the science of man will do less honor to our native country than the former in natural philosophy" (T, xxi).

An examination of the *Abstract* and the first *Enquiry* reveals the same conception of a Newtonian program. In the *Abstract*, Hume claims that the whole of the *Treatise* can be understood by seeing the analysis of causation as a specimen.[7] There he presents once more his major point about formal causes and powers: "it is not anything that reason sees in the cause which makes us infer the effect" (A, 187). Finally, Hume announces the Newtonian program: "We have confined ourselves in this whole reasoning to the relation of cause and effect, as discovered in the motions and operations of matter. But the same reasoning extends to the operations of the mind" (A, 192).

It is noteworthy that in defending his *Treatise* in *A Letter from a Gentleman to his friend in Edinburgh* (1745), Hume showed himself to be aware of the long history leading up to the denial of the Aristotelian position about formal causes and which culminates in Newton's theory of motion. In a passage which sounds very similar to the note he later incorporated in the first *Enquiry*, he says:

I must use the freedom to deliver a short history of a particular opinion in philosophy. When men considered the several effects and operations of nature, they were led to examine into the force or power by which they were performed; and they divided into several opinions upon this head, according as their *other* principles were more or less favorable to religion. The followers of *Epicurus* and *Strato* asserted, that this force was original and inherent in matter, and, operating blindly, produced all the various effects which we behold. The *Platonic* and *Peripatetic* schools, perceiving the absurdity of this proposition, ascribed the origin of all force to one primary efficient cause, who first bestowed it on matter, and successively guided it in all its operations. But all the ancient philosophers agreed, that there was a real force in matter, either original or derived; and that it was really fire which burnt, and food that nourished, when we observed any of these effects to follow upon the operations of these bodies: The Schoolmen supposed also a real power in matter, to whose operations however the continual concurrence of the Deity was requisite, as well as to the support of that existence which had been bestowed on matter, and which they considered as a perpetual creation. No one, till *Descartes* and *Malebranche,* ever entertained an opinion that matter had no force either *primary* or *secondary,* and *independent* or *concurrent,* and could not so much as properly be called an *instrument* in the hands of the Deity, to serve any of the purposes of providence. These philosophers last mentioned substituted the notion of *occasional causes,* by which it was asserted that a billiard ball did not move another by its impulse, but was only the occasion why the Deity, in pursuance of general laws, bestowed motion on the second ball. But, though this opinion be very innocent, it never gained great credit, especially in *England,* where it was considered as too much contrary to received popular opinions, and too little supported by philosophical arguments, ever to be admitted as anything but a *mere hypothesis. Cudworth, Locke* and *Clarke* make little or no mention of it. Sir *Isaac Newton* (though some of his followers have taken a different turn of thinking) plainly rejects it by substituting the hypothesis of an ethereal fluid, not the immediate volition of the Deity, as the cause of attraction. (L, 27–29)

In the *Enquiry Concerning Human Understanding,* Hume announces his Newtonian program in the very first section: "Astronomers had long contented themselves with proving, from the phenomena, the true motions, order, and magnitude of the heavenly bodies: Till a philosopher, at last, arose, who seems, from the happiest reasoning, to have also determined the laws and forces, by which the revolutions of the planets are governed and directed. The like has been performed with regard to other parts of nature. And there is no reason to despair of equal success in our enquiries concerning the mental powers and economy, if prosecuted with equal capacity and caution"

(EHU, 14). Once more it is clear that Hume is applying to the mind what he has learned from the study of matter.

V *Newton's Methods*

If Hume was so impressed with Newton's success, it would only be natural to ask why Newton was so successful. Hume seems to believe that it was the result of Newton's famous four rules of reasoning in philosophy, as they appeared in *Philosophiae Naturalis Principia Mathematica*, Book III, published in 1686. Here are the rules:

> Rule I. *We are to admit no more causes of natural things than such as are both true and sufficient to explain their appearances.* To this purpose the philosophers say that nature does nothing in vain, and more is in vain when less will serve; for nature is pleased with simplicity and affects not the pomp of superfluous causes.

For short, this is usually referred to as the principle of parsimony or simplicity. It will play a crucial role in Hume's philosophy.

> Rule II. *Therefore, to the same natural effects we must, as far as possible, assign the same causes.* As to respiration in a man and in a beast; the descent of stones in Europe and in America; the light of our culinary fire and of the sun; the reflection of light in the earth and in the planets.

This is usually referred to as the principle of uniformity, and it is Hume's specific reference to this principle and to where it appeared that makes us certain that Hume had these principles always in view: "It is entirely agreeable to the rules of philosophy, and even of common reason; where any principle has been found to have a great force and energy in one instance, to ascribe to it a like energy in all similar instances. This indeed is Newton's chief rule of philosophizing. *Principia*, Lib. iii" (EPM, 204).

> Rule III. *The qualities of bodies, which admit neither intensification nor remission of degrees, and which are found to belong to all bodies within the reach of our experiments, are to be esteemed the universal qualities of all bodies whatsoever.* For since the qual-

ities of bodies are only known to us by experiments, we are to hold for universal all such as universally agree with experiments, and such as are not liable to diminution can never be quite taken away. We are certainly not to relinquish the evidence of experiments for the sake of dreams and vain fictions of our own devising; nor are we to recede from the analogy of nature, which is wont to be simple and always consonant to itself. . . . [8]

Rule IV. *In experimental philosophy we are to look upon propositions collected* [inferred] *by general induction from phenomena as accurately or very nearly true, notwithstanding any contrary hypotheses that may be imagined, till such time as other phenomena occur by which they may either be made more accurate, or liable to exceptions.* This rule we must follow, that the argument of induction may not be evaded by hypotheses.

This rule reinforces the important Newtonian point that we cannot be content merely to invent alternative mathematical theories; rather we must devise experiments to test our theories and see which is most consistent with the facts of experience.

In his discussion of the third rule, Newton warned that we could observe gravitational relations of all bodies but "not that I affirm gravity to be essential to bodies; by their *vis insista* I mean nothing but their inertia." Interestingly enough, when Hume expands upon his discussion of necessary connection in the *First Enquiry*, he once more refers to Newton and chides previous philosophers with trying to turn gravity into that mysterious power whose existence Hume denies. This should leave no doubt that what Hume took from Newton was a conception of philosophical method which rules out previous Aristotelian notions as found in both Cartesians and previous empiricists.

I need not examine at length the *vis inertiae* which is so much talked of in the new philosophy, and which is ascribed to matter. We find by experience, that a body at rest or in motion continues for ever in its present state, till put from it by some new cause; and that a body impelled takes as much motion from the impelling body as it acquires itself. These are facts. When we call this a *vis inertiae*, we only mark these facts, without pretending to have any idea of the inert power; in the same manner as, when we talk of gravity,

> we mean certain effects, without comprehending that active power.* It was never the meaning of Sir ISAAC NEWTON to rob second causes of all force or energy; though some of his followers have endeavored to establish that theory upon his authority. On the contrary, that great philosopher had recourse to an etherial active fluid to explain his universal attraction; though he was so cautious and modest to allow, that it was a mere hypothesis, not to be insisted on, without more experiments. I must confess, that there is something in the fate of opinions a little extraordinary. DesCartes insinuated that doctrine of the universal and sole efficacy of the Deity, without insisting on it. MALEBRANCHE and other CARTESIANS made it the foundation of all their philosophy. It had, however, no authority in England. LOCKE, CLARKE, and CUDWORTH, never so much as take notice of it, but suppose all along, that matter has a real, though subordinate and derived power. By what means has it become so prevalent among our modern metaphysicians? (EHU, 73n)[9]

Hume insisted upon taking Newton literally and followed out this proposal with relentless logic.

Hume makes the Newtonian rules of reasoning basic to his philosophical enterprise. In the *Treatise*, his introduction gives the Newtonian rules as follows: "we must endeavour to render all our principles as universal as possible, by tracing up our experiments to the utmost, and explaining all effects from the simplest and fewest causes, it is still certain we cannot go beyond experience; and any hypothesis, that pretends to discover the ultimate original qualities of human nature, ought at first to be rejected as presumptuous and chimerical" (T, xxi). The first section of the *Enquiry Concerning Human Understanding* mentions the rules of universality and simplicity.[10] The *Abstract* refers to the same set of rules: "If in examining several phenomena we find that they resolve themselves into one common principle, and can trace this principle into another, we shall at last arrive at those few simple principles on which all the rest depend.... this author ... promises to draw no conclusions but where he is authorized by experience. He talks with contempt of hypotheses ..." (A, 183–84). Finally, in the *Enquiry Concerning the Principles of Morals* Hume reasserts the same methodology:

find those universal principles, from which all censure or approbation is ultimately derived. As this is a question of fact, not of abstract science, we can only expect success, by following the experimental method, and deducing general maxims from a comparison of particular instances. . . . Men are not [*sic*, read now] cured of their passion for hypotheses, and systems in natural philosophy and will hearken to no arguments but those which are derived from experience. It is full time they should attempt a like reformation in all moral disquisitions; and reject every system of ethics, however subtle or ingenious, which is not founded on fact and observation. (EPM, 174–75)

VI *Hume's Newtonian Program*

Hume's Newtonian program is the attempt to explain human nature on the model provided by Newton for the explanation of phenomena in the physical world. We have already seen in the previous section what Newton's rules of philosophizing were and how Hume self-consciously adopted them in all of his major philosophical works. We can now show in a more detailed way how Hume translated Newton into a philosophical system.

The subtitle of the *Treatise* says that it is an attempt to introduce the "experimental method" into moral subjects. The expression "experimental method" signified in the eighteenth century the Galilean-Newtonian method of analysis as opposed to the Cartesian method. More specifically it means that we begin with analysis of individual objects of which we have direct experience, objects with which we can make observations and experiments. This analysis is then followed by a synthesis or composition, in which we make a generalization and explain additional phenomena on the basis of the generalization. Newton describes it as follows:

From the phenomena of motions to investigate the forces of nature, and then from the forces to demonstrate other phenomena . . . in natural philosophy, the investigation of difficult things by the method of analysis, ought ever to precede the method of composition. This analysis consists in making experiments and observations, and in drawing general conclusions from them by induction. . . . And the synthesis consists in assuming the causes discovered, and established as principles, and by them explaining the phenomena proceeding from them.[11]

If Hume is to follow the Newtonian program, then he must do the following:

(a) Identify or isolate the objects of analysis which we can observe and about which we can conduct experiments. Hume does this when he identifies the objects of analysis as perceptions, specifically differentiated into impressions and ideas. Hume presents the analysis in Book I, Part I, of the *Treatise*. Knowing this is very important. Hume's analysis of mental units into isolable corpuscularian units is an extension of the Newtonian method into moral philosophy; therefore, it is a serious blunder to view Hume's analysis of perceptions simply as a continuation of the Locke-Berkeley tradition or as a simple extension of Cartesianism in modern philosophy. The latter philosophers may have begun with an analysis of the contents of the mind, but they were certainly not analyzing it or its contents in terms of Newtonian corpuscles. Hume's analysis consistently seeks to differentiate itself from what Locke said, from the skeptical purposes of Descartes, from Berkeleian preconceptions and conclusions. What is sometimes referred to as Hume's atomistic analysis, a rather misleading notion, is really Hume's initial and preparatory attempt to identify the specific units on which his analysis commences. However, the analysis goes beyond atomistic separation. It is the principles of connection which Hume seeks to explain. This fact his interpreters too often fail to see.

(b) The second stage of the Newtonian program is to make experiments on the items so isolated for the purpose of arriving at a generalization. Hume proposes these experiments in the introduction to the *Treatise*: "We must therefore glean up our experiments in this science from a cautious observation of human life. . . .Where experiments of this kind are judiciously collected and compared, we may hope to establish on them a science, which will not be inferior in certainty, and will be much superior in utility to any other of human comprehension" (T, xxiii). Hume is not a philosophical phenomenalist who seeks to reconstruct the world in terms of mental units. Hume specifically declines to develop a theory of perception at the beginning of the *Treatise*. The mental units are arrived at after analysis for the purposes of discovering general principles. Hume believes in the common sense public world of physical objects. In fact, Hume goes on to describe how difficult it is to isolate mental units and therefore why experimentation in moral philosophy is so much more difficult than experimentation in natural philosophy. That is why experiments in moral philosophy have to be done judiciously and why they must be supplemented by observation of the nonmental world:

> Moral philosophy has, indeed, this peculiar disadvantage, which is not found in natural, that in collecting its experiments, it cannot make them purposely, with premeditation, and after such a manner as to satisfy itself concerning every particular difficulty which may arise. When I am at a loss to know the effects of one body upon another in any situation, I need only put them in that situation, and observe what results from it. But should I endeavor to clear up after the same manner any doubt in moral philosophy, by placing myself in the same case with that which I consider, it is evident this reflection and premeditation would so disturb the operation of my natural principles, as must render it impossible to form any just conclusion from the phenomenon. We must therefore glean up our experiments in this science from a cautious observation of human life, and take them as they appear in the common course of the world, by men's behavior in company, in affairs, and in their pleasures." (T, xxii–xxiii)

All of these statements would be quite unintelligible if Hume believed that mental things were the only things which existed. Unfortunately this is the misimpression carried away by readers and commentators who fail to note the Newtonian program and what it means to engage in Newtonian analysis.

The same point is made in the first *Enquiry*. Rather than being the only real things, our perceptions are among the most difficult things to isolate: "It is remarkable concerning the operations of the mind, that, though most intimately present to us, yet, whenever they become the object of reflection, they seem involved in obscurity; nor can the eye readily find those lines and boundaries, which discriminate and distinguish them. The objects are too fine to remain long in the same aspect or situation; and must be apprehended in an instant, by a superior penetration, derived from nature, and improved by habit and reflection" (EHU, 13). Analysis of the contents of the mind is, then, a form of introspection practiced by people who live in a physical and public world; it is not a reconstruction of reality based upon self-evident units of experience.

In so far as Hume's experiments involve a specialized and attentive observation of internal phenomena (introspection), and in so far as these observations are designed to confirm a theory about mental states and disconfirm other theories, and in so far as these attentive observations lead to new discoveries as we shall see about the self for example, then Hume's experiments are experiments in the true sense of the word.

(c) The third stage of the Newtonian program is to discover some general principle which explains the relations among the isolated units. So literally did Hume take Newton that Hume found in the mental world a general principle which was analogous to "attraction" in Newton's explanation of relations in the physical world. As Hume puts it when discussing his principles of association, "Here is a kind of ATTRACTION, which in the mental world will be found to have as extraordinary effects as in the natural, and to show itself in as many and as various forms" (T, 12–13). Other philosophers including Hobbes and Locke had spoken about association, but they had never thought of it as an analogue to Newton's theory of gravitation.

The principles of association are Hume's great theory or general principle in terms of which he hoped to explain everything. As he said in the *Abstract*:

> if anything can entitle the author to so glorious a name as that of an "inventor," it is the use he makes of the principle of the association of ideas, which enters into most of his philosophy. . . . It will be easy to conceive of what vast consequence these principles must be in the science of human nature if we consider that so far as regards the mind these are the only links that bind the parts of the universe together or connect us with any person or object exterior to ourselves. For as it is by means of thought only that anything operates upon our passions, and as these are the only ties of our thoughts, they are really to *us* the cement of the universe, and all the operations of the mind must, in a great measure, depend on them. (A, 198)

(d) The fourth stage of the Newtonian program after the articulation of the general principle is to extend that general principle to other phenomena. This is not only an instance of the principle of uniformity, which Hume considered Newton's chief rule of philosophizing, but an instance of what is called the confirmation of a theory by showing that it explains phenomena in addition to those which originally suggested the principle or theory. Throughout Book I of the *Treatise,* where Hume first articulates his general principles, we are reminded again and again that the general principles will be used to explain new and additional phenomena. Even animal behavior is explained by an extension of Hume's principles.

(e) The fifth part of the Newtonian program also has an analogue to Newtonian physics. The reader will recall from the discussion of the third stage that Hume's theory of the association of ideas and impressions is an analogue to Newton's theory of attraction among isolated bodies. Now, Newton's second law states that "the rate of change of momentum is proportional to the applied force, and takes place in the direction in which the force acts." In somewhat simplified layman's terms, momentum is conveyed from one body to another when they collide, and the change which results is mathematically measurable so that we may say that the second body acquires a certain momentum from the first. The analogue to momentum in Hume's theory will turn out to be the principle of the transfer of vivacity.

First, let us note that Hume is aware of Newton's second law and refers to it in that long footnote which we have already quoted at length: "a body impelled takes as much motion from the impelling body as it acquires itself" (EHU, 73n.). Second, we shall see that when Hume differentiates among his perceptions he will mention vivacity. This vivacity is originally a product of external physical objects or internal physiological processes which is somehow conveyed to our mental states. Vivacity is then transferred from one mental state to another according to a certain regularity that Hume claims to have discovered. In this sense, we may talk about Hume's mechanical theory of belief and the passions. Finally, I should note that the transfer of vivacity is not only analogous to the transfer of momentum but reinforces the claim that Hume's theory presupposes the Newtonian theory of external physical objects.

(f) The final part of the Newtonian program is to recognize

the inherent limitations of the reasoning faculty of man. It is not enough to construct mathematically sound hypotheses that account for known phenomena, since there are alternative accounts possible. Experimentation and testing are always essential. Moreover, it is irresponsible to offer speculations about what we do not know as if they were on a par with tested and testable hypotheses. Newton was very conscious of the corrigibility of scientific hypotheses.

Hume took this part of Newton very seriously. Not only was Hume at one with Newton in sharing the modesty of scientific progress, but Hume was cognizant of the claims made about the powers of human reason as the result of scientific successes. Hume recognized that the Newtonian method allows us to discover more and more but cannot offer a glimpse of a system of laws that explains everything. In other words, we cannot pretend to understand even what it means to offer a list of final principles or a final principle. The rationalists had offered a test for a final principle in the form of self-evidence, that is, a system akin to geometric axioms wherein we cannot imagine anything opposed to our self-evident system. Hume consistently attacks this test as illusory and inadequate. He shows himself to be a master at imagining universes in which some cherished principle does not hold. Finally, it is Hume's concern that rationalist pretensions are not only false but serve as a cover for ethical and theological systems that he considers to be pernicious. In attacking the rationalist pretensions, he is also attacking that abstruse philosophy which has been the shelter for superstition, absurdity, and error.

The fact that there are limitations to what we can say about nature even with scientific progress in no way prevents us from making important statements about man and profound statements about philosophical activity, since the latter is a manifestation of the former. As Hume puts it, there is an "impossibility of explaining ultimate principles" (T, xxii), and "we can never arrive at the ultimate principles" (A, 183), for there are "subjects utterly inaccessible to the understanding" (EHU, 11). This impossibility can be explained scientifically once we understand both the nature of the scientific enterprise and the exact nature of the human reasoning faculty. The latter

Hume expects to discover by applying the scientific method to the study of man. Finally, once we understand the limits, the necessary limits to human reasoning, then interestingly enough our desire for explanations which are self-certifying will disappear. The disappearance of the feeling that a special philosophical problem exists is the result of a true understanding of the scientific enterprise, a logical refutation of rationalist pretensions, and a psychological analysis of human nature, in that order. This is what I meant when I said in chapter 2 that Hume's proposal for giving a scientific explanation of philosophy itself was the most brilliant suggestion in all of modern philosophy. Now I believe we are in a position to appreciate more fully what Hume meant when he said "that all the sciences have a relation, greater or less to human nature. . . . Even MATHEMATICS, NATURAL PHILOSOPHY, AND NATURAL RELIGION, are in some measure dependent on the science of MAN; since they lie under the cognizance of men, and are judged of by their powers and faculties. It is impossible to tell what changes and improvements we might make in these sciences were we thoroughly acquainted with the extent and force of human understanding, and could explain the nature of the ideas we employ, and of the operations we perform in our reasonings. . . . we ourselves are not only the beings, that reason, but also one of the objects, concerning which we reason" (T, xix).

Like all moderns, Hume is turning epistemology into our metaphysics; but, unlike other moderns, Hume offers a scientific account of our epistemology. What is thus sometimes considered to be Hume's confusion of psychology and logic is a profound awareness that we can at least explain why we reason as we do even if there are other things we cannot explain. Further, unless we offer an explanation of why we thus reason, we leave open the possibility of misleading and self-destructive claims for other so-called systems.

CHAPTER 4

The Structure of the Treatise

A *Treatise of Human Nature* is divided into an introduction and three books. Each book is further subdivided into parts and sections. In order to understand Hume's philosophy as it is presented in his first and most important philosophical work it is essential to see how the content of each part is related to the content of every other part, how the dominant themes as announced by Hume are developed, and why Hume follows the order he does, that is, why one part comes before or after another. In short, an exposition of Hume's philosophy must give some account of the structure of the *Treatise*. As Hume himself makes explicit in the advertisement to the first two books of the *Treatise*, since the third book was published later, "*The subjects of the* understanding *and* passions *make a complete chain of reasoning by themselves*." Hume's chain metaphor, I contend, is to be taken seriously and literally. This contention may be routine scholarly practice, but it is remarkable if not outrageous that this practice has not been followed in the case of Hume's *Treatise*. So outrageous has the disregard become, that fantastic theories concerning the order of composition have been concocted to explain away the inability of some philosophers to see and explain what Hume is doing. This shall become increasingly clear in this chapter and in the remainder of the book.

I *Introduction*

Hume's *Treatise* begins with an introduction. This may seem obvious at first, but it is completely forgotten by those who launch into an exposition of Hume by immediately talking about perceptions and the fact that perceptions are a great mystery. Beginning with perceptions fits in nicely with the whole tradition of Hume scholarship and the whole of modern philosophy, but it is grossly misleading with respect to Hume.

In his announcement, Hume says "MY *design in the present work is sufficiently explained in the* introduction." To this reader Hume's design is certainly clear and it would probably have been in some respects even clearer to some of Hume's learned contemporaries who would recognize some of the allusions immediately. The first three chapters of this book have in effect been a summary of Hume's introduction to the *Treatise.* The introduction can be interpreted as having three overlapping parts: a declaration of Hume's aims and methods for achieving those aims, a set of assumptions which Hume like any author believes his readers already share, and a third element which I shall call the *Copernican thesis.*

The aim of the Treatise is to explain the principles of "*Logic, Morals, Criticism, and Politics.*" To explain the principles of logic is to explain the nature and limits of human reasoning; this he does in Book I. At the end of Book I, he resummarizes his total aims: "to be acquainted with the principles of moral good and evil, the nature and foundation of government, and the cause of those several passions and inclinations, which actuate and govern us. I am uneasy to think I approve of one object, and disapprove of another; call one thing beautiful, and another deformed; decide concerning truth and falsehood, reason and folly, without knowing upon what principles I proceed" (T, 270–71). The method by which Hume plans to achieve his end is the Newtonian experimental method. This, of course, is the science of man.

The assumptions on which Hume operated were both explicit and implicit. On the one hand, he accepted the common sense view of the world. On the other, Hume was enamored of the great success of physical science. In reconciling these two positions, Hume was doing what most other philosophers in the modern period since Descartes had done. The world of modern philosophy can be contrasted with previous philosophy in many ways, but for our purposes the key distinction concerns the alleged facts of perception. Whereas many of the ancients had believed that man could directly apprehend the structure of the physical world, the moderns recognized that perception was a process mediated by a number of physical events unknown to ancient philosophers and scientists. Interestingly enough, the word for "know" in ancient Greek is the same as the word for "see." In terms of the labels we have used previously, we may contrast the Aristotelian realistic perspective with both the rationalist (Cartesian) perspective and the *via moderna*. Despite their differences, the latter two metaphysical orientations agreed in opposing the Aristotelian view. The Copernican revolution, by challenging the realistic Aristotelian view as naive, gave additional impetus to this metaphysical dispute. For this reason modern philosophers tend to raise the controversy in what looks like purely scientific terms. From one point of view, the scientific revolution of the sixteenth and seventeenth centuries provided a new dimension to an old metaphysical dispute.

Starting with Galileo and Descartes, philosophers argued that our minds and/or brains did not directly apprehend physical objects but rather had access only to experience of some sort which mediated our access to physical objects. This position was stated in a number of ways, frequently with the reference to the difference between primary and secondary qualities, and this in turn had to do with which properties of bodies were mathematically measurable. One contemporary example, an anachronism for Hume's time, of course, is the modern scientific notion that bodies are composed of molecules in motion, such molecules being colorless and moving rapidly in a lot of empty space. We do not experience objects in that fashion; rather, we see solid objects with color, etc. Without attempting fully to articulate or decide philosophical issues here, it is only important to recognize that Hume does accept the philosophical notions and the scientific notions of his day. He thus shares the modern philosophical predicament or world view. Stated in its most simple form, the world of modern philosophy consists of physical objects which cause or produce experience(s) "in" the minds (and/or brains) of subjects or persons. We note that the spatial location of experiences becomes a matter of some controversy. Diagrammed, the world of modern philosophy looks something like this:

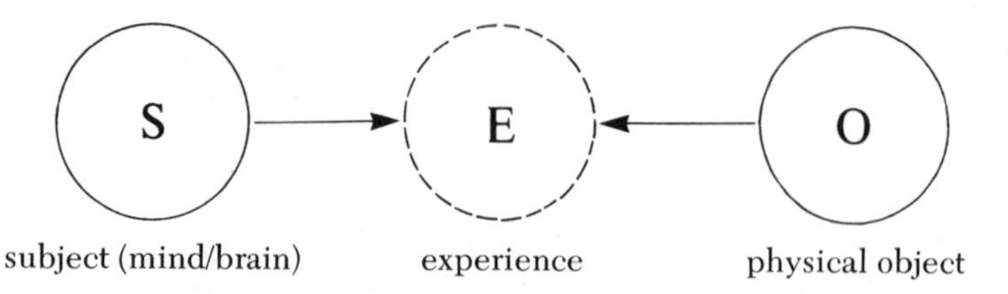

This world view is called dualism, it involves endless philosophical paradoxes, and it is the view of Newton and of Hume. For Newton, the human soul was a sort of substance lodged in the brain as a kind of control box. The sense organs convey impulses from external objects to the brain, and the will or soul in turn moves the body and thereby external objects by means of impulses from its seat in the brain.

A much refined version, but a version, nevertheless, of this view is to be found in Hume. This means that in a sense, problematic though it may be, Hume is a dualist. Endless commentators have tagged Hume as a phenomenalist, or as a man who argues only for the reality of experience and against the reality of physical objects. Interestingly enough, most of Hume's problems are problems about experience. But if Hume is a dualist, then he also believes that physical objects are real. Yet it is precisely this part of his belief or assumptions which readers ignore, and they do this in part by ignoring the introduction to the *Treatise* and not reading past Book I. It is the materialist side of Hume which has to be emphasized because it is precisely this side which is Hume's strength.

It would seem that anyone who starts from common sense and who takes Newton seriously would have to believe in the existence of bodies or physical objects and the fact that physical objects cause us to have the experiences we do have. As Hume puts it neatly, "it is in vain to ask, *Whether there be body or not*? That is a point, which we must take for granted in all our reasonings" (T, 187).[1]

Throughout the *Treatise, Abstract,* and first *Enquiry* Hume continually asserts without argument the existence of an external world which causes the experience of our "internal" world. The medium of this communication is our body, our organs, animal spirits, our brain, etc., declares Hume. "Original impressions or impressions of sensation are such as without any antecedent perception arise in the soul, from the constitution of the body, from the animal spirits, or from the application of objects to the external organs" (T, 275). In fact, "all our perceptions are dependent on our organs, and the dispositions of our nerves and animal spirits" (T, 211). Hume claims that this internal-external distinction is both philosophically acceptable and obviously sound, and therefore not something that has to be argued: "it is universally allowed by philosophers, and is besides pretty obvious of itself, that nothing is ever really present with the mind but its perceptions or impressions and ideas, and that external objects become known to us only by those perceptions they occasion" (T, 67). Experience is both an object of our scrutiny and a source of information about objects. (We are not concerned here with the soundness of this view but only with whether this view is to be found in Hume.)

Not only does Hume assert in general that external objects cause our perceptions and that sometimes our bodies alone give rise to some experiences, but he reasserts this assumption with respect to every individual sense. First, the eyes: "When an object augments or diminishes to the eye or imagination from a comparison with others, the image and idea of the object are still the same, and are equally extended in the *retina*, and in the brain or organ of perception. The eyes refract the rays of light, and the optic nerves convey the images to the brain in the very same manner, whether a great or a small object has preceded" (T, 372). And of course when an organ is defective, we lack the requisite experience: "wherever by any accident the faculties, which give rise to any impressions, are obstructed in their operations, as when one is born blind or deaf, not only the impressions are lost, but also their correspondent ideas" (T, 5). Second, this is also true of taste and smell: "it is upon the application of the extended body to our senses we perceive its particular taste and smell" (T, 237). "The palate must be excited by an external object, in order to produce any relish" (T, 287). Third, the same holds for touch: "an object, that presses upon any of our members, meets with resistance; and that resistance, by the motion it gives to the nerves and animal spirits, conveys a certain sensation to the mind" (T, 230). Finally, Hume discusses hearing indirectly through mentioning sounds which are in part "nothing but perceptions arising from the particular configurations and motions of the parts of body" (T, 192–93).

Not only the usual sensory experiences, but our internal experiences of our passions and pleasures and pains are dependent upon both external objects and internal physiological states: "Some objects produce immediately an agreeable sensation by the original structure of our organs, and are thence denominated GOOD."[2] Again, when discussing the passions, Hume says: "The predominant passion swallows up the inferior, and converts it into itself. The spirits, when once excited, easily receive a change in their direction; and it is natural to imagine, that this change will come from the prevailing affection."[3]

In both the *Abstract* and the first *Enquiry*, Hume reasserts this position. In the former he speaks of impressions as being the "images of external objects." (A, 185) In the latter, he reasserts his point about defective organs.[4]

Not only is it true that Hume believes in external physical objects and in the physiological conditions of our bodies as causes of our experience, but he also believes that the mind is a part of the body. To begin with, perception in general and thought in particular are the result of the motions of external objects and the motions of processes in the brain. "Motion may be, and actually is, the cause of thought and perception" (T, 248). Specifically, Hume assigns to the mind certain organs: "Here then is the situation of the mind, as I have already described it. It has certain organs naturally fitted to produce a passion" (T, 396). In one place he actually identifies the mind with the body: "Bodily pains and pleasures . . . arise originally in the soul, or in the body, whichever you please to call it" (T, 276).

However, the physical and material nature of the external world and our own bodies, minds, etc. is still operating in conjunction with nonmaterial perceptions or experiences. Hume chides the materialists for going too far in conjoining "all thought with extension" (T, 239); he further insists that experiences can "exist without any place" (T, 239). The dualism in Hume is most apparent when he discusses motivation:

"Is there not here, either in a spiritual or material substance, or both, some secret mechanism or structure of parts, upon which the effect depends, and which, being entirely unknown to us, renders the power or energy of the will equally unknown and incomprehensible?" (EHU, 68–69). Hume's dualism is a difficult, perhaps impossible, position to defend. But our concern here is not to judge Hume but to understand him. Hume believed that many of his points could be made even in the face of the obstacles raised by his dualism, and in this we shall see that he is correct. The weaknesses of dualism do not extend to the rest of Hume's philosophy. Finally, it is important to note that dualism also means that Hume believes in an external physical world and in the physical nature of the human body and mind. The whole Newtonian program is an application to the workings of the mind of what Hume has learned about external physical bodies.

The existence of a sometimes bizarre dualism in Hume is a point worth dwelling upon. There are three possibilities: (1) Hume is a complete materialist; (2) he is a phenomenalist (including some form of neutral monism); or (3) he is a dualist. With regard to (1), Hume specifically said that materialists are wrong in equating all thought with extension. With regard to (2), Hume developed a theory in which he claimed that there were two different kinds of impressions (T, 234–40), those which are extended and those which are unextended. Hence, a monism of any kind was rejected by Hume. This leaves only (3), which as we have seen is independently supportable.

Some passages in the *Treatise* seem to suggest a denial of the material world but when examined in context really do not suggest that at all. Perhaps the most notorious is the following:

> "As to those *impressions*, which arise from the *senses*, their ultimate cause is, in my opinion, perfectly inexplicable by human reason, and it will always be impossible to decide with certainty, whether they arise immediately from the object, or are produced by the creative power of the mind, or are derived from the author of our being. Nor is such a question any way material to our present purpose. We may draw inferences from the coherence of our perceptions,

whether they be true or false; whether they represent nature justly, or be mere illusions of the senses. (T, 84)

This passage suggests to some that Hume favors an explanation solely in terms of perceptions without reference to external objects. Certainly this interpretation seems at least plausible. But a closer look reveals something else. Specifically, Hume is claiming that the question of the ultimate cause of impressions is not relevant *here*, meaning the present analysis of how we move from an impression to an idea. Where the impression came from is not his concern at this point. Second, he argues that human reason cannot account for the question of ultimate causes. This argument anticipates his view that we cannot *infer* the object from the impression. Hume plans to account for a belief in a continued and distinct existence by appeal to the imagination. Third, he says that we cannot "decide with certainty," which thereby leaves open the possibility that we can decide in a less-than-certain fashion. Finally, when he says that we may, and in fact do, draw inferences from our impressions without considering their truth, he is not denying that inferences or beliefs can sometimes be true about external nature. The point is innocent enough. The mental process of inference is the same even when we are mistaken about the original impression as in illusions and hallucinations. In this context he is only concerned with the purely mental process of inference independent of all other considerations.

In later contexts it becomes clear that Hume specifically denies a creative power of mind and raises serious doubts about our ability to comprehend the concept of the author of our being or to form any idea of his power. That leaves only the possibility that impressions arise from objects. His "final decision on the whole" is that "matter and motion may often be regarded as the causes of thought, as far as we have any notion of that relation" (T, 250). The conclusion is cautious but it is nevertheless there.

There are contexts where Hume refused to admit any serious difference between the impression and the object (T, 67–68; 239). But this is not to deny that there is some difference between impressions and objects. What Hume has in mind in these contexts is Newton's third rule wherein he insists that bodies have those qualities and only those qualities that we experience. One of the properties we experience is extension, and so bodies are extended.

Hume's theory seems bizarre because of his notion of an extended impression. Further, Hume is creating for himself insurmountable obstacles by arguing for a dualism, problems which he himself saw more clearly than any previous dualist. While those who have tried to extricate Hume from this difficulty are certainly to be commended, it remains that Hume is committed to dualism.

In this context we might mention that Philo's critique of Cleanthes's arguments in the *Dialogues* reveal not an attack on the concept of design or order in general but an attack on how that order is to be conceived. Whereas Cleanthes indulges in a form of argument which is anthropomorphic in making something like human thought or reason the model and source of order, Philo argues that any analogy based upon what we discover in nature must do just the reverse. The point is made in a number of ways. As Philo puts it, "Judging by our limited and imperfect experience, generation has some privileges above reason: For we see every day the latter arise from the former, never the former from the latter" (D, 179–80). This point is perfectly consistent as well with Hume's insistence that any explanation must ultimately be an empirical description of physical facts and not a deduction from purely logical principles. The new science also suggested a new model of scientific explanation. Again, the reader should not be surprised when I describe Hume as a dualist who defends the material foundations of the causes of mental events. Philo reminds us as well that there is "nothing more repugnant to common experience, than mind without body; a mere spiritual substance, which fell not under their senses nor comprehension, and of which they had not observed one single instance throughout all nature" (D, 171). For Hume it is always the material world which serves as the model for explaining the mental world. This should also remind us of Hume's appeal to common sense and his critique of the rationalist view of man, where the latter sometimes seems to require men to become disembodied spirits.

The third overlapping theme of the introduction to Hume's

Treatise is what I call the Copernican thesis. We are already familiar with the so-called Copernican Revolution as it is ascribed to the philosophy of Kant.[5] In one sense the Copernican "turn" in philosophy is traceable to Descartes, but in a more immediate sense it is ascribable to Hume as well; and it may very well be that Kant's formulation of the new direction in philosophy owes much to Hume.

As we know, Copernicus proposed the heliocentric hypothesis to explain the motions of heavenly bodies; that is he argued that the sun was the center of the universe in which the earth was just another planet moving around the sun. Up until then, the dominant Ptolemaic theory had held just the opposite. The Copernican theory seems shocking in that we are not accustomed to thinking of the earth's motion. In fact, we still speak as if the sun were rotating about the earth. Copernicus's view was not immediately accepted but had to wait until the work of Newton to be fully certified among the members of the scientific community. What Copernicus had claimed for his theory as opposed to the Ptolemaic one was a greater simplicity in giving a summary of the known facts. In addition to stressing the value of simplicity, Copernicus called into question the reliability of everyday experience as ordinarily understood. It is crucial to note here that Copernicus does not challenge common sense or what we see but only the description or the interpretation to be given to what we see. Second, Copernicus stressed the fact that a new theory might require a revolutionary change in perspective. Instead of seeing the earth as the passive viewer of the heavenly spectacles, we must now understand that the earth is a participant. Put another way, people had mistaken what they saw as the motion of the sun when in fact it was really the motion of the earth.

From Hume's point of view, we may now say that people mistake as properties of physical objects what are really properties of the human thought process. This kind of mistake is important for a number of reasons including the progress of the sciences. Hume is most concerned about the continuing progress of science and the fact that how we progress depends upon what we think we are doing when we explain the world. It is not that Hume is arguing some weird romantic thesis about man creating reality, nor is he saying that reality is dependent upon man. Rather he is concerned with what in contemporary parlance we call methodology or rules of procedure for grasping more of reality. That is why he says, "it is impossible to tell what changes and improvements we might make in these sciences were we thoroughly acquainted with the extent and force of human understanding" (T, xix). The Copernican thesis is most apparent in his statement about marching "up directly to the capital or center of these sciences, to human nature itself" and in his self-professed aim that in explaining "the principles of human nature, we in effect propose a complete system of the sciences, built on a foundation almost entirely new" (T, xx). Notice that Hume does not say that reality depends upon the man; he says that the sciences depend upon the principles of human nature. Here it might be more appropriate to add that in following the Newtonian program, Hume did not pretend to be the Newton of the social sciences but had the more modest ambition of being its Copernicus: "Here, therefore, moral philosophy is in the same condition as natural, with regard to astronomy before the time of *Copernicus*. The ancients, although sensible of that maxim, *that nature does nothing in vain*, contrived such intricate systems of the heavens, as seemed inconsistent with true philosophy, and gave place at last to something more simple and natural" (T, 282).

Given Hume's aims, presuppositions or assumptions, and the Copernican thesis, how should we expect him to proceed? For a variety of reasons we are not yet capable of describing the biological-physiological activities of the brain, but we are able to experience these activities in part. Hume is thus confident that we can empirically confirm the presence of certain key operations of the human mind. The appeal to a kind of introspection, duly supplemented by the observation of people and animals, confirms the presence of these universal principles of human reasoning. Although he is optimistic about the possibility of confirmation, he never confuses the present empirical confirmation with the physiological or biological reality. He repeatedly reminds us that even his principles are in principle explainable, but not in the present state of our knowledge. Hume's experiments are thus invitations to his readers to see whether the presence of these operations of the mind can be confirmed.

II *Book I: Of the Understanding*

The first sentence of this first book is, "All the perceptions of the human mind resolve themselves into two distinct kinds, which I shall call IMPRESSIONS and IDEAS" (T, 1). This statement raises a number of questions. First, why does Hume begin with a discussion of perceptions?

It is clear from the first paragraph that Hume is presupposing the world view we have previously discussed since he talks about perceptions "entering," being "excited by discourse," and arising "from the sight and touch." In that first paragraph he also makes clear that he means by "perception" what Locke meant by the less precise term "idea." All this reinforces the whole picture of our perceptions (what I have previously referred to as experience) as caused by external physical objects. Thus, a careful reading even of the first paragraph alone should dispel any notion that Hume is a phenomenalist or an idealist trying to reconstruct the whole world in terms of sense experience. It should also be clear that the Newtonian program calls for a precise delineation of the objects to be related and explained. This is why it is necessary to distinguish between impressions, which are what we perceive or experience in the presence of external physical objects or internal physiological states, *and* ideas, which are the images or later thoughts or memories we have of the original experiences themselves. In fact, it is impossible to state the difference between impressions and ideas unless we assume the original presence of some physical object or state. There are other finer distinctions to be drawn, but surely this distinction (so far uninterpreted) is clear and one we still use.

In order to prove this point, I shall reexamine the very arguments Hume presented in the *Treatise*. Hume claimed in section I of Part I of Book I that the major question to be examined there was whether ideas caused impressions or impressions caused ideas. He concluded that impressions were the causes of ideas. His first argument for this conclusion is that both are conjoined. But constant conjunction alone does not determine which is cause and which is effect. The second argument is that impressions are temporally prior to ideas, and thus it is their "*first appearance*" which makes impressions the cause. But how does Hume know that impressions come first? His two examples explain how. First, "to give a child an idea of scarlet or orange, of sweet or bitter, I present the objects, or in other words, convey to him these impressions" (T, 5). To convey an impression one must first present an object in an already public and social world of physical objects. Second, in order "to confirm this" Hume noted that "where the organs of sensation are entirely destroyed" we lose the impression and hence the idea (T, 5). Again, the priority of impressions is established by reference to some physical object or state, namely, an organ of perception.

Hume also speaks about impressions being more *vivid* than ideas, and unfortunately those who attribute some sort of phenomenalism to Hume seize upon this point as unclear. Well, Hume himself admits that vivacity is not a clear differentia, but that is irrelevant here. In fact, given Hume's later plans, it is absolutely essential that ideas are capable of becoming vivid. Here is already a structural point that must be noted. One of Hume's great explanatory principles, the analogue to the transfer of momentum in external physical objects, is the transfer of vivacity among impressions and ideas. All that Hume is doing is anticipating this principle by calling attention to the greater vivacity of impressions. In fact, the original impressions acquire this great vivacity from the external physical objects or internal physiological principles which give rise to the original impressions. Hume will even suggest later a kind of physiological mechanism for the storage and transfer of this momentum or vivacity.

Those who misguidedly attribute phenomenalism to Hume have also seized upon another phrase wherein he says that impressions of sensation arise "in the soul originally, from unknown causes" (T, 7). The key phrase here is *unknown causes.* What such interpreters have in mind, I believe, is an argument which Hume develops much later in Part III of Book I, wherein he argues that we cannot legitimately infer the existence of objects from the existence of perceptions. They then conclude that Hume must be here arguing the same point, in advance, that we cannot know the causes of our perception. While the later use of the concept of vivacity is conveniently forgotten, the later use of an argument against a certain form of inference is misleadingly brought into the picture here.

To begin with, we have already seen that Hume is not going to argue for, or conclude, that objects cause perceptions; rather his entire philosophy presupposes or assumes that objects cause perceptions. This is what is meant by saying that we must take the existence of body for granted. Moreover, we have already pointed out that Hume is prepared to identify the soul with some part of the human body, as when he said of bodily pains and pleasures that they "arise originally in the soul, or in the body, whichever you please to call it" (T, 276). He has used almost the exact same wording in the contested phrase. Most important, if the entire paragraph in which the disputed phrase "unknown causes" appears is read, then it would be noticed that the next-to-the-last remark explains what Hume means quite specifically: "The examination of our sensations belongs more to anatomists and natural philosophers than to moral; and therefore shall not at present be entered upon" (T, 8). By sensations, Hume apparently means those perceptions which arise from the senses. Rather than denying the existence of bodies or physical objects, Hume reiterates his belief in them, but he declines to include the details of those sciences in his discussion. In one sense, those details are irrelevant since his analysis assumes the fact that external objects cause perceptions, but he is only interested in the relations among the perceptions themselves. Another reason is Hume's awareness that anatomists and natural philosophers have not really explained in minute detail the exact nature of the workings of the nervous system. This is still true in our own day, but we hardly question the general truth of such a relationship. Hume will shortly offer a similar disclaimer about the explanation of the mental operations of association which he undoubtedly thinks are due to the operations of the brain: "as to its causes, they are mostly unknown, and must be resolved into *original* qualities of human nature, which I pretend not to explain. Nothing is more requisite for a true philosopher, than to restrain the intemperate desire of searching into causes, and having established any doctrine upon a sufficient number of experiments, rest contented with that, when he sees a further examination would lead him into obscure and uncertain speculations" (T, 13). Finally, as we shall see in our discussion of causation in the next chapter, Hume believes that there are serious methodological obstacles to what we can discover about "secret causes."[6]

Book I is divided into four parts. Part I is concerned with the origin and nature of ideas; Part II, with which we shall not be concerned, deals with the ideas of space and time;[7] Part III deals with knowledge and probability, and more specifically Hume's analysis of causation; finally, Part IV is an amazing collection of Hume's views on the history of philosophy, skepticism, and personal identity.

In Part I Hume advances as a thesis about the origin of ideas his first general proposition, and one of the three major explanatory principles of the *Treatise: "all our simple ideas in their first appearance are derived from simple impressions, which are correspondent to them, and which they exactly represent"* (T, 4). Ideas are caused by impressions. This explanatory principle is not original with Hume, and he himself claims that it is what was meant by Locke when the latter denied the existence of innate ideas.

There are a number of issues raised by this general principle. First, if impressions are the causes of ideas, why does Hume begin the *Treatise* with an analysis of ideas rather than impressions? There are a number of answers. First, Hume has already declined to discuss the physiological mechanisms of perception as not part of his central concern. Moreover, the impressions which are of primary concern to Hume are the passions, but the passions are secondary impressions which frequently require an idea to excite them. Hence, it will be necessary to discuss the nature of ideas in order to understand better how ideas can produce certain passions. Finally, in attacking the rationalist model of human motivation and substituting his own theory, Hume is tactically setting up his discussion so that we can see fully the failure of the rationalist model before he presents his own alternative. The skeptical conclusions of Part IV are a perfect prelude to the Second Book of the *Treatise*, wherein Hume will present his theory of human motivation.

In stating the first principle in this fashion as opposed to the theory of innate ideas, Hume suggests that this principle will be "of more use in our reasonings, than it seems hitherto to have been" (T, 7). What he has in mind is stated more clearly in the *Abstract*: "wherever any idea is ambiguous he has always recourse to the impression which must render it clear and precise. And when he suspects that any philosophical term has no idea annexed to it (as is too common), he always asks 'from what impression that idea is derived?' And if no impression can be produced, he concludes that the term is altogether insignificant."[8] In short, this general principle serves as a kind of test; we shall see Hume use it in Part II with respect to existence; in Part III, with necessary connection; and in Part IV with substance.

The second question we can raise concerns the status of this general principle. Is it an empirical generalization or a rule? It would seem from our previous discussion that it should be some kind of empirical generalization which is in principle falsifiable, and so it would seem from some of Hume's remarks. On the other hand he notes one exception, namely, the case where a man who is familiar with all but one of the shades of a certain color has these shades placed before him in order and is then not only capable of detecting that one of the shades is missing but even to "raise up to himself the idea of that particular shade, though it has never been conveyed to him by his senses" (T, 6).

Hume calls this instance "particular and singular, that is scarce worth our observing, and does not merit that for it alone we should alter our general maxim" (T, 6). Why does Hume consider it unimportant? The admission of the possibility of an exception is consistent with Newton's fourth rule which permits us to accept a hypothesis if it is the best one available "as accurately or very nearly true" and "till such time as other phenomena occur by which they may either be made more accurate or liable to exceptions." Not only is this instance singular, but it is also hardly the kind of idea that the defenders of innate ideas would be concerned about. We might add that even in this case the shade is dependent upon our having had other impressions of the basic color itself, so that in a general sense Hume is still correct. It is for this reason that

I would argue that Hume is making an empirical generalization and that explains why Hume challenges his opponents to bring forth exceptions.[9]

At the same time it is clear that Hume wants to use this empirical generalization as a rule or maxim, in much the same way as the logical positivists were to use the principle of verifiability. Those familiar with contemporary philosophy will recall that the principle of verifiability states that in order for a statement to be considered meaningful, it must be possible to imagine or conceive of a state of affairs which would render the statement either true or false. This principle foundered among other reasons because it itself was not verifiable. It was then defended as a suggested norm, but as such it is hardly binding on those who choose to disregard it. Interestingly enough, Hume's principle, although not as sophisticated—because it concerns ideas or individual words rather than sentences—is immune to the objection which was so fatal to the principle of verifiability. It is because Hume's principle is an empirical generalization rather than a proposal that it can be verified. Moreover, Hume was not concerned to declare certain statements or beliefs meaningless, rather he expected to impale his theological and moral opponents not on the lance of verifiability but on probability. The positivists sometimes specified their principle in such a way that it excluded a large part of science, and when they broadened their principle to include all of science the principle failed to exclude theological statements among others. Hume did not want to declare theological statements to be meaningless but only to show that they were so improbable as to be useless for practical life. Also, Hume took these statements seriously.

The third question about the first general principle is whether Hume is being too restrictive by insisting upon a kind of introspective test for ideas. What about people who do not think in terms of visual imagery, for example? Suppose we do not remember our first experience? In answer, I note that it is clear Hume does not require or hold that all people think in images. He says that we frequently use words instead of ideas or images. Second, he does not insist that we recall the first experience but only that we find the impression from which the idea "is" derived. Notice that Hume did not say the impression from which the idea "was" derived. But, it will be argued, how can a phenomenalist expect us to have the exact same original impression? The answer is that Hume is not a phenomenalist. Impressions are produced by physical objects in a public world, and it is to these objects and natural processes that the ideas refer. If it is objected that Hume speaks about impressions and not physical objects, then I would refer the reader to our summary discussion above about why Hume adopted that procedure. Here I would contend that Hume's psychological analysis is exactly what is needed in order to defend a particular logical thesis about the meaning of concepts. Even more sophisticated theories used at present about the rules by which we originally learned the meaning of expressions rely upon covert psychological theses. The formula has remained the same even though the psychology has become a good deal more sophisticated.

The second general principle which Hume discovers concerns the imagination. According to Hume, the imagination has the ability to reconstruct ideas in a number of interesting ways, and this ability accounts for the creative efforts of individual thinkers. Nevertheless, such thinkers are still limited by their original material. The second of Hume's principles is that of "*the liberty of the imagination to transpose and change its ideas*" (T, 10). Not only is it evident that the mind can recompose ideas into new fictional entities such as fiery dragons, but it is also clear that the imagination can dissolve complex ideas into simpler ones such as one does when he analyzes the idea of an apple into a combination of simpler ideas such as its color, taste, smell, etc. This liberty of the imagination is presented in Part I as a consequence of our ability to distinguish between simple and complex ideas. It is also a consequence of the fact that "all our ideas are copied from our impressions, and that there are not any two impressions which are perfectly inseparable" (T, 10).

This last somewhat cryptic remark is a foreshadowing of what Hume intends to do with this second principle. The notion that our impressions are separable is derivative from the Newtonian position that every body or particle in the universe is in theory separable from every other and that it is only by experience of their impacts on each other that we learn their connection. Hume wishes to apply the same conclusion to our mental states. The conclusion which Hume will reach in Part III is that "the uniting principle among our internal perceptions is as unintelligible as that among external objects" (T, 169). Before he can do that, he must establish an additional thesis about the nature of existence.

In Part II Hume discusses space and time and then tacks on a discussion of existence. His conclusion about existence is that existence is not an additional idea derived from a particular impression. There is no impression of existence, and hence by the first principle of the *Treatise* there is no idea of existence. The idea of the existence of an object is the same as the idea of the object: "To reflect on any thing simply, and to reflect on it as existent, are nothing different from each other" (T, 66–67). We should keep in mind that Hume will distinguish between having an idea and believing in the truth of that idea, but this distinction is not what he means here by the idea of existence.

When we combine Hume's second general principle, that the imagination can transpose and change ideas, with his conclusion that existence is not an additional idea but the same as the idea itself, we obtain the conclusion that "*whatever we can imagine is possible*" (T, 250).

Let us review. The first and second principles together serve to undermine the whole notion of necessary connection. This undermining goes on in Part III. But before this could be done Hume had to present in Part I his two principles, and in Part II his thesis on existence. But we should recall that the thesis on existence is itself a conclusion from Part I, namely, the first general principle. In Part IV Hume spells out the implications of these two principles in his attack on substance which will culminate in his doctrine of the mind itself. It should at least be clear now why Parts I and II, or at least the material in them, are necessary prerequisites for the conclusions in Part III and Part IV.

In Part III, Hume presents his celebrated analysis of causation. We shall devote the next chapter to a discussion of causation, but we can explain a little of the structure of Part III. Hume presents what I shall call a logical analysis of the concept of causation based upon his understanding of

Newton. This we have already discussed in chapter 3. At the same time, Hume knows that his analysis will not be accepted by those still encumbered by the Aristotelian view and its association with the dark concept of power. In order to defuse that criticism before it could get off the ground, Hume presented his two principles in Part I. On the basis of his first principle Hume will challenge his critics to produce the impression of power from which they allegedly derive the idea. He will argue that neither in nature nor in our internal selves can we find any such impression of power. Hence there is no idea of power. With regard to the second principle, that "everything which is different is distinguishable, and everything which is distinguishable is separable by the imagination" (T, 233) he can reach his desired conclusion that "the uniting principle among our internal perceptions is as unintelligible as that among external objects" (T, 169). The whole argument recalls that Hume is arguing from what Newton said about the external world to the internal world. Hume is not arguing from our subjective states to a conclusion about the physical world.

It should be clear that in Part III Hume first offers a logical analysis of causation, which, as we showed in chapter 3, can stand by itself. Only after he has done that does he offer a psychological analysis to explain away the misconceptions of his critics. Part III also shows that Hume's theory of the mind is thus consistent with Newton's world view. And it is in Part III that Hume begins his relentless attack on the rationalist conception about self-certifiability by emphasizing what the minds of men are capable of conceiving. By emphasizing the separability of our ideas, that is, Hume's second principle, he was able to challenge the notion that some things are inconceivable.

In Part III, Hume also presents the third great explanatory principle of the *Treatise*, the principle of the transfer of vivacity. This is, of course, the analogue to Newton's notion of the transfer of momentum. When discussing a psychological point about why we are inclined to make some inferences, and more important, why we are inclined to believe some inferences and not others, Hume says: "*when any impression becomes present to us, it not only transports the mind to such ideas as are related to it, but likewise communicates to them a share of its force and vivacity*" (T, 98). This action is a cause of belief. When he comes to discuss the influence of belief, Hume tells us that this principle of vivacity will be the great explanatory principle of the *Treatise*, far more important and prevalent than the other two principles: "This, then, may both serve as an additional argument for the present system, and may give us a notion after what manner our reasonings from causation are able to operate on the will and passions" (T, 120).

In Part IV, Hume is able to apply his Newtonian analysis of causation to the problem of the existence of the external world, or more precisely our ability to infer the existence of objects from our perceptions. Hume's argument against the validity of this inference is so devastating because he has undermined the Aristotelian causal principles that would have allowed philosophers to argue that a cause can be known simply from its effects. This is one reason why Part IV's conclusions can come only after the full establishment of the conclusions of Part III. Hume next employs the conclusion of this devastating argument to show how the skeptic triumphs over the pretensions of those would-be rationalists who are forever invoking suspect principles of reasoning. Hume obviously enjoyed bearding these lions in their own den. More strategically, Hume is preparing the reader for his theory of motivation by showing the hopeless inadequacy of any rationalist theory of the power of abstract reason as opposed to the biologically based principles of association.

Again in Part IV, as we have seen, Hume employs the first and second principles to challenge the traditional conception of personal identity. Having loosened all of our perceptions, Hume concludes "*that we have no notion of it* [the mind], *distinct from the particular perceptions*" (T, 635). Personal identity is not something we can really understand just as a matter of thought. That is why Hume warns us that "we must distinguish between personal identity, as it regards our thought or imagination, and as it regards our passions or the concern we take in ourselves" (T, 253). What Hume is preparing us for at this point is a solution to the problem of the self which he has worked out as part of his theory of the passions. Here, too, we shall discover that the self is understandable only in terms of the biologically based principles of association. In short, Hume has so arranged the conclusions of Part IV of Book I that problems there raised are to be solved in the next book on the passions.

III *Book II: Of the Passions*

At the beginning of Book II Hume reasserts the Newtonian program in the form of searching for a few universal principles and then proceeds to explain the passions in terms of his theory of the association of ideas and impressions. He also reasserts the basis in physical fact of the passions, "as these depend upon natural and physical causes, the examination of them would lead me too far from my present subject, into the sciences of anatomy and natural philosophy" (T, 275–76). When Hume rewrote this book many years later as a separate *Dissertation of the Passions,* he reasserted that "in the production and conduct of the passions there is a certain regular mechanism, which is susceptible of as accurate a disquisition; as the laws of motion, optics, hydrostatics, or any part of natural philosophy."[10]

From the point of view of Book I, Hume has prepared us to expect two things: an answer to the question of what constitutes personal identity and a theory of human motivation. The self is explained as the object of the indirect passions. The theory of motivation is set out in Part III of Book II, wherein Hume presents a theory on the direct passions and on determinism and the famous statement that "reason is and ought only to be the slave of the passions." This return to the critique of the rationalist model will be important for an understanding of Hume's moral theory in Book III.

The relationship between Book II and Book III will hinge primarily on Hume's theory of sympathy, which is developed in Book II. Sympathy, as we shall see, is not only an example of the association of ideas and impressions but involves both the self and the important third principle of the communication of vivacity. Hume is quick to remind us that the theory of sympathy is analogous to the theory of causal inference he developed in Book I.

Book II is subdivided into three parts. In Part I, section I, Hume presents his general view on the classification of the passions. Within that classification he distinguishes between the direct and the indirect passions. Since the indirect passions more fully exemplify the association of ideas, we should expect Hume to discuss these passions first, and that is what he does. The indirect passions come in pairs, pride and humility and then love and hatred. It is in the context of discussing pride and humility that Hume asserts the "self" to be their object. Having left the problem of the self dangling somewhat at the end of Book I, we should expect Hume to discuss it soon in connection with pride and humility. In fact he does this, and that is why Part I is about pride and humility. In Part II, Hume discusses love and hatred.

At the end of both Parts I and II Hume relates his discussion to animals. He did the same thing at the end of Book I, Part III. Following Newton's second rule of uniformity, wherein we are advised to provide the same explanation for, among other things, "respiration in a man and in a beast," Hume offers as a confirmation, certainly not as a proof, of his position that animal behavior seems to be subject to the same explanation as Hume applies to human beings.

Finally, in Part III Hume presents his theory of the direct passions. Again this arrangement is useful in that it leads naturally into Hume's discussion of morals in the next book, Book III. A more detailed analysis of Book II will be given in chapter 6.

IV *Book III: Of Morals*

Book III is subdivided into three parts. Part I contains Hume's discussion of virtue and vice in general, that is, a general discussion of moral distinctions. Consistent with his Newtonian program Hume first seeks to isolate and identify moral distinctions before attempting to supply some general theory. At the same time, this general discussion following upon the discussion of motivation in the last part of Book II allows Hume to launch into a critique of rationalist moral theories, as when he declares that moral distinctions are not derived from reason. Hume's critique, which has been widely misunderstood, is quite clear when viewed as a part of his general attack on the rationalist position.

As part of his diagnosis, Hume divided the virtues and vices into two groups, the artificial and the natural. Part II constitutes Hume's analysis of the artificial virtues such as justice. Part III constitutes Hume's analysis of the natural virtues and vices. In both analyses Hume raises the Newtonian question of the general principle of morals. His answer is that sympathy is the general principle of morals. Sympathy, as Hume understands it, becomes the unification of his views on judgment, motivation, the association of ideas and impressions, and most of all the communication of vivacity. We shall discuss Book III in greater detail in chapter 7.

CHAPTER 5

The Analysis of Causation

THE most remarkable thing about Hume's celebrated analysis of causation is that few readers seem to agree on what it is. Thus, our first task is to present in succinct fashion the essential Humean position on causation. It is, to be precise, an analysis of causation, or of the causal relation. It is not an analysis of "cause" nor an analysis of "effect," for neither term alone would seem to be comprehensible without the other. Moreover, it is part of Hume's claim in opposition to the Aristotelians that we could not in isolation identify an object as a cause.

Hume's analysis begins with the statement "we must consider the idea of *causation*" (T, 74) and proceeds to identify the origin of the idea. The idea of causation he asserts "must be derived from some *relation* among objects" (T, 75). Thus, Hume's theory of relations is a necessary prerequisite to an understanding of his analysis. Further, when Hume concludes his analysis almost a hundred pages later, the result of the analysis is not a definition but two definitions of the causal relation! How Hume progresses from his theory of relations to his two definitions of causation is the subject of this chapter.

I *Hume's Theory of Relations*

According to Hume the imagination is capable not only of isolating individual ideas, but it also possesses the ability to combine ideas into complexes. Whereas Locke had identified three classes of complex ideas, namely, substances, modes, and relations, Hume rejected substances and modes in favor of relations. The rejection of substances and modes follows from the Newtonian program which recognizes only elementary objects and their relations. Further, Hume makes a distinction between natural and philosophical relations, but since every relation is a philosophical one, it will be convenient to discuss this class first (T, 13–15).

There are an endless number of ways in which *objects* may be compared, and therefore an endless number of ideas of philosophical relation. At the very least, we now know that the philosophical relations of ideas are derived from a comparison of objects. Next, Hume admits that while the possibilities are endless, there are seven general categories into which relations may be classified: resemblance, identity, space and time, quantity or number, degrees of quality, contrariety, and cause and effect. Furthermore, he asserts that resemblance is the most basic relation of all on which all other relations depend, "since no objects will admit of comparison, but what have some degree of resemblance" (T, 14).

The primacy of resemblance as opposed to identity is important. Hume admits that identity is the most universal of relations, since it is exhibited by "every being whose existence has any duration" (T, 14), but it is also to be understood in the "strictest sense" as applying only "to constant and unchangeable objects" (*ibid.*). As a result, resemblance is more basic than identity. Hume gives no indication here of how we come to know or believe that resemblance is present when we compare two ideas or the objects to which they refer. Later in the *Treatise* Hume will assert that this capacity is an unconscious biologically determined one. Later Hume will also tie resemblance to his third great explanatory principle of the communication of vivacity.

The seven philosophical relations (T, 69–74) are divided into two subclasses, constant and inconstant, as shown on the following page. The constant relations (resemblance, degree of quality, contrariety, and quantity) depend entirely on the ideas compared, so as long as the ideas remain the same, the relations will remain invariably the same. For example, as long as our idea of a triangle remains the same, it will always be the case that the three angles of any triangle will be equal to two right angles. The first three of these invariable relations are discoverable at first sight from mere observation and are thus called intuitive. In the case of quantity and/or number we must employ reasoning or demonstration to make a final determination, as in the case above. These four invariable relations give us certain knowledge.

The inconstant relations (identity, space and time, and cause and effect) are variable in the sense that they may change without there being any change either in the objects themselves or in their corresponding ideas. For example, we may change the distance and therefore the spatial relation of two objects by changing their place without actually changing the objects themselves. These relations depend on "a hundred different accidents, which cannot be foreseen by the mind" (T, 69). Moreover, just as the constant relations were divided into two classes, those that depend on immediate awareness and the one that involved a train of thought, so inconstant relations are further subdivided. Both identity and space and time are relations of immediate perception since "both the objects are present to the senses along with the relation" (T, 73). This is more accurately called "perception rather than reasoning."

This leaves causation as the only inconstant relation that involves a form of reasoning, since the mind must reason from a given object to another object which is not always immediately present in experience.

PHILOSOPHICAL RELATIONS

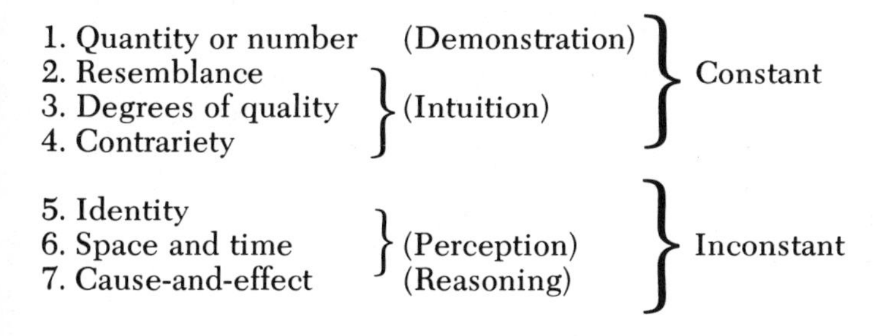

What Hume has presented so far is a format for conceptual analysis, and within that format he has located the causal relation. It is now time to see exactly how he analyzes this relation. Hume has asserted that causation is an inconstant relation since the relation of causation can change without a change in the objects themselves. The truth of this follows from Hume's assertion that "the power, by which one object produces another, is never discoverable merely from their idea" (T, 69). And if we ask Hume how he knows this assertion to be true, the only reply possible is that he asserts the truth of this claim because he has accepted the truth of Newton's physics. In short, Hume's analysis does not conclude with the truth of Newton's physics but proceeds on the assumption of its truth.

Second, Hume has also asserted that causation as a relation allows us to make inferences beyond our present experience. In fact, the relations of identity and contiguity in space and time are themselves dependent upon causation (T, 74) in this respect. Hume will later make use of this point when he discusses the self.

Hume now proceeds to unravel the exact nature of the causal relation. He claims that two elements are found in all cases of causation: contiguity in time and place, and priority in time. Contiguity we should note is just general enough to cover both cases of direct contact and cases of gravitation which are spatially related but where direct contact is not detectable. Hume next considers an alleged third element of the causal relation, necessary connection. Hume's analysis concludes that in the case of the philosophical relation of causation, necessary connection is really just constant conjunction (T, 87–88; 170).

Hume's definition of causation as a philosophical relation is the following: "An object precedent and contiguous to another, and where all the objects resembling the former are placed in like relations of precedency and contiguity to those objects, that resemble the latter" (T, 170). There are thus three conditions in Hume's definition:

1. contiguity in time and place,
2. temporal priority,
3. constant conjunction.

These three conditions are repeated in the first three rules for judging causes and effects:

"1. The cause and effect must be contiguous in space and time.

"2. The cause must be prior to the effect.

"3. There must be a constant union between the cause and effect. It is chiefly this quality, that constitutes the relation" (T, 173).

The question is, where does Hume get his definition?

Perhaps if we look at his examples of causation we may obtain some clue. Hume's favorite example is that of billiard balls. The example comes originally from Malebranche, the French occasionalist philosopher. Both Malebranche and others (including Ockham) had challenged the Aristotelian notion but for primarily religious reasons. These philosophers had argued that if God is omnipotent then there should be no limitation on what God can do and hence for that reason no necessary connection. Hume borrows the example but gives it an entirely new and Newtonian twist. In both the first *Enquiry* and the *Letter from a Gentleman to his friend in Edinburgh* Hume specifically refers to Malebranche and in the very same paragraph introduces Newton's interpretation. Malebranche's billiard balls are a perfect analogue to Newtonian bodies in motion.

Hume writes: "Motion in one body is regarded upon impulse as the cause of motion in another. When we consider these objects with the utmost attention, we find, that the one body approaches the other; and, the motion of it precedes that of the other, but without any sensible interval. It is, vain to rack ourselves with *farther* thought and reflection upon this subject. We can go no *farther* in considering this particular instance" (T, 76–77). In the *Abstract*, there is an even more detailed presentation of the same example:

> Here is a billiard ball lying on the table, and another ball moving toward it with rapidity. They strike; and the ball which was formerly at rest now acquires a motion. This is as perfect an instance of the relation of cause and effect as any which we know either by sensation or reflection. Let us therefore examine it. It is evident that the two balls touched one another before the motion was communicated, and that there was no interval between the shock and the motion. *Contiguity* in time and place is therefore a requisite circumstance to the operation of all causes. It is evident, likewise, that the motion which was the cause is prior to the motion which was the effect. *Priority* in time is, therefore, another requisite circumstance in every cause. But this is not all. Let us try other balls of the same kind in a like situation, and we shall always find that the impulse of the one produces motion in the other. Here, therefore, is a *third* circumstance, viz., that of a *constant conjunction* between the cause and effect. Every object like the cause produces always some object like

the effect. Beyond these three circumstances of contiguity, priority, and constant conjunction I can discover nothing in this cause. The first ball is in motion, touches the second, immediately the second is in motion—and when I try the experiment with the same or like balls, in the same or like circumstances, I find that upon the motion and touch of the one ball motion always follows in the other. In whatever shape I turn this matter, and however I examine it, I can find nothing further. (A, 186–87)

The billiard ball example appears again in the first *Enquiry* (EHU, 28–29).

Hume was aware of the fact that many would find his analysis unacceptable, especially those who still operated within the categories of Aristotelian physics, even when they no longer accepted that physics! This is a case of intellectual lag. His critics were then, and even now, prepared to challenge him for having left something out of the definition, out of the analysis. That missing element was asserted to be necessary connection. In short, the critics will contend that necessary connection is not the same thing as constant conjunction.

What does necessary connection mean? It is clear that two objects can have the relation of contiguity and priority and even a long history of constant conjunction, yet still not be considered causally related. Therefore, Hume's definition cannot be correct. We can all think of examples where one object preceded another and was contiguous for a long time and then it turned out not to be the cause. But Hume would reply that we had discovered some hidden cause, some other mechanism which accounted for the differences, and now we are in a better position to know why the cause works at some times and apparently does not work at others. But when we examine these new causes or circumstances they too turn out to be nothing but particles related in space and time. The possibility of being mistaken is not an argument against Hume's analysis but one of its consequences.

His critics will not be satisfied, for what they demand is Aristotelian essences or formal causes. They contend that every thing has an essence which makes it what it is, and once we know this essence we can understand why a body behaves the way it does and must behave that way. This is the true meaning of cause. Hume's analysis, on the other hand, is predicated on the assumption that Aristotle is wrong and Newton is right. There are no essences or formal causes to be discovered or analyzed. All we can do is record actual constant conjunctions of the impact of one body upon another.

Hume's point is frequently presented by logical positivists as if it were a purely logical point. Borrowing from Hume's own words, they ask, is it not conceivable that a body might behave in a different way from the way in which it has always behaved? This is Hume's second general principle about what is imaginable. As long as we can imagine the opposite or something different, then it follows that there is no logically necessary connection between two objects, between a cause and its effect. Thus we can say that Hume's point is that others have confused logical necessity with causal necessity, or they have confused a relation of ideas with a matter of fact.

However, Hume's point is not a mere logical point. It is difficult to imagine all previous philosophers, including people like Descartes and Leibniz, committing such an obvious blunder. Hume may express his point in this fashion by way of illustration, but his actual position hinges on the correctness of Newtonian physics and not on a logical distinction. For example, we believe that bread nourishes the body, and our evidence rests on a long history of observing the nourishing effects of eating bread. This is a Humean example, and I presume that in his day bread still had some nutritional value. Why does the bread nourish the body? An Aristotelian might contend that given the essence of bread it is logically inconceivable that the bread will not nourish. The logical positivist will contend that, no, it is a mere contingent fact that eating bread nourishes the body. Suppose further that we could find a case where someone ate bread and did not receive nourishment (assuming we had some test for this). We might postulate that something is wrong with that person's physiology. Suppose we check him out and find that he is normal. Then, the argument would go that the bread was deficient. But here an Aristotelian is perfectly just in his contention that the bread was not really bread after all, for if it were bread then it would have given nourishment. Here it can be assumed that giving nourishment is part of the essence of bread. Given this Aristotelian assumption, it is a logical impossibility for the bread not to nourish.

The logical positivist would be unhappy about this reply, and he would contend that bread can still be bread and be deficient. The object looks, smells, and tastes like bread. It even has the chemical composition of bread, so it must be bread. The assumption made by the positivists, and likely to be shared by a good many of us including Hume, is that a thing is what it appears to be and not some secret power which it displays only when interacting with some other thing. In short, we deny Aristotelian essences. But if this is what our point comes to, then we are making an ontological point about what we take the world to be, and we make this point based upon our belief that some scientific theory is correct. In this particular case we are not only accepting the correctness of Newtonian theory in general but we are also accepting Newton's third rule that the properties of bodies are the properties they appear to possess. In short, Hume's point is an ontological one and not a mere logical point. What is conceivable and what is inconceivable depends upon what one already believes about the nature of the world. That is why it was so important to stress the Newtonian program before examining what Hume said. It was not a conclusion on Hume's part when he argued against real connections among distinct existences; it was one of his Newtonian presuppositions.

I am willing to speculate that a good many of Hume's admirers are not aware of the fact that Hume's critique of necessary connection is convincing because we have accepted the Newtonian vision in place of the Aristotelian one. More often than not, these admirers are ignorant of the historical details involved and probably acquired their appreciation of Hume by reading back into him the later Kantian distinction between analytic and synthetic propositions. That is, they have always tended to view Hume's position as a technical point in logic. Kant, of course, understood the original historical context and the ontological implications of Hume's position.

II *Secret Causes and Counterfactuals*

It would be only natural to ask Hume whether he recognizes the possibility that external physical objects whose "essence" he says and assumes "is unknown to us" (T, xxi) might not have properties we are presently unaware of. Hume's reply is, of course, that bodies may have properties we do not now recognize. But he refuses to grant that we really understand what these qualities are or what we are saying when we call them powers akin to Aristotelian essences: "I am indeed, ready to allow, that there may be several qualities both in material and immaterial objects, with which we are utterly unacquainted; and if we please to call these *power* or *efficacy*, it will be of little consequence to the world. But when, instead of meaning these unknown qualities, we make the terms of power and efficacy signify something, of which we have a clear idea, and which is incompatible with those objects, to which we apply it, obscurity and error begin then to take place, and we are led astray by a false philosophy" (T, 168). It is important to notice that Hume is claiming that the Aristotelian essence as a power is *incompatible* with physical objects. His second claim is that those who invoke these essential powers cannot really explain what they mean.

The two foregoing claims he repeats throughout his works: "When we say we desire to know the ultimate and operating principle, as something, which resides in the external object, we either contradict ourselves, or talk without a meaning" (T, 267). Not only does this hold for external physical objects but it applies as well to the structure of our human bodies: "Could men anatomize nature, according to the most probable, at least the most intelligible philosophy, they would find, that these causes are nothing but the particular fabric and structure of the minute parts of their own bodies and of external objects; and that, by a regular and constant machinery, all the events are produced about which they are so much concerned."[1]

Hume's position may then be explained as follows. First, he grants that there are causes, secret causes or qualities, with which we are not presently familiar, and this is because they are at present too remote or minute or unreachable by our ordinary experimental means. Secret in this context means unknown. We are all familiar at this date with the notion of the atomic properties of matter, and atomism was one of Hume's presuppositions as well. "Look around the world . . . you will find it to be nothing but one great machine, subdivided into an infinite number of lesser machines . . . to a degree beyond what human senses and faculties can trace and explain" (D, 143). Or again, "philosophers, observing that, almost in every part of nature, there is contained a vast variety of springs and principles, which are hid, by reason of their minuteness or remoteness" (EHU, 86–87). Second, Hume contends that it is unlikely that the currently hidden or unknown causes operate in a manner different from the way in which observable causes operate. That is, he assumes that the Newtonian laws for macroscopic objects will also hold for microscopic objects, and that all interaction consists of particles in motion colliding with each other. "But as to the causes of these general causes, we should in vain attempt their discovery. . . . These ultimate springs and principles are totally shut up from human curiosity and enquiry. Elasticity, gravity, cohesion of parts, communication of motion by impulse; these are probably the ultimate causes and principles which we shall ever discover in nature" (EHU, 30). Until the twentieth century, scientists continued to assume that there was one universal set of laws holding for both macroscopic and microscopic objects.

With the development of quantum mechanics by Heisenberg and others, this assumption came to be challenged. Quantum physicists have shown that a different set of laws operates on the microscopic level, but Hume's contention about essential powers still holds. In fact, within quantum mechanics there is in a sense even less predictability than in the Newtonian system, and there certainly are not any Aristotelian essences. For a philosopher, or anyone else, to argue that there is something more is an act of intellectual presumption of unprecedented proportions. Third, Hume wishes to contend that the existence of Aristotelian essences is incompatible with modern science, and that is why it is not simply a matter of being remote but a matter of not belonging at all. Essences are *never* discoverable: "in no single instance the ultimate connection of any objects is discoverable, either by our senses or reasons, and . . . we can never penetrate so far into the essence and construction of bodies, as to perceive the principle, on which their mutual influence depends."[2]

If we press the Aristotelian to explain what he means by an essence, we do not receive a description of any property or imaginable property of a body. What we receive is a description of what we can do with propositions which contain references to such powers. That is, we receive a description of what we would be able to infer. In short, an Aristotelian essential power can only be defined negatively in terms of what we do not have and as a property of logic or language rather than as a property of things. We might be tempted to say that Hume is then making a logical point when he denies essential powers, but it should be recalled that the Aristotelians are asserting something about the world even if they cannot explain it as other than a point of logic, and that Hume certainly believes he is asserting something about the nature of external objects. The best description of what the Aristotelians have in mind is to be found in the *Dialogues*:

> It is observed by arithmeticians, that the products of 9 compose always either 9 or some lesser product of 9; if you add together all the characters, of which any of the former products is composed. Thus, of 18, 27, 36, which are products of 9, you make 9 by adding 1 to 8, 2 to 7, 3 to 6. Thus 369 is a product also of 9. . . . To a superficial observer, so wonderful a regularity may be admired as the effect either of chance or design; but a skillful algebraist immediately concludes it to be the work of necessity, and demonstrates, that it must for ever result from the nature of these numbers. Is it not probable, I ask, that the whole economy of the universe is conducted by a like necessity, though no human algebra can furnish a key which solves the difficulty? And instead of admiring the order of natural beings, may it not happen, that, could we penetrate into the intimate nature of bodies, we should clearly see why it was absolutely impossible, they could ever admit of any other disposition? (D, 191)

From this statement as quoted several of the most astute Hume commentators have been led to conclude that Hume does believe in some kind of hidden absolute necessity.[3] But in the very next paragraph Hume declares this conclusion to be an egregious mistake and confusion: "I shall venture to add an observation that the argument *a priori* has seldom been found very convincing, except to people of a metaphysical head, who have accustomed themselves to abstract reasoning, and who finding from mathematics, that the understanding frequently leads to truth, through obscurity, and contrary to first appearances, have transferred the same habit of thinking to subjects where it ought not to have place" (D, 191–92). Notice that Hume says *to subjects where it ought not to have place.* It is not that Hume believes in the possibility of a hidden essential necessity; rather he sees this as a misguided application of the properties of mathematics to the properties of the world. Here we should recall Newton's fourth rule and the critique of both Descartes and even Galileo for assuming that nature must conform to some preestablished mathematical system. Mathematics is a tool for explication, but it is not a limit on what we can discover only by experimentation. Hume seems to have taken this view to heart.

On this basis we can sharply distinguish between Hume and one of his medieval precursors, Nicholas of Autrecourt. The latter had argued the sophisticated but still purely epistemological point that our knowledge of cause and effect was only probable. But Nicholas continued to accept the Aristotelian notion of science as demonstration. The causes are powers even if we cannot be sure in our judgments about them. Hume, on the contrary, wants to argue not just the epistemological point but the ontological point as well that causes simply do not operate in nature as conceived within the Aristotelian framework. It is not that essences are forever hidden; rather there are no essences. This is not to deny the existence of causality but to substitute the Newtonian for the Aristotelian view.

One of the more interesting problems in contemporary philosophy of science is the problem of so-called counterfactual or subjunctive conditionals. There seems to be a difference between a statement of a physical law and a mere statement of constant conjunction, even though both kinds of statements are universal, that is, of the form "All A is B" (more technically, "for any x, if x is an A, then x is a B). Let us see if we can characterize "lawlike" statements so as to distinguish them from statements of mere constant conjunction. One way of making the distinction is to argue that "lawlike" statements express *nomic* universality or a strong connection between A and B, whereas statements of constant conjunction express only a loose connection or *de facto* universality. The adjective *de facto* is usually contrasted with *de jure*, and there is a historical sense in which nomic universals were considered *de jure*, the sense being that they were part of God's plan for the universe and willed by God. There were those who believed that moral commands (here *de jure* expresses a legal or moral connotation) were on the same footing with scientific laws or nomic universals. We may anticipate at this point that if Hume's analysis leads to a rejection of nomic universality, then we should expect his ethical theory to involve a corresponding rejection of absolute moral commands.

In addition, it is asserted that there is something a nomic universal statement can do which a *de facto* universal statement cannot do and that is support or justify an inference to a subjunctive or contrary-to-fact conditional statement. For example, the statement "If *c* is a piece of copper, and if *c* had been heated, then *c* would have expanded" is a subjunctive conditional. We believe it to be true even if *c* is never heated, and we believe that the subjunctive conditional is supported by, or inferable from, the nomic universal statement "copper always expands when heated." On the other hand, the statement "all the ravens in the zoo at time *t* are black" is a mere statement of constant conjunction which will not alone justify the subjunctive conditional "if *r* is a raven, and if *r* had been in the zoo at time *t*, then *it* would have been black."

This leads to the question, what makes a statement universal in the nomic sense, that is, how do we identify a nomic universal? First, the statement must be unrestricted as to time and space. The universal statement about copper appears to have this form; that is, *as far as we know*, copper expands when heated in any place or time. Second, the statement must be true not only of known objects but for all objects of the same type that will ever be encountered. This means that the examined instances must not be known to have been exhaustively examined and that the number of instances could be augmented *as far as we know*. It is thus clear that a nomic universal, or lawlike statement, is so by virtue of its relation to other statements which we claim to know.

Critics of Hume's analysis of causation as based upon constant conjunction claim that *de facto* universals cannot support subjunctive conditionals. Even if all known ravens are black, few if any of us would be willing to assert that the color of a raven is unrestricted or unrelated to time or place, and few would be willing to infer that in the future all ravens will be black. Put more formally, the universal statement "all ravens are black" does not support the subjunctive conditional, "if r is a raven, and if r had been in the zoo at time t, then r would have been black." As far as we know, there are factual statements about the variations in color of a bird's plumage and the genetic derivation of color, and the environmental factors which affect genes, such as x-rays, to severely limit what we would be willing to infer.

But what this criticism shows so far is that a statement which is lawlike, or nomic, is so designated because of our willingness to infer a subjunctive conditional, and this inferability is not a property of the statement itself but is dependent upon the existence or nonexistence of other statements known to be true. But then neither of these other statements alone can support a subjunctive conditional without the others. There is nothing to indicate so far that individual statements in isolation from others can be identified as nomic. Nomic universality thus seems to be explicable in terms of a *set* of related *de facto* universals. If this is so, then Hume's analysis is not inadequate since it can be easily amended to include the notion of a set of constant conjunction statements. Causal statements as a subclass of universal statements never seem to be more than statements of constant conjunction. Even when we bring in consideration of indirect evidence in support of a statement, the indirect evidence turns out to be the truth of other statements which are *de facto* universals.

Nevertheless critics of Hume's analysis have persisted in arguing that lawlike, or nomic, universals can only be analyzed if there are modal categories of logic such as "physical necessity" or "necessary connection" where these are not explicable in terms of constant conjunction alone. These arguments take several forms. First, there are those who flatly assert that modal notions are ultimate and therefore inexplicable. This is a kind of rationalist insistence on a priori notions or a kind of Aristotelianism which insists upon seeing a rigid structure built into events. However, such an insistence remains metaphysical and finds no counterpart in actual physical laws or scientific practice. Second, there is a large body of modal logic which is designed to exclude certain cases from the designation of nomic universality. This is certainly consistent with Hume's position in that any exclusion of a universal statement from the class of nomic statements would meet with Hume's approval. He considers that class to be empty. Third, and most interesting, those who insist upon the modal categories assume that it is possible to treat each universal law as a unit or entity itself even though they have not been successful so far in performing the logical operation of isolation.

The third possibility is the most interesting in that it shows Hume's opponents to be operating on the very ontological assumption that he denies. The idea of isolating a law is identical to the Aristotelian notion of discovering an essence or formal cause. Hume, of course, denies that this is possible. In fact, if we continue to think of scientists as discovering in a quasi-Newtonian manner functional relations of interdependence among bodies in motion, then no matter what we discover as the constant relation of two types of body, it is always conceivable that other types of body can at a different time and place modify the original functional relation. It is not that Hume denies the possibility of discovering constant relationships among subsystems of interactions; rather he insists that within a larger or different context other systems can modify the original subsystem. Hence, there is a sense in which Hume would deny the *ultimate* character of any lawlike statement. If Hume's view is correct, then it is impossible to isolate a nomic, or lawlike, statement. All we ever have are statements of wider or narrower generality.

The inability to isolate a lawlike statement does not preclude the possibility of identifying some statements as laws if we wish merely to claim that they are part of the set we mentioned above, but each unit of the set remains a mere *de facto* universal statement of constant conjunction.

A fourth possibility is to argue for a distinction between fundamental lawlike statements and derivative lawlike statements, wherein the fundamental statements refer to no specific or particular object or spatiotemporal location. The derivative lawlike statement is supposed to be specific, and it is alleged that these are derivable from the former. But not only has the derivation never been carried out (and this would amount in Hume's language to "demonstrating a matter of fact"), it does not even seem possible to derive statements such as Kepler's laws from so-called fundamental laws alone. This would seem to reinforce Hume's point that such regularities can only be discovered empirically and thus have some sort of irreducible empirical element.

If we look at the actual practice of science itself, as opposed to the metaphysical demands of either Platonists or Aristotelians who believe in an essence, we shall find a host of statements designated by scientists themselves as laws but which do not exhibit the characteristics that Hume's critics demand. This important fact has prompted some to argue that we can only explicate the meaning of law by noting the conditions under which *de facto* universals are "accepted" as laws, and this requires reference to the "Cognitive attitudes manifested toward a statement because of the nature of the available evidence."[4] I think that this argument is quite right, but what it does in an interesting sort of way is to reinstate in a more sophisticated fashion the Humean idea that a purely formal analysis is inadequate, that the formal analysis must be supplemented by the consideration of the activities of the knower, or the user of the statement. In Hume's terminology, the philosophical relation must be supplemented by reference to the natural relation. This we shall examine in the discussion of natural relations.

III *Rules of Reasoning*

On the basis of his analysis of causation, Hume arrives at a list of rules for causal reasoning. We have already seen the first three rules, and they constitute the composite definition of causation as a philosophical relation. It is important to stress the composite nature of the definition, for in examining an alleged case of causation the case must conform to all three rules. We have already seen one alleged counterexample, namely, the case of the counterfactual. In that case it was argued that Hume's definition failed to cover an important case or make the requisite distinction. In reply to that objection I contended on Hume's behalf that either counterfactuals were based on the suspect category of an Aristotelian essence or they were reducible to cases where we required a set of *de facto* universal statements or constant conjunctions. This notion of a set of statements of constant conjunction is perfectly compatible with Hume's third rule. This response is confirmed by what Hume says in his sixth rule: "when in any instance we find our expectation to be disappointed, we must conclude that this irregularity proceeds from some difference in the causes" (T, 174).

A second alleged case which Hume's definition fails to cover concerns cases where causes are supposed to be simultaneous with their effects instead of preceding them. Hume rejects such cases on the grounds that if we made causes simultaneous with their effects then this would annihilate time: "For if one cause were co-temporary with its effect, and this effect with *its* effect, and so on, it is plain there would be no such thing as succession, and all objects must be co-existent" (T, 76). Hume does not rule out the possibility that some causes might be simultaneous with their effects. I believe that cases of simultaneous cause and effect may be redescribed so as to make it clear that the cause precedes the effect. For example, it is said that a hand is moving the pencil or causing it to move and the motion of the hand and the pencil are simultaneous. It is perhaps more plausible to argue that the hand is not the cause of the pencil's motion; rather both the hand and the pencil are caused to move by prior physiological events within the nervous system, etc. of the person whose hand is involved.

A third alleged counterexample concerns our ability to discover a cause after a single instance.[5] Does this not rule out the necessity for constant conjunction? First, the objection confuses what Hume says about causation as a natural and as a philosophical relation. Psychologically we do not require repetition in many instances before we believe in the connection. This question is to be distinguished from the question of whether we are logically entitled to assert a causal connection after one instance. Hume's reply is that we can discover or infer causes after one instance in a particular case because we can generalize from causality in general and not just a repetition in one series of cases. Hume's fourth rule is designed to cover just this case: "The same cause always produces the same effect, and the same effect never arises but from the same cause. This principle we derive from experience, and is the source of most of our philosophical reasonings. For when by any clear experiment we have discovered the causes or effects of any phenomenon, we immediately extend our observation to every phenomenon of the same kind, without waiting for that constant repetition, from which the first idea of this relation is derived" (T, 173–74).

The final alleged counterexample to Hume's definition concerns the necessity for spatial contiguity. Sometimes Hume specifically requires it and sometimes he seems to leave it out. The answer to this is that Hume demands spatial contiguity for objects in the external physical world and for physiological conditions, but he does not and cannot require it for mental states, which lack extension.[6]

The foregoing were attempts to criticize Hume's definition for being too narrow and excluding some important cases. The following examples are supposed to show that Hume's definition is too broad and allows causation where it does not exist. These examples usually involve the failure to apply all of Hume's criteria at the same time. First, there are the endless cases where two things seem constantly conjoined, such as the increase in college enrollment and the increase in crime. It is obvious that such examples say nothing about spatial contiguity or priority and should not even be taken seriously. The second favorite example concerns the alleged constant conjunction of night and day.[7] But it is impossible to state what spatial contiguity means here, and certainly there is no general relation of temporal priority. Although particular days precede particular nights and vice versa, there is no way of saying that night always precedes day or day always precedes night. Third, there are always the cases where there is constant conjunction of two events and we already know that they are not causally connected. Known counterexamples are hardly a refutation of Hume because they obviously violate the condition of constant conjunction. To argue we might be mistaken is not a conclusion to be used against Hume; it is a restatement of one of his major points.

Perhaps the most famous and interesting counterexample is that of the occasionalist clocks.[8] Imagine two clocks, A and

B, where A is five minutes ahead of clock B. Every state of clock A is followed by a similar state of clock B, but it is obvious that clock A is not the cause of clock B's states.

The diagram is useful because it shows that it is impossible to state any general relation of temporal priority between the two clocks. Clock B may be viewed as five minutes behind clock A as in the example, but it is just as easy to conceive of clock B as eleven hours and fifty-five minutes ahead of clock A. The alleged counterexample fails to meet the requirement of temporal priority. Finally, it is clear that it is a known counterexample and thus cannot be used against Hume, because it already violated constant conjunction.

In addition to the rules of causal reasoning, Hume also develops a theory of probability based upon his examination of causation. Hume claims that there are three general types of arguments: demonstrations ("knowledge" in the *Treatise*, 124), proofs, and probability (EHU, 56). Demonstrations involve the relations of ideas, they do not rely upon experience, and are thus certain. Proofs concern causal arguments based upon a complete and uniform history and are thus free from doubt and uncertainty. That the sun will rise tomorrow is a conclusion free from doubt and uncertainty. In probable arguments the evidence is attended with uncertainty. I presume that weather forecasting would be a good example of a probability type argument for Hume. Hume further distinguishes between probability of chances, wherein we have no basis for deciding that one possibility is greater than another, as in trying to decide which side of a die will come up, and the probability of causes, wherein we operate with a kind of frequency theory of probability. In the latter case, Hume claims that we assume that the uncertainty is due to the operation of a multiplicity of causes or "contrary causes" (T, 132). In both instances, Hume's brief discussion shows a great deal of sophistication, but what he shows for the most part is that our analysis of probability rests upon the assumption of a causal order.

One has only to compare Hume's discussion of probability with John Locke's to see huge differences, and this insight explains why Hume insists on a difference between a proof and a probability. I think this insistence is due in part to the Newtonian perspective in Hume and the residual Aristotelianism in Locke, who still looks upon science as producing demonstrations if we but only knew those secret powers. Proofs are not only different from probabilities, but they can no longer be considered demonstrations in any sense.

IV *Justifying (Explaining) Our Rules*

Having described at length what he took to be our rules of reasoning, and having based that examination on what he had learned from Newtonian science, Hume was in a unique position to ask a question which would not really have occurred to anyone else. Given the fact that we have these rules, what justification is there for these rules? When a philosopher operates within the Aristotelian perspective, he assumes that each body has its essence such that if we knew that essence we would know why the body acts as it does and why it could not possibly act in any other way. In such a system all knowledge would be demonstrative. In a demonstrative system, we may arrange our beliefs in an interlocking system wherein the less general beliefs are derived from the more general, and the most general principles of all have the form of self-evident axioms. In short, within the Aristotelian perspective, there must be self-certifying rules of reasoning on which all others are based. Philosophers who accept this world view, whatever their other differences, see their function as articulating these self-evident first principles. The examples of Descartes and Spinoza come immediately to mind. Not only would self-evidence be a property of the first principles of knowledge but the test of self-evidence would apply to ethical first principles as well. Here Leibniz comes to mind. To know the essence of something is to know why it has to be that way. To ask for the justification of a rule or first principle is eventually to see why it, too, must be that way. One way of expressing this point is to say that such principles or rules are such that we cannot conceive of the opposite being true. It is not simply that the opposite is improbable; it is rather that the opposite or contrary state of affairs is inconceivable. This is what the test of self-evidence amounted to up to the time of Hume.

When Hume challenged the Aristotelian system by explicating the implications of the Newtonian system, he found that there were no formal causes, thus no essences. Therefore, what we know is based upon experience. There are no real connections among the distinct existents of this world other than those connections we discover, and then we do not really observe or comprehend anything other than constant conjunction. Let us say then that the first conclusion of the Newtonian analysis of causation is that there is no necessary connection.

If there is no necessary connection between any two existents, then we can always imagine, or even conceive of, the opposite state of affairs. Self-evidence is ruled out as a justificatory test for any set of rules or any individual rule. The traditional justification of the rules has been removed.

At the same time Hume subscribes to one of his own rules: he believes in the so-called uniformity of nature, in the fact that the future will resemble the past, in the fact that unexamined instances will resemble examined instances. In fact, Hume says as much in his fourth rule: "The same cause always produces the same effect, and the same effect never arises but from the same cause. This principle we derive from experience, and is the source of most of our philosophical reasonings" (T, 173). Now how can we justify this rule? Having spelled out the rules, Hume can ask for their justification. Reason in any of the requisite senses and especially in the most crucial sense of the self-certifying procedure of demonstration is incapable of providing an answer to this question. This is what Hume means in one context by his skepticism: "the philosophy contained in this book is very sceptical and tends to give us a notion of the imperfections and narrow limits of human understanding. Almost all reasoning is there reduced to experience" (A, 193).

It should now be clear that when Hume calls for the justification of this important rule he is asking that question within a very special context. I note this because Hume has become famous for allegedly having raised the so-called problem of induction. The problem concerns what warrant we have for believing that the future will be conformable to what we know about the past; and Hume is supposed to have shown that we have no such warrant. There are some serious questions about whether this is really a problem at all and if it can be stated coherently. But our concern is with whether Hume conceived of it as a problem.[9]

It is clear that in the *Treatise, Abstract,* and first *Enquiry* such inference is not a problem. In the *Treatise,* it is his aim to show that reason in its capacity of seeing "*ultimate connection*" (T, 91) is unable to operate in the case of causal relationships. Nor will reason in the form of demonstrative inference be able to make the inference. His conclusion is that the logical analysis of causal inference would never lead us to make inferences unless there were some natural psychological mechanism which was operative. It is not the legitimacy of the inference which is at issue but the question of how we make it.

In the *Abstract*, Hume claims that this principle "will admit of no proof but from experience. But our experience in the past can be a proof of nothing for the future but upon a supposition that there is a resemblance between them. This, therefore, is a point which can admit of no proof at all, and which we take for granted without any proof" (A, 189). Here Hume is even more explicit that the wrong kind of answer is being given, an answer based upon the Aristotelian claim that demonstrative reason applies to the physical world.

In the first *Enquiry*, Hume concludes that "it is not reasoning which engages us to suppose the past resembling the future" (EHU, 39). In short, the whole question of conceiving rules of reasoning as things which require proof is to adopt the wrong model of scientific explanation.

Historically speaking, there are three ways of handling first principles, corresponding to the three models of explanation we identified above. The first way is to argue that first principles are self-evident. This is the rationalist or Platonic point of view. One form of self-evidence is that of the axiom, wherein we cannot conceive of the opposite. This, as Hume has shown, is entirely inadequate for our first principle of the uniformity of nature. A second model, the Aristotelian, is based on the claim that first principles are synthetic, not axiomatic, and that they are abstracted from experience, from the structure of reality itself. In this context, Hume's challenge that arguments from experience cannot be justified on the assumption of the uniformity of nature is an explicit denial of the Aristotelian model. It is regrettable that the critique of the Aristotelian model has been taken as some kind of claim that there is a problem of induction.

The third general way of presenting the status of first principles is to argue for the fact that these principles are already implicitly accepted and must be accepted because of human psychological makeup. Hume claims that we are psychologically so constructed that we operate with these first principles. This way of discussing the status of first principles, as far as I can tell, was originally applied by Hobbes and then Hutcheson to ethical first principles, and Hume has extended this notion to every other sphere. In this sense Hume's science of man is one of the historically legitimate modes of philosophizing. Finally, the science of man is consistent with common sense, for common sense already displays these principles at work.

V *Causation as a Natural Relation*

Having distinguished causation as a natural relation from causation as a philosophical relation, and having discussed the latter, it is now time for us to address ourselves to the former. Hume offers as an empirical thesis the view that logic is not independent of psychology but, in fact, derives from psychology: "Thus though causation be a *philosophical* relation, as implying contiguity, succession, and constant conjunction, yet it is only so far as it is a *natural* relation, and produces an union among our ideas, that we are able to reason upon it, or draw any inference from it" (T, 94). In numerous places, Hume reasserts his view that all reasoning is psychologically and biologically determined: "It would have been easy to have made an imaginary dissection of the brain, and have shown, why upon our conception of any idea, the animal spirits run into all the contiguous traces, and rouse up the other ideas, that are related to it" (T, 60). Belief is more explicitly explained as due to "the course of my animal spirits and passions" (T, 269). The association of ideas or natural relations may be conscious operations but they have their unconscious counterpart in the operations of our bodies: "But our wonder will, perhaps, cease or diminish, when we consider, that the experimental reasoning itself, which we possess in common with beasts, and on which the whole conduct of life depends, is nothing but a species of instinct or mechanical power, that acts in us unknown to ourselves; and in its chief operations, is not directed by any such relations or comparisons of ideas, as are the proper objects of our intellectual faculties" (EHU, 108).

While the ultimate operations of the brain are mechanical or biological and thus not something of which we can be directly conscious, there is a conscious counterpart to this process which we know as the association of ideas. This conscious inferential process is explained in Newtonian fashion in terms of Hume's third great explanatory principle, the transfer of vivacity.

As we have already indicated, Hume's logical analysis of causation explains it in terms of contiguity, priority, and constant conjunction. The Aristotelian objection to this logical analysis is that it fails to account for the essential power of bodies or their necessary connection. Hume has argued that this necessity does not exist except as constant conjunction. Since his opponents insist that it is real, Hume then offers an explanation of how necessary connection becomes psychologically annexed to the logical or philosophical concept of causation. Three things must be noted here. Hume always, and carefully, distinguishes between the two questions:

"First, For what reason we pronounce it *necessary*, that every thing whose existence has a beginning, should also have a cause?

"Secondly, Why we conclude, that such particular causes must *necessarily* have such particular effects; and what is the nature of that *inference* we draw from the one to the other, and of the *belief* we repose in it?" (T, 78).

The first question is a logical one, and Hume answers it in the negative by demolishing the arguments of Hobbes, Clarke, and Locke. There is no necessity in nature in the Aristotelian sense of formal causes or essential powers. This we have already made clear above, but it is a point which is easily missed. Hume never denied the existence of causes; in fact his whole set of rules is predicated on the existence of a rigid causal network. What he denies is Aristotelian necessity: "I never asserted so absurd a Proposition *as that any thing might arise without a cause*." [10]

The second point to be noted is that the genetic explanation of how we come to believe in necessary connection is always given after Hume has shown that there is no logical basis for insisting upon necessary connection. The third point is that the relation between causation as a natural relation and causation as a philosophical relation is not a necessary logical one.

Not only do we not discover any necessary connection in nature, but Hume also attacks Locke's idea that we can find an analogue to necessary connection within ourselves. He does this in both the *Treatise* (T, 157) and the first *Enquiry* (EHU, 64–73): "We are ignorant, it is true, of the manner in which bodies operate on each other: Their force or energy is entirely incomprehensible: But are we not equally ignorant of the manner or force by which a mind, even the supreme mind, operates either on itself or on body?" (EHU, 72).

What we find when we analyze a particular causal inference from the purely psychological aspect is the following. We perceive something as an impression; perhaps we see smoke, and we remember from past experience that smoke has constantly followed fire. We infer fire, which at the moment is only an idea since we do not see it directly. We thus have a present impression and an inferred idea based upon past regularity. Now what happens is that the vivacity of the impression is transferred to the inferred idea. This makes the inferred idea more vivid than a mere thought and explains why we believe. "*When any impression becomes present to us, it not only transports the mind to such ideas as are related to it, but likewise communicates to them a share of its force and vivacity*" (T, 98). This also explains why ideas in memory are more vivid than mere imagined ideas, for sometimes we make inferences when both objects are not present, and then it is still the case that vivacity is transferred from the more vivid remembered idea to the inferred idea. We should recall that the original vivacity is preserved in some mechanical biological way in the brain. We should also note that Hume does not confuse the vivacity of inferred ideas, and therefore our belief in them, with the truth of the idea so inferred. An idea, which by definition stands for an object not immediately present, is believed if vivacity is transferred to it from a present impression of something different, either its cause or effect, or from a vividly remembered idea. An idea or inference is true if there can be found an impression to confirm it. Thus, in our previous example, I believe that there is a fire before I even see it because vivacity is transferred from the present impression of smoke, which I am confronting directly. But the inferred existence of fire is not true unless I actually observe the fire at a later time. The observation of the fire, of course, is not an inference but the having of an impression.

Hume's argument makes sense as long as we remember that impressions are of objects and that Hume is not giving some fanciful phenomenalistic reconstruction of reality. It should also be clear that the believed inference might turn out to be false if we discover later that the smoke was not caused by fire, but this in no way invalidates the existence of the belief. Beliefs may be false if the inferred object does not exist, but the belief itself is real.

The existence of two definitions of causation, or two analyses, has been a source of great perplexity and debate. Let us review the order of Hume's exposition. In Book I, Part III, sections 1 and 2 state the problem in terms of the theory of relations. Having then identified priority, contiguity, and constant conjunction, Hume raises two questions: "First, For what reason we pronounce it *necessary*, that every thing whose existence has a beginning, should also have a cause? Secondly, Why we conclude, that such particular causes must *necessarily* have such particular effects; and what is the nature of that *inference* we draw from the one to the other, and of the *belief* we repose in it?" (T, 78).

Section 3, "Why a cause is always necessary," constitutes Hume's attack on the rationalist position of an a priori account of causation, specifically, necessary connection. Hume concludes that causation is discovered empirically, not by an a priori argument. This conclusion naturally leads to the second great philosophical tradition, wherein it is argued that in the Aristotelian model necessary connection is discovered empirically, but it is still a necessary and objective feature of the world. In order to respond to this second philosophical tradition, Hume asks us to examine particular cases to see if we can make this discovery: "The next question, then, should naturally be, *how experience gives rise to such a principle*? But as I find it will be more convenient to sink this question in the following, *Why we conclude that such particular causes must necessarily have such particular effects, and why we form an inference from one to another*? we shall make that the subject of our future enquiry" (T, 82).

Sections 4 through 6 give the breakdown of particular causal inferences. In section 6, Hume isolates constant conjunction and raises the next issue: "the next question is, Whether experience produces the [inferred] idea by means of the understanding or the imagination; whether we are determined by reason to make the transition, or by a certain association and relation of perceptions" (T, 88–89).

Sections 7 through 13 constitute Hume's exposition of the principle of vivacity and how much it can explain. As I have said earlier, Hume was not content merely to identify the contents of common sense but wished to explain it in Newtonian terms as well.

In section 14, Hume returns to the idea of necessary connection and gives us his two answers. Philosophically, causation consists of contiguity, priority, and constant conjunction. However, there is a tendency on the part of people to project their *natural* propensities (the ones encouraged by common sense) onto the objective world. That is why they attribute necessity to it. Here the natural definition, or analysis, attempts to capture this very natural but essentially illicit process.

When we examine the first *Enquiry*, we find not only the same double analysis, but in a footnote Hume spells out that the purpose of the double analysis is to account for this natural process of projection:

As to the frequent use of the words, Force, Power, Energy, etc., which every where occur in common conversation, as well as in philosophy; this is no proof, that we are acquainted, in any instance, with the connecting principle between cause and effect, or can account ultimately for the production of one thing to another. These words as commonly used, have very loose meanings annexed to them; and their ideas are very uncertain and confused. No animal can put external bodies in motion without the sentiment of a *nisus* or endeavour; and every animal has a sentiment or feeling from the stroke or blow of an external object, that is in motion. These sensations, which are merely animal, and from which we can *a priori* draw no inference, we are apt to transfer to inanimate objects, and to suppose, that they have some such feelings whenever they transfer or receive motion. With regard to energies, which are exerted, without our annexing to them any idea of communicated motion, we consider only the constant experienced conjunction of the events; and as we *feel* a customary connexion between the ideas, *we transfer that feeling to the objects* [italics mine]; as nothing is more usual than to apply to external bodies every internal sensation, which they occasion. (EHU, 77–78n)

Strictly speaking, only the philosophical definition is official as indicated by its reappearance in all of Hume's works. The natural definition is a genetic account of a natural human tendency, as well as an example of Hume's continuing attempt to account for common sense views.

As we have seen again and again, Hume begins by noting that common sense is correct but naive so that it must be corrected and methodized; next, he proceeds to incorporate the sophistications of philosophy, but the usual philosophical analyses are inadequate; finally he offers an account of common sense beliefs which provides what the philosophers have left out but only by moving to the level of the science of man as portrayed by the Newtonian program.

We may now summarize Hume's double treatment of causation:

There may two definitions be given of this relation, which are only different, by their presenting a different view of the same object, and making us consider it either as a *philosophical* or as a *natural* relation; either as a comparison of two ideas, or as an association between them. We may define a CAUSE to be "An object precedent and contiguous to another, and where all the objects resembling the former are placed in like relations of precedency and contiguity to those objects, that resemble the latter." ... "A CAUSE is an object precedent and contiguous to another, and so united with it, that the idea of the one determines the mind to form the idea of the other, and the impression of the one to form a more lively idea of the other." (T, 169–70)

The same definitions in the same order are given in the *Enquiry*.[11]

Now that we have recognized Hume's double analysis and the reasons for it, we may immediately dismiss all criticisms which claim that Hume offers a bewildering variety of definitions. It is sometimes said that Hume's psychological account of how the notion of necessary connection is mistakenly annexed to the concept of causation is itself a causal explanation. This is hardly surprising. Having just defined what causation means, Hume is certainly entitled to employ the concept. Many who accuse Hume of this apparent circularity assume that he has denied the existence of causation. This assumption is absurd, especially in the light of his Newtonian program. Moreover, if it is true that man is so constructed as naturally and unavoidably to give causal explanations, then it must be that Hume has to give a causal explanation of why we give causal explanations. Rather than presenting a circular argument, Hume is giving us the consistent application of an empirical hypothesis and, I might add, exemplifying the subtlety of the *Treatise*.

The first and most obvious objection to any psychological analysis of causation is that it is either irrelevant or commits the genetic fallacy. However, we have seen that Hume's psychological analysis is not a substitute for a logical analysis but a supplement to it. Secondly, Hume was well aware of the distinction between the genesis and the validity of a proposition. As he puts it, to discover "the principle of human nature which ... makes us draw advantage from that similarity which nature has placed among different objects" is not the same thing as to discover what "gives this mighty authority to experience" (EHU, 36). But much more important, Hume denies that one can justify this principle if by justification one means showing that the principle is self-evident; and it is not Hume but his opponents for whom this is a problem. All one can do, according to Hume, is to explain the origin of the principle.

It is sometimes asked if psychology itself does not presuppose the validity of the causal principle, and if so, how can the assumption of the validity of a principle serve as a proof of that principle? The answer is that Hume does not use psychology as a justification in the sense of proving the validity of the causal principle. As Hume puts it, we cannot even assume that men will always reason in causal terms, all we can say is that men in fact do reason that way as of now. According to Hume, "If the mind be not engaged by any argument to make this step, it must be induced by some other principle of equal weight and authority, and that principle will preserve its influence as long as human nature remains the same" (EHU, 41–42).

One objection made by both Passmore and Popper is that Hume's analysis is inadequate in not recognizing the basis in human needs of anticipating repetition.[12] Mere constant conjunction is not going to make us take causal connection seriously unless we are predisposed to take constant conjunction as a serious matter. This objection is a confusion of causation as a philosophical relation with causation as a natural relation. As a philosophical or logical relation we need constant conjunction. But as a natural relation we find causal reasoning to be something we do automatically and as a response to our needs. Hume concludes: "Nature must have provided some other principle, of more ready, and more general use and application; nor can an operation of such immense consequence in life, as that of inferring effects from causes, be trusted to the uncertain process of reasoning and argumentation" (EHU, 106).[13]

Hume's use of the word "habit" has had a confusing effect upon his readers. We naturally tend to think of a habit as something which is acquired over a period of time as the result of external conditioning. Hence when Hume says that we project the past into the future as the result of habit, and at the same time he says that we cannot in any one instance see a real connection between a cause and an effect, we are left wondering what it is that is projected. The normal use of the word "habit" seems to make Hume's position contradictory.

However, a closer look at how Hume uses the term will remove the apparent contradiction. For Hume, "habit" in the sense here referred to is a species of instinct which is triggered by experience. In fact, in the lengthy discussion of probability in the *Treatise*, Hume contrasts a perfect habit with an imperfect habit. The perfect habit is an instinctual propensity of the imagination to project immediately the past into the future even the very first time. "The supposition, *that the future resembles the past*, is not founded on arguments of any kind, but is derived entirely from habit, by which we are determined to expect for the future the same train of objects, to which we have been accustomed. This habit or determination to transfer the past to the future is full and perfect; and consequently the first impulse of the imagination in this species of reasoning is endowed with the same qualities" (T, 134). It is this perfect habit which is a natural relation, a human instinct. "Habit is nothing but one of the principles of nature, and derives all its force from that origin" (T, 179). It is only later in the presence of contrary experiences that the habit becomes imperfect and requires us to weigh the conflicting evidence. This philosophical activity is the philosophical relation at work: "Contrary experiments produce an imperfect belief, either by weakening the habit, or by dividing and afterwards joining in different parts, that *perfect* habit, which makes us conclude in general, that instances, of which we have had no experience, must necessarily resemble those of which we have" (T, 135).

The last major objection to Hume's psychological analysis is that it presents no adequate basis for opposing those who are either irrational or who make inferences on the basis of prejudice.[14] The Humean answer is more than adequate. To begin with, Hume contends that all people reason in terms of cause and effect and the general rule of the uniformity of nature. We would say that induction is a universal rule of practice: "If belief consisted merely in a new idea annexed to the conception, it would be in a man's power to believe what he pleased. We may, therefore, conclude that belief... depends not on the will, but must arise from certain determinate causes and principles, of which we are not masters" (T, 624). In short, we cannot choose to be irrational.

Second, we would have to distinguish between a particular

belief and a general rule. In the case of a particular belief we must distinguish between why somebody believes something and whether that belief is true. If the belief is not true and it concerns something within our experience, then it is a rather simple matter to observe the fact in question and expose the error. Obviously the difficult and interesting cases concern some general principle or generalization which cannot be handled so easily.

When we deal with general beliefs, we distinguish between two different sets of rules, those we may employ in very specific circumstances or disciplines and the more general rules upon which even the former are based and judged. In cases of conflict or error we may expose the error of the lower-level principles by appeal to the higher level principles: "I must distinguish in the imagination between the principles which are permanent, irresistible, and universal; such as the customary transition from causes to effects, and from effects to causes: And the principles, which are changeable, weak, and irregular; such as those I have just now taken notice of. The former are the foundation of all our thoughts and actions, so that upon their removal human nature must immediately perish and go to ruin. The latter are neither unavoidable to mankind, nor necessary, or so much as useful in the conduct of life" (T, 225). Hume was especially adept at undermining his philosophical opponents with this distinction.

Aside from the obvious cases of confusing which rules apply where or simple-minded inconsistency, mistakes in reasoning boil down to mistaken generalizations. And the difference between a good generalization and a bad generalization is the amount of evidence available for it. When we consider other people to be prejudiced it is not because their beliefs are not based upon past experience or causal generalizations but because there is enough evidence available to call that generalization into question. So the real issue is not whether people use general rules but whether they have been *careful* and diligent in the use of general rules. It is in terms of a wider generalization that the narrower one is considered incorrect. If a man believes that all swans are white because all the swans he has seen have been white, we do not say he is irrational. He has been careless, perhaps, in not noting that birds in general come in different colors and it is thus possible that swans might come in some other color. As Hume states: "The following of general rules is a very unphilosophical species of probability; and yet it is only by following them that we can correct this, and all other unphilosophical probabilities" (T, 150). Education consists presumably in conditioning or training people to acquire the habit of being more careful and thorough, to say nothing of the sheer additional information imparted in order to make the generalizations more evidential.

In his discussion of the reasoning of animals in the first *Enquiry*, Hume presents a rather detailed list of the reasons some people are better reasoners than others. Most of the list concerns wider experience and carefulness. The list also mentions "Bypasses from prejudice, education, passion, party, etc." (EHU, 107n.). That there are nonrational devices for enlivening a belief or general rule of thumb would not surprise Hume in view of his theory of the imagination. But even these devices can only work by a kind of conditioning which is based upon habit but in a much more subtle fashion. Modern psychological theory contains no new information to challenge Hume's contention that such influences are the result of conditioning. What is acquired by conditioning can be unacquired or removed in the same fashion. Rather than being a problem, Hume's empirical hypothesis about the fundamental nature of the reasoning process, if correct, not only accounts for prejudice and seeming irrationality but offers the only hope of being able to reeducate people.

Finally, it should be noted that Hume even offers a physiological account for both common errors and philosophical errors: "As the mind is endowed with a power of exciting any idea it pleases; whenever it dispatches the spirits into that region of the brain, in which the idea is placed; these spirits always excite the idea, when they run precisely into the proper traces, and rummage that cell, which belongs to the idea. But as their motion is seldom direct, and naturally turns a little to the one side or the other; for this reason the animal spirits, falling into the contiguous traces, present other related ideas in lieu of that, which the mind desired at first to survèy. This change we are not always sensible of" (T,

60–61). This kind of physiological explanation is useful as a reason for the lack of attention displayed by some persons. Lack of attention is, along with a lack of broad enough experience, the principal cause of error. According to Hume, "The posture of the mind is uneasy; and the spirits being diverted from their natural course, are not governed in their movements by the same laws, at least not to the same degree, as when they flow in their usual channel" (T, 185).

I conclude by noting that Hume's explanation of the biological causes of correct and incorrect reasoning is consistent with his differentiating on the logical level between good and bad reasoning. He does not confuse the two types of issues. But in distinguishing the two types of issues it is still possible for Hume to argue that the answer to one question depends upon the answer to another question. We say that someone reasons well or badly depending upon whether he follows the rules, and then we describe those rules. We may then raise the question of what makes those rules the rules they are. Here Hume can argue that when those rules are fully articulated, no one can really imagine an alternative set of rules. But, as Hume goes to great pains to point out, this does not mean that those rules are self-certifying in the rationalist's sense. Finally, we can argue as Hume does that those rules are built into human nature, and if someone asks for more than that then he either is asking for the impossible, which is self-certification, or he does not know for what he is asking. This was why Hume said in the introduction to the *Treatise*: "we are no sooner acquainted with the impossibility of satisfying any desire, than the desire itself vanishes. When we see, that we have arrived at the utmost extent of human reason, we sit down contented; although we be perfectly satisfied in the main of our ignorance, and perceive that we can give no reason for our most general and most refined principles, beside our experience of their reality" (T, xxii). What Hume has tried to do, and with a great deal of success, is to push our knowledge to the very limits:

> One who concludes somebody to be near him, when he hears an articulate voice in the dark, reasons justly and naturally; though that conclusion be derived from nothing but custom, which infixes and

enlivens the idea of a human creature, on account of his usual conjunction with the present impression. But one, who is tormented he knows not why, with the apprehension of spectres in the dark, may, perhaps, be said to reason, and to reason naturally too: But then it must be in the same sense, that a malady is said to be natural; as arising from natural causes, though it be contrary to health, the most agreeable and most natural situation of man. (T, 225–26)

CHAPTER 6

The Passions

I *Introduction*

BOOK II of the *Treatise* is in many respects the most important for exemplifying the major themes of Hume's philosophy. By its discussion of the mechanism of association it serves as a confirmation of Hume's explanation of the mechanics of causal belief. At the same time, it prepares the way for Hume's moral theory by explaining the mechanism of sympathy. Again, it serves as explanation for the concept of the self which proved so problematic in Book I. Finally, by outlining his theory of human motivation Hume completes his project of undermining both the rationalist model in general and rationalist moral theories. Thus, an understanding of the passions is essential for an understanding of all the philosophical issues in Hume's *Treatise.*

II *Classification of the Passions*

In Book I, Hume had divided the impressions into two classes, those of sensation and those of reflection. In Book II, this same distinction is made and called a distinction between original impressions and secondary impressions. Original impressions are impressions of the senses and internal or bodily pleasures and pain. They are purely physical in origin, and they are called original because they arise from these direct physical sources without any antecedent. Secondary impressions are secondary in the sense that they are preceded by either an original impression alone or by ideas, which are themselves derived from original impressions. It is among the secondary impressions that Hume locates the passions.

The secondary impressions may also be divided into two classes, the calm and the violent. The calm impressions include both the moral sense, the sense of virtue and vice, and the aesthetic sense, the sense of beauty and deformity. We may already anticipate Hume's moral theory by noting that the moral sense comprises impressions which arise from, or are caused to come into existence by, previous original impressions and/or ideas. Clearly, then, when we discuss Hume's moral theory we shall be interested in the circumstances under which the moral sense is activated.

The violent impressions include the passions. Hume notes that the distinction between calm and violent is relative. This, like the distinction of vivacity, is a tactical distinction used by Hume in his discussion of human motivation. The violent impressions or passions are subdivided into the direct and the indirect. The direct passions come in contrasting pairs and include desire and aversion, grief and joy, and hope and fear. They arise immediately from the original impressions of pleasure and pain. Later Hume will argue that in some cases they arise without an antecedent. The indirect passions, which are Hume's major concern, include pride and humility as well as love and hatred. They arise from the original impressions of pleasure and pain in conjunction with other qualities. Hume's major concern is with these other qualities.

HUME'S CLASSIFICATION OF THE PASSIONS

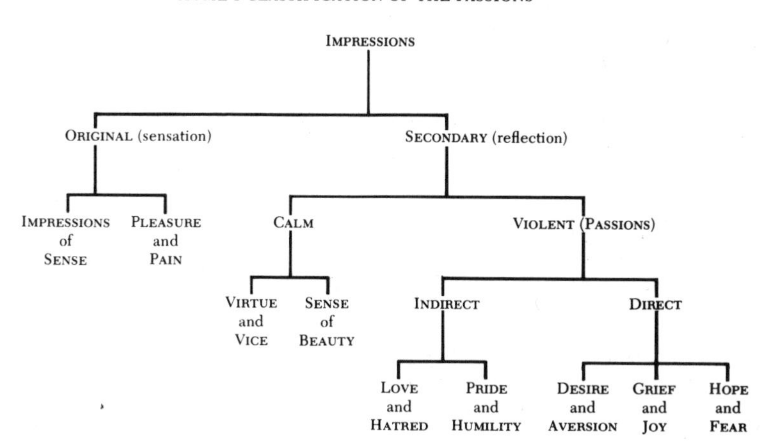

In analyzing the passions, Hume distinguishes between the cause of the passions and what he calls the object of the passions. With respect to the cause, he is concerned with what he calls the quality of the cause and the subject of the cause. True to his Newtonian orientation, Hume contends that "*it is not by a different principle each different cause is adapted to its passion*" (T, 282).

Hume discusses primarily four passions, the pairs pride and humility and love and hatred. Most of what he says can be understood by concentrating on pride and humility. The objects of the passions are relatively easy to deal with. Although otherwise different, pride and humility have the same object, namely, the self; the object of love and hatred is some other self. Whenever we are feeling pride or humility, it is because of ourselves or something intimately related to ourselves. At the same time, it is not always that we feel pride and humility simply by reflecting upon ourselves. The passion has to be excited by some cause. The cause is that idea which excites the passion, whereas the object is that idea which follows from, or is caused by, the passion. The indirect passions are, therefore, impressions which occur between two ideas.

The cause has both a quality and a subject. For example, if we are proud of the beauty of our house, then we can identify the house as the subject of the cause, and we can identify the beauty as that quality of the cause which excites our pride.

Three principles account for the causes of the passions. The first principle is the association of ideas. The cause of a passion, at least an indirect passion, is always an idea. Therefore, resemblance, contiguity, and causation as associations among ideas can cause a passion. The second general principle is the association of impressions. This is not to be confused with the association of ideas. Impressions may only be associated by resemblance so that one passion such as anger, which resembles envy, will easily allow us first to feel anger and then immediately feel the associated passion of envy. Third, and most important for the passions, there is a double association of ideas and impressions wherein both previous principles unite and reinforce each other. For example, when one man is injured by a second man, the first not only feels anger at the second but he feels uneasy whenever a thing or idea associated with the second man occurs to him.

A further example of the double association should make Hume's theory clear. Let us return to the example of pride felt because of our beautiful house. The beauty of the house, the quality of the cause of our passion of pride, is pleasurable independent of all other considerations. Therefore the quality of the cause of the passion gives rise to a feeling of pleasure or pain independent of all other considerations. Second, in order to give rise to our passion, the subject of the cause of the passion, our house, must be related to ourselves in order to produce the passion. In short, the causes of the passions have two properties: they are independently a source of either pleasure or pain, and they are related to our selves. The passions, in turn, have two corresponding properties: each passion is itself either a pleasurable or painful feeling or impression, and each passion produces the idea of our selves. This double impulse or coincidence explains why the indirect passions are so powerful.

As we shall see when we discuss motivation, the passions are what motivate us. Hence, anything which can cause a passion is a potential source of human motivation.

Having loosened all of the components of our passional life, we should now raise the question of how these passions communicate with each other. This requires Hume's third great explanatory principle, the communication of vivacity. In fact, Hume's discussion of the double relations of ideas and impressions is a prelude to his explanation of how vivacity is communicated. The idea which is the cause of the passion gives rise to an impression of pleasure or pain. It sounds odd to some that Hume should be arguing that an idea can communicate vivacity to an impression, since we were told that impressions cause ideas. However, we were also told that passions are secondary impressions which in the case of pride and humility require a preceding idea. This preceding idea had its own original impression. Some may well ask how the idea could have retained this vivacity since impressions were supposed to be more vivid than ideas. But if we recall that there is a physiological mechanism at work of which we are not conscious, and that in describing the passions Hume is merely describing the conscious counterpart of what is going on in the body, we may understand how vivacity as stored-up momentum can be retained. This is crude but perfectly consistent, and it reinforces the point that Hume's theory is unintelligible unless we continually remind ourselves of the biological basis. "As these depend upon natural and physical causes, the examination of them would lead me too far from my present subject, into the sciences of anatomy and natural philosophy" (T, 275–76).

Let us return then to the main argument. There is an idea which gives rise to an impression of pleasure or pain. This impression of pleasure or pain is associated by resemblance with other impressions of pain and pleasure such as pride or humility. The impression of pride and humility in turn gives rise to the idea of the self. The transition or transfer of vivacity is thus from the first idea to the first impression; from the first impression to the second impression; from the second impression to the second idea. This transfer of vivacity, Hume takes pride in reminding us, is analogous to the transfer of vivacity which he used in explaining belief: "There is evidently a great analogy between that hypothesis, and our present one of an impression and an idea, that transfuse themselves into another impression and idea by means of their double relation: Which analogy must be allowed to be no despicable proof of both hypotheses" (T, 290). Hume also takes this opportunity to inform us that virtue and vice produce the indirect passions.

III *The Self*

Since the self is the object of pride and humility, it is important to discuss it. The notion of the self is one of the most disputed aspects of Hume's philosophy, and yet no other issue affords us such an opportunity to display the interconnectedness of Hume's theses and misinterpretations which result from the failure to consider all of Hume's *Treatise* as a total theory. Since Hume's celebrated analysis of the self is an example of how his doctrines are treated in isolation from his philosophy as a whole, we must preface our discussion with a more general discussion of the context in which Hume raises this issue.

Part IV of Book I begins with a summary of skepticism and then moves through the attempts of both the ancient and the modern philosophers to offer an account of our beliefs which can withstand the onslaught of the skeptics. Hume's general conclusion is that reason as traditionally conceived, that is, as operating by means of the rationalist model, is totally incapable of performing this function. It is only the operations of the imagination, especially in the transfer of vivacity, which can adequately account for our beliefs. Notice that the beliefs are never called into question, the only issue concerns an adequate account of these beliefs.

With regard to explaining our beliefs about how objects and/or perceptions are related to each other, Hume says that there are three views. First, the vulgar, or common sense, view is that there is a real connection. This corresponds to what we have called the Aristotelian view that there is an objective and necessary structure which we apprehend. Hume claims that this is false. Second, there is the view of what Hume calls the philosophers, wherein connections are explained either in ancient terms as substances and accidents or in more modern terms as the result of a special faculty of the mind or as occult qualities in objects. This view can be either Aristotelian or Platonic (Cartesian, rationalist, etc.). Hume claims that this view is also false. Third, we have the true philosophy which is the acceptance of the vulgar, or common sense, beliefs but only on condition that these beliefs are accounted for by reference to the activities of the imagination, namely, habit, custom, and the transfer of vivacity. This view is what we have previously identified as the *via moderna*. It has always been the main strength of the *via moderna* to call attention to the confusion of the properties of the mind (or language) with the properties of things. What is unique to Hume is that he tries to explain, not just identify, the activities of the mind, and of course his explanation is in Newtonian terms.

In Part IV, Hume goes on to demolish the traditional and modern notions of substance in general and then discusses the question of the substance of the mind. In the section entitled "Of the immateriality of the soul," immediately preceding that on personal identity, Hume argues that we must "separate the question concerning the substance of the mind from that concerning the cause of its thought" (T, 248). With regard to the latter question, Hume's answer is that "matter and motion may often be regarded as the causes of thought" (T,

250), especially in view of Hume's position that local conjunction in space is not always necessary for the causal relation. Thus, an extended material object may be the cause of an unextended mental object or perception. This, as Hume says, "gives the advantage to the materialists" (T, 250). If matter can cause thought, and if we do not need substances, then it also follows that "the question concerning the substance of the soul [mind] is absolutely unintelligible" (T, 250). It should now be clear that Hume is attacking the Cartesian, Lockean, and Berkeleian insistence on the existence of a knowing mind. Even before we arrive at the discussion of personal identity Hume's position is a foregone conclusion.

The whole discussion of personal identity is predicated on the assumption that the common sense view is basically correct, but it still has to be explained. The philosophers have not given the correct explanation. The opening words of the section are, "There are some philosophers who imagine we are every moment intimately conscious of what we call our Self" (T, 251). It is against these philosophers that Hume is arguing, and not against the beliefs of common sense.

Identity is a relation found "only in philosophy" (T, 13), for common sense operates only in terms of the natural relations of resemblance, contiguity, and causation. This should remind us that Hume originally identified identity as a philosophical relation. The common man operates with resemblance and not identity. Since identity is philosophical, Hume clearly differentiates it from the common sense view: "This relation I here consider as applied in the strictest sense to constant and unchangeable objects; without examining the nature and foundation of personal identity, which shall find its place afterwards" (T, 14). When in the later section Hume distinguishes two senses of identity, he is recalling both the philosophical view which is strict and therefore could not possibly account for our common sense view of identity, and the loose sense of personal identity which depends upon resemblance and causation (T, 260–62). Resemblance and causation are natural relations as well. It is not Hume's purpose to berate common sense for accepting the loose sense of identity; it is rather his purpose to show that the transfer of vivacity accounts for the common sense view which clearly depends upon natural relations. The natural relations are produced by association, and thus the glory of it all is that it exemplifies the correctness of Hume's Newtonian program of explanation.

There is never any prospect of calling into question the existence of the self or the common sense view of the self in a social and public world. Before he even offers his own explanation, Hume talks about the self as if we already knew what it meant. He begins by saying, "When I enter most intimately into what I call *myself*," and then adds, "if any one upon serious and unprejudiced reflection, thinks that he has a different notion of *himself*, I must confess I can reason no longer with him" (T, 252). Strictly speaking, Hume is not discussing the whole concept of the self but the existence of a knowing mind, or one part of the self. Finally, it should be noted that the statements in which Hume says that it is perceptions which compose the mind are not affirmations of an idealist or phenomenalist position but rather a denial of a substantial Cartesian mental faculty as an addition to our perceptions. We should always keep in mind that it is matter in motion which *causes* these perceptions, and the brain is as material in nature as the rest of our bodies.

The most misunderstood part of Hume's analysis is that Hume explicitly mentions that he has two discussions of the self: "We must distinguish between personal identity, as it regards our thought or imagination, and as it regards our passions or the concern we take in ourselves" (T, 253). Hume thus clearly warns the reader that the discussion of personal identity in Book I is to be distinguished from the discussion of identity in Book II on the passions. A few commentators have seen the distinction but have failed to see the relationship between the two. There is a direct relation, for as Hume says, "our identity with regard to the passions serves to corroborate that with regard to the imagination" (T, 261).

In addition, we must note that Hume makes a number of statements about the self, the idea of the self, the impression of the self, ourselves, myself, the identity of the self, personal identity, etc., in a number of different contexts, each with a specific purpose. But there is a consistent theory behind his remarks.

The most important distinction is between the self and the

idea of the self. Those who insist upon seeing Hume as a phenomenalist or an idealist trying to reconstruct reality in terms of sensations miss this point completely. We have already seen in previous chapters the material or physical foundations of both external physical objects and our bodies including the brain or mind. Hume may be a dualist, but his dualism has a firm foundation in material events. It should therefore have been obvious from the start that for Hume the self, as distinguished from the idea of the self, is a composite of both body and mind, and that even the mind is to a large extent material. This is not only a presupposition on Hume's part but something he makes explicit in several places. He speaks of "the qualities of our mind and body, that is *self*" (T, 303). Finally, we should recall Hume's common sense and therefore public or social perspective. From the latter point of view Hume can invite others to introspect. In short, a sense of the self in a public or social world is already presupposed by Hume's analysis.

The failure to distinguish between Hume's concept of the self and the idea of the self leads to horrendous misinterpretations. One commentator has gone so far as to say that Hume "says that people are nothing but bundles or collections of different perceptions."[2]

Hume's discussion of the self has both a negative and a positive side. The negative side, which is primarily what he develops in Book I, is an attack on both the Cartesian doctrine of the mind as a simple and individual substance and the Lockean view of consciousness as reflected thought. Hume denies both of these theories, and the basis of his denial is rather simple. Anyone who introspects carefully will fail to find any such items. We can never observe the mind observing. All we can perceive is the individual perception: "For my part, when I enter most intimately into what I call *myself*, I always stumble on some particular perception or other, of heat or cold, light or shade, love or hatred, pain or pleasure. I never can catch *myself* at any time without a perception, and never can observe any thing but the perception" (T, 252). Two things should be noted about Hume's discovery. First, it is a discovery made by the kind of introspective technique or experimental technique Hume has been using since the beginning of the *Treatise*. Despite the shortcomings of Hume's technique and the ridicule directed against it, it is nevertheless true that Hume was the first philosopher to challenge successfully the belief in a substantial self. Second, Hume has been criticized for assuming in the above statement that we have a concept of the self. Of course he does, for the purpose of his negative analysis is not to discuss the self but the idea of the self. This is no contradiction, but only a case of readers' failing to see what Hume is about.

Since the mind consists of individual and separable perceptions, both ideas and impressions, the identity which we ascribe to it is fictitious, but fictitious in the innocuous sense in which we ascribe a continuous identity to a plant or to an animal or to a government, all of which obviously change over time. This is a useful and benign sort of fiction. The only question concerns the nature of the identity. How do we come to use or to discover this identity? With respect to our identity in the thought or imagination, Hume claims that we discover it in retrospect, that is, after the fact we see causal connections between our perceptions and our body. It is difficult for Hume to explain this, because his theory depends upon human action, and human action is more understandable in terms of the passions. But the essence of his theory is that we discover ourselves through causation "by the making our distant perceptions influence each other, and by giving us a present concern for our past or future pains or pleasures (T, 261).

When it comes to the passions, Hume can make his theory much clearer, and in fact this success underscores Hume's critique of the rationalist model. The self or rather the idea of the self in the passions is the same as in the imagination, for it is "that succession of related ideas and impressions, of which we have an intimate memory and consciousness" (T, 277). We note first that the idea of the self is not self-consciousness or a substantial mind but a collection. More accurately, the idea of the self refers to a collection of other ideas and impressions. This collection is related primarily by causation. Finally, it is intimate in the sense that each person can introspect his own collection in his own body or mind. Once again, the discussion of the idea of the self presupposes the existence of the self.

What is peculiar about the self as discussed in the passions is that it becomes for Hume an impression. Here he says, "the idea, or rather impression of ourselves is always intimately present with us" (T, 317). Is this a slip or a contradiction? Hume has already made clear in the discussion of the passions that there is a transfer of vivacity from the original exciting idea to the indirect passion which is an impression and thence to the self which in the case of pride and humility is the object of the passion. The transfer of vivacity allows the idea of the self to acquire the vivacity of an impression. Moreover, the self refers to a series of ideas and impressions to which it can communicate its vivacity and which already contain vivid impressions. As Hume said, when I introspect I find only a collection that consists of, among other things, passions, which are impressions. It is only as a creature who acts and feels that we discover our identity, not as disembodied reasoners.

We may sum up as follows. First, as selves we are composites of minds and bodies. Second, the mind does not consist of an immaterial substance nor is it a form of self-consciousness. Rather, the mind consists of a series of isolable ideas and impressions. This is the Newtonian program at work. Third, the idea of the self, therefore, is the idea of that series when that series is considered as related by resemblance and causation. Fourth, when we discover this idea, the idea of the series, we discover it in retrospect and this discovery constitutes our identity in thought or the imagination. Fifth, the idea of the self can itself be, on occasion, one of the ideas in the mind. This condition can be confused by some with self-consciousness, but Hume is always quick to point out that it is just an isolable idea. Sixth, and lastly, when the idea of the self is produced by a passion, we have a vivid conception of ourselves because of the transferred vivacity, and this conception is what is meant by identity as it concerns our passions.[3]

When Hume returned to his discussion of the self in the appendix to the *Treatise*, he repeated the same arguments, but he added a somewhat cryptic remark: "In short, there are two principles, which I cannot render consistent; nor is it in my power to renounce either of them, viz., *that all our distinct perceptions are distinct existences*, and *that the mind never perceives any real connection among distinct existences.*

Did our perceptions either inhere in something simple and individual, or did the mind perceive some real connection among them, there would be no difficulty in the case. For my part, I must plead the privilege of a sceptic, and confess, that this difficulty is too hard for my understanding. I pretend, not, however, to pronounce it absolutely insuperable. Others, perhaps, or myself, upon more mature reflections, may discover some hypothesis, that will reconcile those contradictions" (T, 636).

This statement has been taken by some to indicate that Hume is both dissatisfied with his theory of the self and that he believes his own theory contains a contradiction. But a closer look at the paragraph reveals no contradiction. To begin with, the two italicized statements are not contradictory statements. They do not contradict each other, because they both represent important principles in Hume's philosophy. The real contradiction is between each of these principles and the assumption or theory of a simple, substantial, and unitary self. In fact, since there are two statements, there must be two contradictions, for each italicized statement is contradictory with the assumption of a simple and unified self. And, indeed, this is what we find, for at the end of the paragraph Hume speaks of "those contradictions." Hume is dissatisfied, to be sure, but not because there is a contradiction in his views.

"The soul, as far as we can conceive it, is nothing but a system or train of different perceptions—those of heat and cold, love and anger, thoughts and sensations—all united together but without any perfect simplicity or identity. Descartes maintained that thought was the essence of mind—not this thought or that thought, but thought in general. This seems to be absolutely unintelligible, since everything that exists is particular; and therefore it must be our several particular perceptions that compose the mind. I say compose the mind, not belong to it. The mind is not a substance in which the perceptions inhere."[4]

IV *Sympathy*

Having seen Hume's notion of the double association of ideas and impressions in the operation of the passions, the importance of the transfer of vivacity, the analogy of belief and the passions, and having clarified the nature of the self, we are now in a position to understand Hume's theory of sympathy.

In his examination of the causes of pride and humility, the last cause Hume discusses is our reputation, our character, or our name. In order to account for this cause, Hume invokes the sympathy mechanism. In sympathy we begin with a belief about the emotions of some other person, a belief which is the product of an inference based upon the external features which we know are customarily related with that internal emotion. The belief is an idea which requires vivacity in order to be converted into an impression or emotion which is similar to the one being felt by the person observed. This is of course what we commonly mean by sympathizing with others. The source of vivacity which sympathy requires is found by Hume in the impression of the self. Sympathy may thus be defined as the process in which "the ideas of the affections of others are converted into the very impressions they represent" (T, 319).

Hume offers the following example. Our fame that is the result of the praise we receive produces a pleasant feeling in us. The exact relationship of the praise to our pride can only be understood in terms of sympathy. When we are pleased by the praise of others, it is because we observe the admirer and feel his pleasure. His pleasure, of course, is produced by qualities in us which are the objects of his admiration. In technical terms, our idea of his emotion, an emotion produced by qualities in ourself, becomes an emotion or impression directed toward these very same qualities.

This process is an example of the double relation of ideas and impressions. The idea which is the cause gives rise to an impression of pleasure. The first impression is associated with other impressions which are pleasant such as pride; the impression of pride then gives rise to the idea of the self. The transition is thus from an idea to an impression; from the first impression to a second resembling impression; from the second impression to the second idea. In sympathy, the second idea, namely, the idea of the self, acquires the vivacity of the second impression, thereby arousing the corresponding affection within ourselves.

Again and again, Hume stresses that sympathy is an inferential process. He emphasizes that the inference in sympathy is analogous to the inference in a causal judgment. Both inferences give rise to a judgment about a matter of fact. Hume stresses that we do not, and cannot directly, observe the emotion of another person. That emotion must be inferred from the appearance or language of the other person: "When any affection is infused by sympathy, it is at first known only by its effects, and by those external signs in the countenance and conversation, which convey an idea of it" (T, 317). Since we can never directly inspect someone else's emotions, it may be asked how the foregoing inference can be based upon a history of constant conjunction. Hume's answer is that we know about the frequent conjunction of our own emotions and our appearance and language, and we extend this conjunction to other persons because others resemble us. "Now it is obvious, that nature has preserved a great resemblance among all human creatures, and that we never remark any passion or principle in others, of which, in some degree or other, we may not find a parallel in ourselves. . . . this resemblance must very much contribute to make us enter into the sentiments of others, and embrace them with facility and pleasure" (T, 318). The inference might be invalid in a strictly technical sense, but what argument is incapable of doing for us nature has provided in the makeup of cur passional life. In contemporary jargon, Hume's argument for other minds is the one based upon analogy, and he is arguing that we cannot help believing in the conclusion. This is one more instance of Hume's critique of the rationalist model.

Sympathy is also analogous to causal inferences, in that it involves the principle of the transfer of vivacity. In a causal inference, the conclusion is believed because vivacity has been transferred from the original impression to the inferred idea. In sympathy, the vivacity of our own person is transferred to the idea of the sentiments and passions of others. The inference is assisted by the presence of the relations of resemblance and contiguity.

Hume finds an additional analogue to the understanding in his analysis of sympathy, that is, the operation of general rules. Such generalizations take the form of a general rule which provides our judgments with a degree of uniformity even in the presence of contrary observations. Such general rules owe their influence on the imagination, of course, to vivacity. This, in fact, is how Hume explained the influence of frequency in cases of probability. The same is true of the passions: "*General rules* have a great influence upon pride and humility, as well as on all the other passions.... Custom readily carries us beyond the just bounds in our passions, as well as in our reasonings" (T, 293). Specifically, we form a notion of the subject's condition rather than relying exclusively on countenance and conversation. The imagination, assuming that there have been previous cases, then moves from the cause to the usual effect or passion. Sometimes this happens even in the absence of the affection: "Though there be an exception in the present case, yet the imagination is affected by the *general rule*, and makes us conceive a lively idea of the passion, or rather feel the passion itself, in the same manner, as if the person were really actuated by it" (T, 371).

V *The Influencing Motives of the Will*

After everything that Hume has said in the *Treatise*, his theory of motivation appears as an obvious consequence. There are, however, a few important qualifications, which Hume adds in the final part of Book II. These qualifications are not only indications of the subtlety of Hume's analysis, but they also circumvent some of the criticisms traditionally made of Hume's analysis.

Contrary to many assertions made about him, Hume is not a hedonist, that is, he does not believe that the only source of human motivation is the desire to obtain pleasure and to avoid pain. When Hume first described the direct passions, he said that they arise from the ideas of pleasure and pain. That description is largely but not completely true. In the first context in which he discussed the direct passions he was concerned only with contrasting them with the indirect passions when the latter were his major concern. When he came to discuss the direct passions themselves, he qualified his original characterization of the direct passions and said:

> *Desire* arises from good considered simply, and *aversion* is derived from evil. The *will* exerts itself, when either the good or the absence

of the evil may be attained by any action of the mind or body. Beside good and evil, or in other words, pain and pleasure, the direct passions frequently arise from a natural impulse or instinct, which is perfectly unaccountable. Of this kind is the desire of punishment to our enemies, and of happiness to our friends; hunger, lust, and a few other bodily appetites. These passions, properly speaking, produce good and evil, and proceed not from them, like the other affections." (T, 439)

In short, Hume does not believe that the only desires or motives we have are for pleasure and pain; he asserts that sometimes we desire things without the prospect of pleasure or pain, and the latter are the results of satisfying the impulse but not the motive to, or explanation of, the impulse, and that acts of benevolence are just as impulsive as any of the other direct passions.

What is the relation between the passions and the will? According to Hume the *will* is "*the internal impression we feel and are conscious of, when we knowingly give rise to any new motion of our body, or new perception of our mind*" (T, 399). Hume says that the will is an impression, that it is indefinable like the impressions we have described as pride, humility, love, hatred; and that the will is not itself a passion. This statement is important.[5] What Hume means here is that the will is not an entity or even an impression with a continuous identity. It is an impression which is caused by the passions. Therefore, whenever the passions give rise to any action of the mind or body, the passions are conscious impressions or impressions we are conscious of. This is what we call the will. It is in this sense that the passions are the causes of "the direction of the will" (T, 413). Since we cannot define an impression, we are forced to describe the circumstances under which it exists.

In fact, this description of the circumstances under which an impression exists, especially in the case of the secondary or reflective impressions, is an important part of Hume's analysis. Given his Newtonian program, it is essential for Hume to isolate the units about which he seeks to describe relationships. Therefore he isolates the passions as impressions. All of this appears a little artificial, for it is impossible to understand Hume's theory of the passions without the accompanying circumstances which surround each passion so isolated. It is much easier to see what Hume has in mind when he describes the accompanying circumstances, such as the ideas which precede and follow each isolable impression or passion. Pride is understandable once we are told what objects and qualities lead to it and the fact that the idea of the self is its object.

Two points are worth making here. When Hume says that will is controlled by the passions, this is just another way of his saying that will is nothing more than our being conscious of the passion causing our actions. It is therefore hardly surprising that he says that reason cannot be a motive or direct the will. It is also clear that Hume means this to be an empirical thesis which anyone can confirm by introspection and which is in principle disconfirmable. Second, Hume's analysis of motives or passions as causes is also a dispositional analysis. Motives or passions for Hume are not simple occurrences.[6] True, he does describe them as impressions and thereby gives the reader the notion that passions as motives are occurrences, but Hume also describes the passions as occurring under certain circumstances, and also as being influenced by general rules. Hence, when fully understood, Hume's analysis of passions is a dispositional analysis. The same can be said of Hume's analysis of belief.[7]

The Newtonian program as he conceived of it compels Hume to identify each element of his analysis, and this he does at the risk of making his elements static. But Hume's analysis tends of its own nature to become dispositional. When he discussed belief in the appendix to the *Treatise*, he reasserted that belief is nothing but a peculiar feeling, but at the same time he goes out of his way to say that beliefs are also identifiable because "the *effects* of belief, in influencing the passions and imagination, can all be explained from the firm conception" (T, 626). Hume then compares the belief feeling to the will in saying, "it is only annexed to it [the idea], after the same manner that *will* and *desire* are annexed to particular conceptions of good and pleasure" (T, 625).

What misleads many readers is the presumption that Hume's analysis is phenomenalistic. They forget, ignore, or misunderstand the material foundation of all of Hume's analyses.

Hume reminds us that the passions ultimately depend upon "natural and physical causes," but the "examination of them would lead me too far from my present subject, into the sciences of anatomy and natural philosophy" (T, 275–76). In the *Dissertation of the Passions*, Hume was more explicit in stating that "some objects produce immediately an agreeable sensation by the original structure of our organs"[8] and that in the conflict of passions one can swallow up the other because "the spirits, when once excited, easily receive a change in their direction."[9] Passions as understood and described by Hume are not simple occurrences; they are the conscious counterparts of complicated biological happenings.

The dispositional nature of the passions is also brought out when Hume discusses in a more qualified way how the passions can influence behavior or determine behavior. Sometimes the passion is hardly something of which we are conscious: "There are certain calm desires and tendencies, which, though they be real passions, produce little emotion in the mind, and are more known by their effects than by the immediate feeling or sensation" (T, 417). Moreover, in trying to understand the behavior of an individual person, it is foolish to think that passions have an immediate and unalterable effect on behavior or that information which causes a passion to be operative works in any simple and immediate fashion. The explanation has to be in terms of tendencies because of two factors—the presence of a multiplicity of desires and the character of the person involved, meaning his habits as conditioned over a long period by general rules:

> Men often act knowingly against their interest: For which reason the view of the greatest possible good does not always influence them. Men often counter-act a violent passion in prosecution of their interests and designs: It is not therefore the present uneasiness alone, which determines them. In general we may observe, that both these principles operate on the will; and where they are contrary, that either of them prevails, according to the *general* character or *present* disposition of the person. What we call strength of mind, implies the prevalence of the calm passions above the violent; though we may easily observe, there is no man so constantly possessed of this virtue, as never on any occasion to yield to the sollicitations of passion and desire. From these variations of temper proceeds the great diffi-

culty of deciding concerning the actions and resolutions of men, where there is any contrariety of motives and passions. (T, 418)

The will therefore is controlled by the passions. The passions have their origin ultimately in the physical makeup of human beings. The physical world both in external objects and in the operations of the body is completely controlled by causal relationships. It is in short determined. Hence, the same can be said of the will and the relationship between the passions and human behavior. Determinism applies to human behavior as much as it does to inanimate objects. This application follows from Hume's Newtonian analysis. It is confirmed according to Hume by the introspective technique which allows us to see the constant conjunction of certain passions and the resulting bodily behavior. Whatever philosophical problems exist for determinism on the ontological level, they do not exist for Hume on the human level. Human behavior, he argues, as a matter of empirical observation, is subject to causal laws. Hume also has no trouble in disposing of the specious argument that we do not feel determined or compelled in our behavior. Causal connection or physical necessity depends upon constant conjunction, not some mysterious link. If there is no link in nature or external physical objects and inanimate objects, why should we expect to find this link in human behavior? Again, it is worth noting that Hume's argument is a generalization from what we find in the external world to what we find if we look to the internal world.

It is also a foregone conclusion that reason is not a motive in Hume's system. Having spent most of Book I showing the impotence of demonstrative reasoning and the fact that even causal reasoning depends for its efficacy upon the psychological and biological makeup of men, it is sheer anticlimax for Hume to say that "reason alone can never be a motive to any action of the will; and *secondly*, that it can never oppose passion in the direction of the will" (T, 413). Of course reason is important as a source of information for our passions and as a way of influencing us in the choice of means necessary to achieve a desired end. And in a sense reason can help in the resolution of the conflict among competing ends, but ultimately it is the passions which decide.[10]

There is no way of arguing with Hume on philosophical grounds. His conclusions are the obvious results of his premises, and his premises are based upon an empirical thesis about human nature. The fact that ordinary language might not sanction everything he says or that other philosophical systems are scandalized by his theories is all quite irrelevant. In fact he is quite deliberate about challenging the whole of the tradition of ethics in making these assertions: "Every rational creature, it is said, is obliged to regulate his actions by reason. . . . On this method of thinking the greatest part of moral philosophy, ancient and modern, seems to be founded"; and the purpose of Hume's analysis is "to show the fallacy of all this philosophy" (T, 413).

No doubt Hume's theory raises the specter in the minds of some of no ethics at all, of a world in which each man satisfies his impulses without regard for others. That such a possibility exists is not an argument against Hume's system, since Hume is concerned with the facts, not with justifying any cherished preconceptions. This is why the science of man is such a revolutionary conception of philosophy. If Hume is wrong, then he can only be wrong about the facts.

Hume offers his thesis and then tries to explain in part how others could have mistaken the conflict among passions for a conflict between reason and passion. He claims that such philosophers confuse the operation of reason with the operation of a calm passion. We should recall that at the beginning of his discussion of the passions, Hume noted that passions could be distinguished as either calm or violent, but that this was only a rough distinction. Calmness can refer to the degree of felt strength of a passion. This, however, is not always a sure indication, for the "force of our mental actions in this case, no more than in any other, is not to be measured by the apparent agitation of the mind" (T, 631). Further, Hume has designated the calm impressions as composing the feelings of virtue and vice. These moral feelings are capable of causing the indirect passions. In fact, "*vice* and *virtue* . . . are the most obvious causes of these passions" (T, 295). Finally, "these indirect passions, being always agreeable or uneasy, give in their turn additional force to the direct passions, and increase our desire and aversion to the object" (T, 439). Hence it is clear how in the case of our being influenced by vice and virtue we think that we are being influenced by reason: "When any of these passions are calm, and cause no disorder in the soul, they are readily taken for the determinations of reason, and are supposed to proceed from the same faculty, with that, which judges of truth and falsehood. Their nature and principles have been supposed the same, because their sensations are not evidently different" (T, 417).

There is also the more interesting case of a man taking a long time to decide on a course of action by considering all of the alternatives and carefully calculating the consequences of the alternatives. Still it is true that this deliberation can only terminate when he has worked out the hierarchy of his desires or needs. It is rather easy to think that this is reason at work without passion. Being rational in this case is no different from the kind of care we talked about in connection with those who are wise and careful in their use of reason. In both instances, this kind of care is a result of conditioning and education and wider experience. But when all is said and done, we are animated by our passions.

Hume's ethical theory, as we shall see, is a direct consequence of his theory of motivation. "But it is certain we can naturally no more change our own sentiments, than the motions of the heavens; nor by a single act of our will, that is, by a promise, render any action agreeable or disagreeable, moral or immoral; which, without that act, would have produced contrary impressions, or have been endowed with different qualities. It would be absurd, therefore, to will any new obligation, that is, any new sentiment of pain or pleasure; nor is it possible, that men could naturally fall into so gross an absurdity" (T, 517). Now it should be clear why Hume reduces the will to the operation of the passions and also why the self is not a form of self-consciousness sitting in judgment on the rest of our experience. Hume's ethical theory, as we shall see, is the first fully secular ethical theory in the modern period. This is why, in part, he attacks religion as a foundation for ethics. It is also why he goes back to the classical world to find his models. It may be true as Hume says that reason is the slave of the passions, but it is a Greek slave to passions with a fondness for Roman virtues.[11]

CHAPTER 7

Moral Theory

I *Introduction*

IN chapter 2, I outlined the dominant themes of Hume's philosophy as consisting of an acceptance of common sense, a critique of the rationalist view of man and human reason, a proposal for a science of man in which Newton's rules were taken as the model of that science, and the consequent important relation between logic and psychology. If this overall view is correct and if the intervening chapters have been plausible as an interpretation of other elements of Hume's philosophy, then what might we anticipate will be the nature of Hume's moral theory?

First, we should expect Hume to accept the common sense notions about morality, that is, the reality and significance of moral distinctions and the common list of what constitutes right conduct and what constitutes wrong conduct. Hume does just exactly that. What he will be concerned about is not the correctness of routine practice but how we are to understand and explain common sense views of morality. Just as he pointed out in Book I that the vulgar are correct but unsophisticated, so we should expect the same view to be given in Book III. At the same time, Hume was very critical of alternative philosophical accounts of common sense beliefs, and his major objection to such accounts is that they utterly fail to explain how common sense views can actually influence practice. Thus we should expect a critique of alternative philosophical accounts of morals based on the charge that they fail to account for the influence of common sense moral beliefs on our actual behavior.

The critique of alternative philosophical accounts chiefly

means a critique of the rationalist view. I have tended mainly to identify the rationalist view with the Cartesian or Platonic tradition; but it is now important to see that, as is so often the case for Hume, the Aristotelian tradition is close to the rationalist view. Despite their important differences, both the rationalist view of discovering a priori what the eternal verities are and the Aristotelian view that there is an objective structure—that all structure is objective in the sense of being in the object that is grasped or abstracted by reason—agree that reason is the key to understanding or accounting for moral distinctions.

Hume's critique of the view that moral distinctions are discovered by reason is twofold. First, he identifies two forms of reason, demonstrative and matter of fact. Demonstrative reason as a source of moral relations is rejected on the grounds that such moral relations are unintelligible and could not influence conduct even if they existed. Common sense demands that moral knowledge have a relationship to conduct. Matter-of-fact reason is also incapable of explicating moral distinctions. This view of reason is Aristotelian in the sense later represented by Thomas Reid, who claimed that it is based on the assumption that there is an objective ethical structure embedded in relationships which are totally independent of man and which human reason can allegedly grasp. Hume rejects the notion that there is an objective ethical structure independent of man. This rejection, of course, does not rule out objectivity.

What Hume offers as an acceptable alternative account is a secularized version of the *via moderna.* Ethical or moral facts are explainable but only as a combination of elements, including not only facts of nature but the presence of human beings. Moral distinctions are not independent of man either in the a priori or Aristotelian senses. The contribution of the knowing and feeling mind must be taken into account. That is why Hume will stress that moral distinctions are analogous to secondary qualities like color. To discover that an action is virtuous or vicious is like discovering that an object is red; that is, it is not an inference to a quality in objects but the perception of a quality, which depends upon the presence of man. Just as objects do not have color when not perceived, so actions do not have moral qualities unless a human being is involved. None of this, of course, implies that facts, reason, and objectivity are irrelevant.

The denial of the existence of a priori or of Aristotelian objective moral entities leads to the denial of moral laws in the old sense as holding in all times and places. One may make generalizations, but such generalizations are reflections of human experience, not the revelation of eternal rules. The seemingly vague generalizations of common sense can be explained but at another level. The denial of such moral relations and especially of objective moral entities is similar to Hume's denial of essences.

The mention of treating moral distinctions as secondary qualities brings us to the third factor in Hume's philosophy, the science of man. Science is understood by Hume in the Newtonian sense; and Hume is quick to remind us of the analogy between his analysis of moral distinctions and the new science: "this discovery in morals, like that other in physics, is to be regarded as a considerable advancement of the speculative sciences" (T, 469). Once more we understand why man is the center of the sciences.

If Hume follows his Newtonian program, then we should expect him first to isolate or identify the elements of his analysis. This is what he does in Part I of Book III. That is, he describes the moral sentiments. Next, he should seek to study the causes or general principles which explain the interactions among moral sentiments and other entities. This, too, is what Hume does, and thus it is not surprising that moral sentiments are embodied in our common sense decisions but explainable only on the model of the transfer of vivacity as exemplified in the process of sympathy. Sympathy, we should recall, is a form of attraction.

The final element is the relation of logic and psychology. The Aristotelian and rationalist view of science and explanation is demonstration from first principles, a shared view independent of disagreements about where those first principles are obtained. Thus it is part of the classic view that ethical statements can ultimately be understood only as part of a deductive system derived from self-evident ethical axioms, usually expressed by means of the special moral word "ought."

A typical moral syllogism is the following:

(a) If I promise to do something, then I ought to do it.
(b) I promised to return the book.
(c) Therefore, I ought to return the book.

Presumably the moral axioms are all like (a) above. Hume has consistently rejected the notion that all explanation must be of this demonstrative kind. On the contrary, an adequate explanation for Hume can be nothing but the widest empirical generalization we can discover in human experience. Hence the logic of moral statements does not proceed from self-evident, moral "ought" statements but from empirical generalizations about how people actually behave. For Hume, all moral statements are derivable from statements about human psychological makeup.

Hume begins Book III of the *Treatise* by stressing the continuity of his moral theory with his philosophy as a whole: "the present system of philosophy will acquire new force as it advances; and . . . our reasonings concerning *morals* will corroborate whatever has been said concerning the *understanding* and the *passions*" (T, 455).

II *Moral Sentiment*

The question as posed by Hume is, "*Whether it is by means of our* ideas *or* impressions *we distinguish between vice and virtue, and pronounce an action blameable or praiseworthy?*" (T, 456). There are two issues. First, there is the issue of distinguishing, which means recognizing or perceiving, vice and virtue. Second, there is the issue of our pronouncements, meaning our moral judgments. So the first question is whether the perception of a moral distinction is the perception of an idea or an impression. The second question is whether moral judgments refer to ideas or to impressions. Thus, it is important to distinguish between Hume's remarks about moral sentiments or perceptions and his remarks about moral judgments, which, as we shall see, are reports about moral sentiments. Failure to make this distinction will make a shambles of any interpretation of Hume's moral theory. It is obvious that Hume makes this distinction at the very beginning of his discussion. Moreover, it should be clear that if there is such a thing as a moral impression, then there obviously must be a moral idea, since every impression causes its corresponding idea. It also follows that if there are meaningful moral ideas, they must either have a preceding impression or be a relation among ideas. Thus it sounds rather odd for Hume to ask if moral distinctions or perceptions are either ideas or impressions.

It is odd only until we realize the context in which Hume is operating. Recall Hume's standing antagonism to rationalist systems of anything, to pretentious philosophical claims for what reason can do, and recall how in his discussion of the passions, Hume announces the major theme of his moral theory: "Nothing is more usual in philosophy, and even in common life, than to talk of the combat of passion and reason, to give the preference to reason, and to assert that men are only so far virtuous as they conform themselves to its dictates. . . . On this method of thinking the greatest part of moral philosophy, ancient and modern, seems to be founded"; it is Hume's purpose "to show the fallacy of all this philosophy" (T, 413). If moral distinctions are the product of the activities of reason, then in Hume's technical language moral distinctions must be ideas, for reason is concerned only with ideas.

Hume proceeds to argue that moral distinctions are not derived from reason. As we have already seen in Book I and Book II of the *Treatise*, ideas cannot influence behavior unless they are converted into impressions. Moral distinctions are supposed to influence behavior. Therefore, moral distinctions must be impressions. Hence, moral distinctions cannot be ideas. There may be moral ideas, but moral ideas are not moral distinctions. Such moral ideas can become moral distinctions only by being converted into impressions through some process of vivacity transfer.

Some philosophers had argued that moral distinctions are discovered by reason, specifically, the same sort of intellectual activity involved in demonstrative reason. In short, they believed in self-evident and self-certifying moral axioms. Hume argues in rebuttal that demonstrative reason is concerned with the comparison of ideas, and the comparison of ideas produces demonstrative relations in four cases: "there remain only four, which depending solely upon ideas, can be the objects of knowledge and certainty. These four are *resemblance, contrariety, degrees in quality, and proportions in quantity or number*" (T, 70). In Book III, Hume challenges philosophers who would introduce a concept of moral relations comparable to these four: "There has been an opinion very industriously propagated by certain philosophers, that morality is susceptible of demonstration. . . . Upon this supposition, vice and virtue must consist in some relations. . . . Point out distinctly the relations which constitute morality or obligation. . . . If you assert, that vice and virtue consist in relations susceptible of certainty and demonstration, you must confine yourself to those *four* relations, which alone admit of that degree of evidence; and in that case you run into absurdities, from which you will never be able to extricate yourself" (T, 463). His two arguments against moral relations or a *new* moral relation are, first, that the moral relation is unintelligible; second, such relations would be applicable to animals and inanimate objects. As an example, Hume notes that an oak tree drops a seed from which a second oak tree springs. The first oak is the parent of the second oak. If the new tree grows taller than the parent tree and overshadows it, it robs the parent of sunlight and causes its death. This relation is no different from that of a child who murders its parent. Yet we blame the child but not the tree. It matters not that the tree is insensible of the relation, for as an objective state of affairs the relation or duty holds even if no one is aware of it.

Moral distinctions are not derived from causal reasoning either. This is a rebuttal of the Aristotelian view. Since Hume insists that there are two and only two kinds of reasoning, "nor is there any third operation of the understanding" (T, 463), he must show that causal reasoning is also no source of moral distinctions, in other words, that moral distinctions are not solely properties of objects. This function should not be confused with our ability to make causal inferences about moral distinctions. Hume is talking about what goes on when we directly perceive a moral situation.

Since it is clear that moral distinctions are not ideas, they must be impressions. Hence moral distinctions are derived from a kind of moral sense. Hume goes on to compare moral distinctions to secondary qualities; that is, moral distinctions are not objective properties of bodies but properties which exist because of the interaction of human beings with such bodies. In this respect a moral distinction is like the perception of a color. Bodies are not green in themselves; rather greenness results from a body interacting with an animate being having a nervous system. It is also clear that when we see a body as green, we are not perceiving a relation of ideas and we are not inferring it to be green; rather we have a direct impression of its greenness. Of course, we can infer a color if the body is not directly visible, but such inference is not what Hume means here by a moral distinction. Just as Hume emphasized the dependence of our knowledge on the activities of the knower in logic, so the same point can be made in moral theory. And just as nature manages somehow to establish some sort of harmony in the logical world, so the same sort of harmony seems to operate according to Hume in the moral world: "Vice and virtue, therefore, may be compared to sounds, colors, heat and cold, which according to modern philosophy, are not qualities in objects, but perceptions in the mind: And this discovery in morals, like that other in physics, is to be regarded as a considerable advancement of the speculative sciences; though, like that too, it has little or no influence on practice. Nothing can be more real, or concern us more, than our own sentiments of pleasure and uneasiness; and if these be favorable to virtue, and unfavorable to vice, no more can be requisite to the regulation of our conduct and behavior" (T, 469).

If moral distinctions are impressions, then the only remaining job is to describe the circumstances which distinguish these impressions from others. First, the impression of virtue is pleasurable or agreeable, and the impression of vice is painful or uneasy. Second, moral impressions can only be caused by the actions of human beings, not by animals or inanimate objects. Third, moral impressions are involved only when viewed from the social or general point of view. According to Hume, "It is only when a character is considered in general, without reference to our particular interest, that it causes such a feeling or sentiment, as denominates it morally good or evil" (T, 472). Finally, Hume notes that the sentiments of virtue and vice, as he has already shown in Book II, are causes themselves of the indirect passions of pride and humility, love and hatred. This explanation reveals, of course, how moral sentiments can influence behavior.

It is now time for Hume to apply the Newtonian rules of simplicity and universality. The remaining question is, what is the general principle of morals? *"From what principles is it derived, and whence does it arise in the human mind?"* (T, 473). Hume proceeds to make a list of the virtues, divide them into natural and artificial, and then seek the general principle which explains why we consider them to be virtues.

In giving his analysis of one artificial virtue, justice, Hume makes an all-important distinction between the original nonmoral motive for performing a virtuous act and the growth of a later moral motive. The natural obligation to perform an act is the original nonmoral motive for behaving in a certain way. In the case of the artificial virtues (which include justice, allegiance, the laws of nations, and chastity) the original nonmoral motive, and therefore the natural obligation, is self-interest. In time we come to perform an act from a purely moral motive, that is, with sole consideration of its being either virtuous or vicious. In the latter instance, of course, we refrain from an act. This choice leads to the question of why we come in time to attribute a moral obligation to justice and all of the artificial virtues.

According to Hume, we attribute a moral obligation to justice and the other artificial virtues because of a sympathy with the public interest:

> We never fail to observe the prejudice we receive, either mediately or immediately, from the injustice of others; as not being in that case either blinded by passion, or bypassed by any contrary temptation. Nay when the injustice is so distant from us, as no way to affect our interest, it still displeases us; because we consider it as prejudicial to human society, and pernicious to every one that approaches the person guilty of it. We partake of their uneasiness by *sympathy*; and as everything which gives uneasiness in human actions, upon the general survey, is called Vice, and whatever produces satisfaction, in the same manner, is denominated Virtue; this is the reason why the sense of moral good and evil follows upon justice and injustice. And though this sense, in the present case, be derived only from contemplating the actions of others, yet we fail not to extend it even to our own actions. The *general rule* reaches beyond those instances, from which it arose; while at the same time we naturally *sympathize* with others in the sentiments they entertain of us. *Thus self-interest is the original motive to the* establishment *of justice: but a* sympathy *with public interest is the source of the* moral approbation, *which attends that virtue*. (T, 499–500)

The foregoing is not only Hume's explanation of the general principle of morals but it also constitutes Hume's theory of moral obligation. The fact that Hume has a theory of moral obligation is plain enough, and it is clear that it depends upon sympathy. Those who fail to note the existence of such a theory have also failed to note the extreme importance of sympathy in Hume's moral theory. Hume's theory of moral obligation is totally naturalistic and follows from his psychological theory as he developed it in Book II of the *Treatise*. To disagree with Hume's theory or to find it inadequate requires that a challenge be directed to the accuracy of his psychological theory of man. Interestingly, there is no way to do this without engaging in psychological analysis. This constitutes, I contend, an incontrovertible argument for the crucial role of psychological theory in any ethical theory. To contend that there is somehow a fundamental fact of moral responsibility or that obligation in the moral sense is independent of human nature is to invoke that moral theory of relations which Hume went to such pains to refute.[1]

In Part III of Book III, Hume discusses the natural virtues and vices, and, in keeping with the methodological rules of universality and simplicity, he finds that sympathy also produces the sentiment of morals in these cases.

III *Moral Judgment*

So far we have been primarily concerned with Hume's theory of moral sentiment. It is now time to turn to Hume's theory of moral judgment. For Hume, a moral judgment is of the form "x is virtuous," where x may be replaced by the name of a human action; "virtuous" is the moral predicate and it refers to a moral sentiment. The relation of the moral sentiment to the moral judgment is thus confirmatory.[2]

We may begin by distinguishing between an experience and the description of that experience. There is one property which descriptions have that original experiences cannot have, and that is truth value. Descriptions may be true or false; experiences can be neither. Descriptions (judgments, statements, sentences, propositions) are true if they accurately portray the experience. The representational aspect of a description is therefore crucial. Descriptions imply a reference to standard conditions; they are capable of confirmation or disconfirmation; and they constitute knowledge. These distinctions may be formulated within Hume's theory as the distinction between impressions and ideas. Impressions are original existences or experiences, and therefore neither true nor false. Ideas represent impressions; they are the copy, so to speak. That is why it was so important to stress at the beginning of this book that the representational aspect of ideas is what counts as a specific difference, not vivacity, although the latter is important for other reasons. This is also why Hume criticizes Locke's misleading use of the term "idea" as being too broad. Further, ideas form judgments in Hume's theory, and as he says, we frequently use words instead of ideas. Finally, all judgments involve reference to standard conditions and to confirmation.

The same distinction can be made within Hume's moral theory. Moral distinctions (or moral sentiments) are impressions. Impressions are nonreferential and therefore neither true nor false. For every impression, there is a corresponding idea. Hence there is a moral idea. If there are moral ideas, then there must be moral judgments. Such judgments must be either true or false, made under standard conditions, and capable of confirmation or disconfirmation. Hume does speak about moral ideas. He raises the question of "*why we annex the idea of virtue to justice, and of vice to injustice*" (T, 498). Further, as we have seen, virtue and vice as ideas are causes of the indirect passions of pride and humility, which require such an idea according to Hume's double association theory of ideas and impressions.

When we observe something directly, we do not make judgments about it or reason about it; we just see it. On the other hand, in the absence of the experience we do make judgments or have ideas about it. In moral judgments, Hume claims that we make judgments about the tendencies of actions to produce moral qualities: "Moral good and evil are certainly distinguished by our *sentiments*, not by *reason*: But these sentiments may arise either from the mere species or appearance of characters and passions, or from reflections on their tendency to the happiness of mankind, and of particular persons. My opinion is, that both these causes are intermixed in our judgments of morals. . . . Though I am also of opinion, that reflections on the tendencies of actions have by far the greatest influence, and determine all the great lines of our duty" (T, 589–90). Moral judgments are for the most part causal judgments. "Wherever an object has a tendency to produce pleasure in the possessor, or in other words, is the proper *cause* of pleasure, it is sure to please the spectator, by a delicate sympathy with the possessor" (T, 576–77).

In all perceptual judgments it is necessary to specify standard conditions to insure confirmation and the communication of information through the uniformity of perspective. Moral judgments are no exception, claims Hume:

> In general, all sentiments of blame or praise are variable, according to our situation of nearness or remoteness. . . . But these variations we regard not in our general decisions, but still apply the terms expressive of our liking or dislike, in the same manner, as if we remained in one point of view. Experience soon teaches us this method of correcting our sentiments, or at least, of correcting our language, where the sentiments are more stubborn and inalterable. . . . Such corrections are common with regard to all the senses; and indeed it were impossible we could ever make use of language, or communicate our sentiments to one another, did we not correct the momentary appearances of things. (T, 582)

It should also be obvious that moral judgments may be inferred from nonmoral judgments describing the circumstances under which moral qualities occur. This in fact is just what Hume's whole analysis of morals is designed to show.

There is one important property worth noting. As we have shown, reason for Hume can never be a motive to any action. Therefore, no judgment can of itself motivate us. This would be true of moral judgments as of any other. That is why Hume is so careful to say that it is "morals" which "excite passions, and produce or prevent actions" (T, 457). That is, it is the moral sentiment which produces the passion. However, Hume does add that reason can influence action in two indirect ways: "Either when it excites a passion by informing us of the existence of something which is a proper object of it; or when it discovers the connection of causes and effects, so as to afford us means of exerting any passion" (T, 459). If this influence is so, then there should be an analogous way in which moral judgments can guide behavior.

The analogue is provided for in Hume's theory by sympathy. The predicate of a moral judgment is an idea. A moral sentiment is an impression. The transition from the moral idea to the moral impression must be accounted for if the belief in moral judgments is to result in action. The transition from the moral judgment to the moral sentiment is accomplished through sympathy. "The bare opinion of another, especially when enforced with passion, will cause an idea of good or evil to have an influence upon us, which would otherwise have been entirely neglected. This proceeds from the principle of sympathy or communication; and sympathy, as I have already observed, is nothing but the conversion of an idea into an impression by the force of imagination" (T, 427). Sympathy is a form of causal inference. In sympathetic inference we begin with an idea of someone's condition; next we infer through causation the existence of some affection; finally, the inferred idea of this affection is converted into the very impression it represents. Analogously, there are three stages in which we come to believe a causal inference. First, an object is present to the memory or senses; second, by the force of custom we infer a commonly associated object; finally, such a conception is attended by the belief feeling. The belief feeling, of course, is what influences action. Sympathy operates for moral judgment in precisely the same manner as belief operates for the other judgments of the understanding. Now I think we can at least appreciate what Hume meant when he said "that our reasonings concerning *morals* will corroborate whatever has been said concerning the *understanding* and the *passions*" (T, 455).

There are a host of misunderstandings which surround Hume's moral theory, but interestingly enough almost all of them involve the same error of taking what Hume says about moral sentiment and assuming that he meant it to apply to moral judgments. There are endless interpretations of Hume depending upon which particular statement is focused upon. Since I have documented these elsewhere,[3] I shall choose just one. Hume says "passions, volitions, and actions, are . . . original facts. . . . It is impossible, therefore, they can be pronounced either true or false, and be either contrary or comformable to reason" (T, 458). This has been interpreted by one commentator as evidence for the assertion that Hume does not believe that moral judgments can be either true or false.[4]

Finally, it is worth noting that Hume is not a strict utilitarian. First, he denies that approval is always based upon utility: "there is another set of mental qualities, which, without any utility or any tendency to farther good, either of the community or of the possessor, diffuse a satisfaction on the beholders" (EPM, 250). Second, certain qualities are good not simply because they are useful but because utility causes us to have the moral sentiment. The moral sense explains why utility pleases.

IV *Hume's Rejection of 'Ought' as a Moral Category*

Nothing in Hume's moral theory has attracted more attention among moral philosophers of late than his famous is-ought passage. This is natural in view of the fact that one of the most persistent issues of contemporary moral theory is the possibility of inferring moral judgments from factual nonmoral judgments. Another way of stating this issue is to inquire into the possibility of inferring "ought-judgments" from "is-judgments." It is generally thought that the first person to deny the possibility of this inference was David Hume.[5] The denial is supposed to be articulated in the last paragraph of the section of *A Treatise of Human Nature* entitled "Moral Distinctions not derived from Reason." Hereafter I shall refer to this paragraph, the "is-ought paragraph," as (I-O). My purpose is to show that in (I-O) Hume makes no such denial, and to outline the implications of this revelation.

The complete text of (I-0) follows:

> I cannot forbear adding to these reasonings an observation which may, perhaps, be found of some importance. In every system of morality, which I have hitherto met with, I have always remarked, that the author proceeds for some time in the ordinary way of reasoning, and establishes the being of a God, or makes observations concerning human affairs; when of a sudden I am suprised to find, that instead of the usual copulations of propositions, *is*, and *is not*, I meet with no proposition that is not connected with an *ought*, or

an *ought not.* This change is imperceptible; but is, however, of the last consequence. For as this *ought,* or *ought not,* expresses some new relation or affirmation, it is necessary that it should be observed and explained; and at the same time that a reason should be given, for what seems altogether inconceivable, how this new relation can be a deduction from others, which are entirely different from it. But as authors do not commonly use this precaution, I shall presume to recommend it to the readers; and am persuaded, that this small attention would subvert all the vulgar systems of morality, and let us see, that the distinction of vice and virtue is not founded merely on the relations of objects, nor is perceived by reason. (T, 469–70)

Hume says four things about "ought." First, he says it is a relation; second, he specifically calls it a new relation; third, he asks that this relation be observed and explained; finally, he requests an explanation for the deduction of this new relation from "others," which presumably stands for other relations. The other relations, Hume claims, are entirely different from "ought." The nature of "others" is thus crucial for explaining "ought."

What does Hume mean when he says that other moral theorists make "ought" a relation? According to Hume, all mental activities are perceptions. Perceptions are of two kinds, impressions and ideas. This distinction gives rise to the question: are moral distinctions or perceptions of virtue and vice impressions or ideas (T, 458)? If moral distinctions are ideas, then moral distinctions are derived from, or are, objects of reason. Reason is of two kinds: comparing ideas (relations of ideas) and inferring matter of fact (T, 463). Thus, when Hume speaks of "ought" as a relation, he is considering the view that moral distinctions are perceived as relations of ideas.

Hume asserts that "there has been an opinion very industriously propagated by certain philosophers, that morality is susceptible of demonstration" (T, 463). Here Hume probably is referring to Locke and other members of the English tradition of rational morality such as Clarke, Cudworth, and Wollaston. If morality is demonstrable then moral distinctions are relations of ideas (T, 463). This follows from the fact that demonstrative reason discovers only relations of ideas.

Demonstrative reason discovers only relations. But that reason, according to this hypothesis, discovers also vice and virtue. These moral qualities, therefore, must be relations. When we blame any action, in any situation, the whole complicated object, of action and situation, must form certain relations, wherein the essence of vice consists. This hypothesis is not otherwise intelligible. (T, 464)

Hume raises two objections to the view that moral distinctions are perceived as relations of ideas. First, these relations are never specified so as to be intelligible or to exclude absurd cases such as animals or inanimate objects; second, relations are not obligatory, that is, "no relation can ever alone produce any action" (T, 466).

Hume eliminates two suggested relations. First, rightness as a relation of actions to eternal laws of fitness is eliminated because of the first and second objections. So long as the relation is independent of human perception it is also applicable to the behavior of animals. One counterargument is that animals do not have the reason to see the moral turpitude but that "man, being endowed with that faculty, which *ought* to restrain him to his duty, the same action instantly becomes criminal to him" (T, 467). This second suggested relation of "ought" is eliminated by Hume on the grounds that the relation must exist independently of reason, which can only find the relation and never produce it. Animals are still guilty even if they do not know it. Applicability to animals is a "decisive" argument against moral relations (T, 468).

Hume specifically denies that moral distinctions are relations of resemblance, contrariety, degree of quality, or proportion in quantity and number (T, 464). Earlier in the *Treatise,* Hume had referred to these same four relations as the objects of science (T, 70, 73). In the paragraph preceding (I-O), he says "morality consists not in any relations which are the objects of science" (T, 468).

He further argues against the possibility of treating "ought" as a special or "new" relation. If "ought" were a new relation, it would have to be experienced in some way, as any concept must be in Hume's epistemology. No such experience seems likely, says Hume:

Should it be asserted, that the sense of morality consists in the

> discovery of some relation, distinct from these [four relations of science], and that our [Hume's] enumeration was not compleat, when we comprehended all demonstrable relations under four general heads: To this I know not what to reply, till some one be so good as to point out to me this new relation. It is impossible to refute a system, which has never yet been explained. (T, 464)

What does Hume require of this new relation? He requests that it be "pointed out" and "explained." What did Hume require in (I-O)? He requested that the new relation of "ought" be "observed" and "explained." Obviously, (I-O) simply repeats the same argument.

Hume's repetition of the same argument in the *Enquiry Concerning the Principles of Morals* is even clearer. Those who speak of "moral relations" are confused. They cannot specify the relation, and when they compare moral relations to the relations of science, they involve themselves in absurdities (EPM, 288). Moral relations cannot be deduced from, or made analogous to, contrariety or any of the relations of science.

Earlier, I called attention to the fact that the nature of "others" was crucial for explaining "ought." I take "others" to mean other relations, namely, the four relations of science. Hume is denying that "ought" is demonstrable in the way that the relations of science are demonstrable, and he is denying that we can deduce "ought" from contrariety or from any of the other relations of science.

Other interpreters have assumed that "others" refers to "is" and that Hume is discussing the deduction of "ought" from "is." What gives most plausibility to this view is a statement from the previous paragraph that "vice and virtue are not matters of fact, whose existence we can infer by reason" (T, 468). This statement has been misinterpreted to mean that moral distinctions are not matters of fact. Hume does not deny that moral distinctions are facts; he insists that they are facts. "It [morality] consists not in any *matter of fact*, which can be discovered by the understanding. . . . Here is a matter of fact; but 'tis the object of feeling, not of reason" (T, 468–69).

The important word in this context is "discover." If we directly perceive fire, then we may infer the existence of heat even if we do not now feel the heat. The inference is valid if we can confirm the existence of the heat at a later time by direct observation. It is the actual perceptual confirmation that Hume calls a discovery.[6]

We discover moral distinctions in the same way that we discover that tomatoes are red, that fire is hot, and that snow is cold. We discover moral distinctions as directly perceived secondary qualities. Of course, this in no way implies that moral distinctions are not inferable from other elements when the distinction is not itself present for direct inspection.

In the last sentence of (I-O), Hume arrives at three conclusions. However, in order to understand this part of (I-O), we must recall Hume's earlier discussion of the dispute between the vulgar and the philosophers (T, 192–93). The vulgar believe in the continued and distinct existence of the immediate objects of perception. The philosophers distinguish between perceptions and objects and also seek to infer the object from the perception by means of a cause-and-effect inference.

Hume rejects that part of the vulgar view which attributes a distinct and continued existence to our perceptions, but he admits that the attitude of the vulgar by which we identify our perceptions with objects is inevitable and that we must accept it in practice (T, 214). Hume also accepts the philosophers' contention that perceptions are dependent "upon the mind," but he denies the philosophers' contention that we infer objects from perceptions.

How does the dispute between the vulgar and the philosophers affect Hume's moral theory? First, the rejection of "ought" subverts the vulgar systems of morality. The vulgar believe that we have an immediate perception of independent and continuously existing objects. Moral relations, if they existed and if they formed a system of eternal rational measures of right and wrong, would have to be independent of human perception. Such relations would then apply to animals and to inanimate objects. Applicability to nonhuman objects is a decisive argument against moral relations. Consequently, the same argument would undermine the vulgar moral theory that there are moral objects existing independent of human perception.

The foregoing interpretation of the "vulgar systems of morality" is compatible with Hume's general epistemology, with what he says in the remainder of the section of the *Treatise* with which we are dealing, and with the immediately preceding paragraph where Hume reintroduces the dispute between the vulgar and the philosophers by mentioning the "modern philosophy."[7] Here he is not using the term "vulgar" in a purely pejorative sense, since he, too, accepts a version of the vulgar view.[8]

The second and third conclusions of the last sentence of (I-O) are even more obvious than the first. If Hume denies that we can explain moral distinctions in terms of relations of ideas, then vice and virtue are not relations. Having shown that an immediate moral perception is not a matter-of-fact inference to a mysterious quality and that there is no incomprehensible demonstrative moral relation (see T, 476) and having defined reason as either demonstrative or matter-of-fact inference, Hume concludes that moral distinctions are not "perceived by reason." This is simply the conclusion to a section whose very title is almost a *verbatim* repetition, "Moral Distinctions not derived from Reason."

All previous moral theories, claims Hume, attempt to explain moral distinctions as relations of ideas perceived by reason. These moral relations are not descriptions of impressions, that is, "is" judgments, as Hume would have it; rather, they are examples of a "new relation" of "ought." Hume challenges the introduction of this "ought" relation on the grounds that it is never observed, it is never explained without covering absurd cases, and it is not like any of the relations that are capable of deduction, namely, the relations of science. The conclusion Hume reaches is that "ought" is to be rejected as a moral category.

The denial of "ought" as a moral category is a serious business. Rather than accept such a drastic conclusion as Hume's meaning, we might look for other interpretations. Perhaps Hume wishes only to dramatize for us the necessity of deriving "ought" from "is." We should, therefore, look for a special kind of inference from facts to moral concepts.[9] The search for a special mode of inference is fruitless. Aside from the previous arguments, which show that Hume is not even discussing the derivation of "ought" from "is," Hume specifically denies any third mode of inference: "As the operations of human understanding divide themselves into two kinds, the comparing of ideas, and the inferring of matter of fact; were virtue discovered by the understanding; it must be an object of one of these operations, nor is there any third operation of the understanding, which can discover it" (T, 463).

We are accustomed to identifying the moral "ought" with obligation, but this practice seems implausible in the case of Hume.[10] Certain curious consequences follow from the identification of "ought" with obligation. If "ought" were equivalent to "is obliged," we would have to show that "is obliged" is a state that cannot be factually described, in order to make moral concepts or judgments inferentially independent of facts. If this cannot be done, then the distinction between "is" and "ought" becomes pointless. For if obligation is a factual state of affairs, then we could make inferences to and from it. Finally, and most important, we would have to show that the moral "ought" is what Hume means when he speaks of obligation.

Hume's treatment of obligation makes such an identification impossible. Being obliged is a state of affairs where we are actually motivated to perform an act (T, 465). To be under an obligation is not to be in a state where we ought to do something, but where we are obliged or actually motivated to perform an act. To have a motive is presumably a state of mind capable of factual analysis.

One might object that Hume really wishes "ought" to be construed as a moral sentiment which as a matter of fact is obligatory. How do we discover that obligations motivate us to perform an act? Hume views the relationship of obligation to action as one of cause and effect: "there is no connexion of cause and effect, such as this [obligation] is supposed to be, which is discoverable otherwise than by experience.... It is only by experience we learn their influence and connexion" (T, 466). Granted that the influence of obligation on action is a matter of cause and effect discovered by experience and supposing that "ought" is a moral distinction or sentiment which is obligatory, we must conclude that "ought" would be discovered by cause-and-effect inferences based upon experience. There is another reason why "ought" cannot be equated with obligation. Obligations are motives. The influencing motives of the will are the passions. Since nothing can oppose one passion except another passion, it makes no sense for any moral philosophy to command passion to obey any other principle. The passions recognize no "ought." According to Hume:

> Every rational creature, it is said, is obliged to regulate his actions by reason; and if any other motive or principle challenge the direction of his conduct, he *ought* to oppose it. . . . On this method of thinking the *greatest part of moral philosophy, ancient and modern,* seems to be founded. . . . In order to show the fallacy of all this philosophy, I shall endeavour to prove first, that reason alone can never be a motive to any action of the will; and secondly, that it can never oppose passion in the direction of the will. (T, 413; italics mine)

The similarity of this paragraph to (I-O) in mentioning "ought" and previous moral theories is strikingly obvious. In short, Hume is rejecting any normative conception of morals.

It is not the word "ought" that Hume objects to but the interpretation of it as a special moral relation. "Ought" has many uses having nothing to do with moral contexts. Finally, as we have seen, if the moral "ought" is equated with obligation then "ought" would be equivalent to a factual state of affairs in Hume's theory.

The widely accepted interpretation of (I-O) is that the paragraph is concerned with the deduction of "ought" from "is." I have shown above that this interpretation is mistaken. One variation of this interpretation is the claim that Hume is denying the inferability of moral judgments from nonmoral judgments. If what I have said above about (I-O) is correct, then this variation is also mistaken.

The variation is also important because it represents an outstanding instance of how Hume's statements about moral sentiments are confused with his statements about moral judgments.[11] It is this confusion which largely accounts for the misinterpretation of (I-O).

That (I-O) is not concerned with moral judgments but with moral sentiments is best seen in two ways. First, the entire section deals with a single problem: the attempt to show that moral distinctions or sentiments are perceived not as relations of ideas but as impressions. Second, the conclusions of (I-O) all deal with the analysis of moral distinctions as impressions.

Since (I-O) concerns moral sentiments and not moral judgments, we may inquire into the cause of the confusion. At least one reason is that the *paragraph is almost always read or quoted in an incomplete manner.*[12] Usually, the last sentence quoted is: "For as this ought . . . how this new relation can be a deduction from others, which are entirely different from it" (T, 469). The part of the paragraph that remains unquoted or unread is the part that shows that the paragraph concerns moral sentiments.

Aside from the confusion of judgment and sentiment, the incomplete quotation can in itself be a source of misinterpretation. Consider the following. Hume tells us that "ought" is a relation. Next he tells us that moral distinctions are not relations. The omission of the latter part may lead a reader away from the obvious conclusion, namely, that "ought" cannot express what we mean by moral distinctions.

Once we accept the view that moral distinctions are impressions, we must also accept the fact that we can make inferences about such distinctions and even infer their existence from accompanying circumstances. Those who would deny this inferability must show that Hume does not give a factual analysis of distinctions or that he implies that such an analysis cannot be given. In the first place, Hume gives a factual, nonmoral analysis of moral distinctions in the following section of the *Treatise* entitled, "Moral Distinctions derived from a moral sense." In the second place, his entire moral theory is directed toward uncovering the principles that will permit the inference in question (T, 473; E, 289).

That Hume does give a factual analysis of moral distinctions is a fact that has not escaped some of those who have misinterpreted (I-O).[13] These readers, however, rest content with the assertion that Hume simply commits the error against which he has argued. I do not think they realize the gravity of the accusation. I have given an interpretation of (I-O) that not only avoids charging Hume with such an obvious blunder, but is also perfectly consistent with the remainder of Hume's moral theory and his philosophy in general.

Hume's rejection of "ought" as a special moral category is

far more revolutionary than his rejection of the traditional concept of causal necessity. The former rejection stands as an unanswered challenge to the whole tradition of normative ethics. It is a challenge because he questions the intelligibility of normative ethical theories. It is unanswered in that there is not a single normative theory of ethics, including contemporary nonnaturalistic theories of ethics, that has ever specified any test by which we could confirm it or disconfirm it. One can no longer chant the refrain that "ought is not deducible from is" because this view presupposes the very thing that is to be proved, and it is the very thing that Hume rejects, namely, the existence of peculiarly normative entities.

In place of a normative conception, Hume holds the view that ethics is an empirical science. If ethics is an empirical science, then no ethical theorist has to explain the particular ethical views of any person or community. Moreover, any linguistic analysis of common ethical usage is as irrelevant to ethical science as a linguistic analysis of astrological concepts is to astronomy.

The above implications could be stated and defended independently of Hume and of (I-O), but our willingness to accept the normative conception of ethics is so deeply embedded that, when someone such as Hume challenges it, we take the challenge as a classic defense. (I-O) is not the foundation of normative ethics but its death warrant. Perhaps the shock value of this revelation will lead us to reconsider what might be the most important issue in twentieth-century moral philosophy.

CHAPTER 8

The Enquiries

IN 1748, Hume published *Philosophical Essays concerning Human Understanding.* The title was changed in 1758 to *Enquiry concerning Human Understanding*, which is how it has been known ever since. Much has been written about the relationship between this so-called first *Enquiry* and the *Treatise.*[1] In order to understand the relationship of this *Enquiry* to the *Treatise* and to Hume's philosophical development, it is necessary to mention two other works written by Hume. The *Enquiry concerning the Principles of Morals* was published in 1751, and the dissertation *Of the Passions* appeared as part of *Four Disserations* in 1757. These three works, together with important additions and deletions, comprise the restatement of the philosophical issues of the *Treatise.* It is my contention that the changes in Hume's outlook and the separation of his earlier work into three separate works as well as the substantive additions and deletions can be explained by difficulties in the *Treatise* itself, along with other information of a less philosophical nature. In order to show the evolution of Hume's thought, at least briefly, I shall begin with the first *Enquiry*. Several questions will be raised but not immediately answered. The answers to these questions can be given by showing the further development of Hume's position in both the second *Enquiry* and the dissertation *Of the Passions*.

I Enquiry concerning Human Understanding

The first *Enquiry* corresponds roughly, but only very roughly, to the first book of the *Treatise*, "Of the Understanding." Nevertheless, as Antony Flew has convincingly shown, the first *Enquiry* must be read as a serious philosophical work in its own right, not as a mere rehash of the *Treatise.* There are two additions to the *Enquiry* of material not previously published, the sections on "Miracles" and "A Particular Providence and of a Future State." Both of these essays are philosophical dynamite, and they go a long way toward clarifying some of the implications of what Hume only hinted at in the *Treatise.* We now know that at least the essay on miracles was originally intended to be a part of the *Treatise* but was withdrawn for reasons which Hume expressed in a letter to Henry Home, the future Lord Kames, in 1737:

> Having a franked letter I was resolved to make use of it; and accordingly enclosed some "Reasonings concerning Miracles", which I once thought of publishing with the rest, but which I am afraid will give too much offence even as the world is disposed at present. . . . I beg of you to show it to nobody, except to Mr. Hamilton, if he pleases; and let me know at your leisure that you have received it, read it, and burnt it. . . . Your thoughts and mine agree with respect to Dr. Butler, and I would be glad to be introduced to him. I am at present castrating my work, that is, cutting off its nobler parts; that is, endeavouring it shall give as little offence as possible, before which I could not pretend to put it in the Doctor's hands. This is a piece of cowardice for which I blame myself, though I believe none of my friends will blame me.

(Butler was an important philosopher in his own right, one who influenced Hume, and Butler was a future Bishop.)

So far it seems clear that what Hume has to say about miracles is consistent with, and perhaps a development of, some of the basic themes of the *Treatise.* It is also worth noting that during the period of time between the publication of the *Treatise* (1739–40) and the publication of the first *Enquiry*, Hume had been denied the Chair of Ethics and Pneumatical Philosophy at the University of Edinburgh, presumably on the grounds of his reputation as an atheist and despite a letter he wrote (which was later made public,) in which he denied the charge. There is thus good reason to believe that Hume felt it was time to take off the kid gloves in his battle with his theological opponents.

There is another kind of addition to the first *Enquiry.* Section VII, "Of Liberty and Necessity," is a rewritten version of Book

II, Part III of the *Treatise*, not a part of Book I. Hume apparently felt that the material of that book had a clear connection with the material of the *Enquiry* which he wanted to emphasize.

If we examine the *Enquiry* beyond the first section, which reasserts the same program of the introduction to the *Treatise*, and the brief reintroduction to the theory of the origin of ideas and the association of ideas, what we find in the rest of the book is the working out in clear unadulterated fashion the implications of the Newtonian analysis of causation. Unencumbered for the most part by Hume's own positive theory of the transfer of vivacity, we see Hume spelling out the arguments against the demonstrative conception of causality, against the notion of a necessary connection among events, against the Lockean argument that we have an internal idea of power—an argument which he develops at much greater length in the *Enquiry* than in the *Treatise*—and finally the theological implications of Newton's conception of causality as Hume understood it. Not content with these implications, Hume draws the further implication that causality as thus understood applies to human behavior as well. The fact that the sections on miracles, all the theological sections of the *Enquiry*, and the section on liberty and necessity are added to the *Enquiry* can thus be explained as Hume's attempt to dramatize, in as clear a fashion as possible, what he understood to be the implications of Newton for philosophy, for theology, and for his new science of man. Even in the *Abstract*, Hume concentrates on the causal argument. Much to his dismay, Hume's *Treatise* and the revolutionary program outlined therein were never appreciated in his lifetime; in fact, they were never understood. Unable to make an impression with his originality, Hume apparently decided to take the one thing his learned readers did think they understood, namely Newton, and give them the shock of their intellectual lives. Probably as an answer to Thomas Reid, who had charged that Hume's negative conclusions about religion were the result of the theory of ideas which Reid claimed Hume had acquired from Locke, the first *Enquiry* is an exercise in showing how theology falls before the Newtonian ax and not before the theory of ideas.

More specifically, in his Newtonian analysis, Hume asserts

that we cannot infer the existence of any object of which we cannot form an idea and that no examination of an effect can lead to an inference about the nature of the cause unless we have also exprienced the cause. This follows from the rejection of the Aristotelian notion that an efficient cause must embody the same essence as the effect. For all we know, there may be a God, but we certainly cannot prove his existence by any causal argument. Hume states:

> I much doubt whether it be possible for a cause to be known only by its effect (as you have all along supposed) or to be of so singular and particular a nature as to have no parallel and no similarity with any other cause or object, that has ever fallen under our observation. It is only when two *species* of objects are found to be constantly conjoined, that we can infer the one from the other; and were an effect presented, which was entirely singular, and could not be comprehended under any known *species*, I do not see, that we could form any conjecture or inference at all concerning its cause. (EHU, 148)

Again, in the section on providence, Hume hammers away at the notion of a final cause and gives us a glimpse of what is to come in the *Dialogues*.

> It must evidently appear contrary to all rules of analogy to reason, from the intentions and projects of men, to those of a Being so different, and so much superior. In human nature, there is a certain experienced coherence of designs and inclinations; so that when, from any fact, we have discovered one intention of any man, it may often be reasonable, from experience, to infer another, and draw a long chain of conclusions concerning his past or future conduct. But this method of reasoning can never have place with regard to a Being, so remote and incomprehensible, who bears much less analogy to any other being in the universe than the sun to a waxed taper, and who discovers himself only by some faint traces or outlines, beyond which we have no authority to ascribe to him any attribute or perfection. (EHU, 146)

Hume's attack on a Newtonian-based theology in the *Enquiry* may be summarized as follows. Since there is no necessity for the original motion, there is no necessity for a first cause. Since there is no formal or final cause, we cannot, even if there really is a God, infer God's properties from his alleged effects, namely, the world. The design argument rests upon the cosmological argument, so that if the latter is unconvincing, the former will be as well. The lack of a formal cause prevents us from drawing any specific conclusions about the nature of the cause if any.

Much has already been said elsewhere about Hume's handling of the question of the existence of miracles.[3] Suffice it to say that Hume's position is quite exasperating to many readers. I think that it, too, can be explained in Newtonian terms. Hume is attempting in that section a kind of philosophical *tour de force.* With his previous arguments Hume has removed the ground from the theologians who also claimed to be Newtonians, and there were many. The only recourse, if Hume's attack is successful, is to fall back on miracles. But miracles contradict design. To believe in order is to disbelieve in miracles. Since there are no two ways about it, Hume's purpose clearly is to show that no self-respecting Newtonian could accept such a contradictory position. One might even speculate that Hume presented the argument against miracles both because he knew the Newtonian theologians would go along and because this made the attack on the arguments for God's properties all the more uncomfortable to the reader. In effect, Hume's challenge is that you cannot have it both ways.

There is a similar ironic element in Hume's examination of the question about man's freedom. Hume argued against the popular Lockean notion that necessity was discoverable by attending to the relation between our will and our bodily movements. Hume's position was that all we could attend to is the constant conjunction. In the section on liberty and necessity Hume considers the popular belief that we are free because we "feel no such connection of the motive and the action" (EHU, 92). Obviously those who offer this argument against determinism had not consulted those who offered the previous Lockean argument in favor of some form of necessary connection. Hume's position remained the same throughout, namely, that there is an observed constant conjunction and this is all we need to justify a belief in determinism. There are also some embarrassing consequences for theism if, as Hume argues, determinism is applicable to human behavior. If God created us as we are, and if we are determined to be wicked, then God is responsible for our wicked behavior. A more naturalistic moral theory offers no embarrassment if determinism is true.

The ironic element in the treatment of freedom explains in part the curious fact that Hume does not really establish that there are causes of our motives, only that our motives cause our behavior. This weaker position is also to be found in the *Treatise.* Hume did believe that our motives are caused by our passions and that our passions have a physiological basis, but this is as far as he cared to discuss the matter.

So much for the additions. What about the deletions? There are deletions only on the assumption that we are considering the first *Enquiry* as a parallel to the first book of the *Treatise.* From that point of view, there are two topics of the *Treatise* not discussed at all in the *Enquiry*, nor for that matter are they discussed in the second *Enquiry* on morals or in the dissertation *Of the Passions.* They are the argument for how the imagination comes to believe in body, the continued and distinct existence of our perceptions through constancy and coherence; and the theory of personal identity. The unanswered questions at this point are, why they do not appear in the first *Enquiry,* and why they do not appear later at all. They do not appear in the first *Enquiry*, in large part, because they are not needed as part of Hume's exposition of the Newtonian analysis of causation. But more of this later.

COMPARISON

	Treatise	*Enquiry*
1.	Introduction	sec. 1, "Different Species of Philosophy"
2.	Book I, Part I, sec. 1	sec. 2, "Origin of Ideas"
3.	Book I, Part I, sec. 4	sec. 3, "Association of Ideas"
	relations	omitted
	Part II, "Space & Time"	omitted
4.	Part III, sec. 1 and 2	sec. 4, "Sceptical Doubts"
	sec. 3 and 4	omitted

5. sec. 6–9	sec. 5, "Sceptical Solutions"
6. sec. 11–13	sec. 6, "Probability" (greatly curtailed)
7. sec. 14	sec. 7, "Necessary Connection"
sec. 15 (rules)	omitted
8. [Book II, Part III, sec. 1–3]	sec. 8, "Liberty and Necessity"
9. Book I, Part III, sec. 16	sec. 9, "Reason of Animals"
	*sec. 10, "Miracles"
	*sec. 11, "Providence and a Future State"
12. Part IV, sec. 1, 2, 4	sec. 12, "Academical or Sceptical Philosophy"
personal identity	omitted
existence of body	(problem raised but not answered as in *Treatise*)

*additions of new material

II Enquiry concerning the Principles of Morals

A comparison of Hume's second *Enquiry* with the third book of the *Treatise*, "Of Morals," reveals some equally interesting changes. First, Hume has jettisoned his idea-impression terminology and theory and speaks instead of moral sentiment. He still invokes the Newtonian program, but he does not employ the frame of reference of his own positive theory as he had presented it in the *Treatise.* Quite possibly the disappearance of the idea-impression terminology can be viewed as Hume's answer to critics like Reid, who charged that Hume's views on morality are the result of the Lockean theory of ideas. If the same conclusions can be presented without the idea-impression theory, then those conclusions will have to be examined on their own merit and not dismissed with a misguided charge about philosophical antecedents.

Second, although Hume restates his theory about the relation of reason to moral sentiment, he presents most of the same arguments of the *Treatise* in a clearer form; he places them in the first appendix rather than at the beginning of his analysis.

Tactically, this is a more effective way of making his case, and he recognized this: "if we can be so happy, in the course of this enquiry, as to discover the true origin of morals, it will then easily appear how far either sentiment or reason enters into all determinations of this nature" (EPM, 173). This second difference is related to the next few differences I shall note. Hume retained the view that no ethical theory can move men unless it is built upon a firm theory of what is crucial to human nature and consistent with determinism. This in no way implies the doom of ethics, for Hume finds that there is a common humanity. Ethical naturalism does not require the priority of self-love. This brings us to the third difference, the apparent influence of Butler's views on Hume's later ethical theory. Bishop Butler had argued quite effectively in the *Analogy of Religion* that the distinction between selfish and benevolent motives is usually misrepresented. To argue that men are benevolent because benevolence gives them a selfish pleasure is to misuse both the concepts of benevolence and of selfishness. To be selfish is to be indifferent, or hostile, to the interests of others. To be benevolent is to be vitally concerned for, and sensitive to, those interests. It may be, and in fact is, true that we have benevolent impulses whose satisfaction gives us pleasure, but this attitude is hardly the same thing as selfishness. Hume adds a special second appendix wherein he discusses self-love and makes these very points in his own way, consistently with his ethical theory.

The fourth and major difference between the second *Enquiry* and Book III of the *Treatise* is Hume's rejection of the sympathy mechanism. I say sympathy mechanism and not sympathy because he still uses the word "sympathy," but he now uses it in a different way and makes it synonymous with the sentiment of humanity, which is the new general principle of morals. In making humanity the general principle of morals, Hume says the following: "everything which contributes to the happiness of society, recommends itself directly to our approbation and good will. Here is a principle which accounts, in great part for the origin of morality: And what need we seek for abstruse and remote systems, when there occurs one so obvious and natural" (EPM, 219). What Hume means is explained in a footnote: "It is needless to push our researches so far as to ask, why we have humanity or a fellow feeling with others" (*ibid.*, n.). In short, there will be no attempt to explain our humanity by reducing it to the sympathy mechanism, and Hume leaves us in no doubt about this:

> It is but a weak subterfuge, when pressed by these facts and arguments, to say, that we transport ourselves, by the force of imagination, into distant ages and countries, and consider the advantage, which we should have reaped from these characters, had we been contemporaries; and had any commerce with the persons. It is not conceivable, how a *real* sentiment or passion can ever arise from a known *imaginary* interest; especially when our *real* interest is still kept in view, and is often acknowledged to be entirely distinct from the imaginary, and even sometimes opposite to it. (EPM, 217)

The foregoing, of course, is a perfect description of the sympathy mechanism in the *Treatise*. There are several reasons, spelled out in this statement above, why Hume rejects it, and the difficulties mentioned became apparent to Hume, as I shall show below, when he wrote the last part of the *Treatise*. One point worth noting here is that the reduction of ethics to human psychology does not require a reduction to self-love. As Butler helped Hume to see, humanity can be just as natural to man as selfishness.

Many commentators have not taken the rejection of sympathy seriously, and their single reason is that Hume recognizes the existence of benevolence even in the *Treatise*.[4] What these commentators have failed to notice is that, although there is a recognition of benevolence in the *Treatise*, Hume has specifically rejected it there as the general principle of morals. In the second *Enquiry* he specifically says that benevolence and humanity may now be the general principle of morals.

You will recall that Hume claims in the *Treatise* that there is no original motive to moral actions, that is, no original moral motive. There is a natural motive which is nonmoral, the so-called natural obligation. This natural obligation is sophisticated self-interest. The moral obligation only develops later and is grafted onto the natural obligation through the process of sympathy. In the second *Enquiry*, Hume is still insisting that there must be an original nonmoral motive, but he no longer invokes the sympathy mechanism. Instead he argues that benevolence corrected by general rules will perform the same function.

In the *Treatise*, Hume considered three candidates for the original nonmoral motive: self-interest, private benevolence, and public benevolence. The kind of self-interest which Hume rejects as the original motive to the performance of just acts is that uncorrected self-interest which, "when it acts at its liberty, instead of engaging us to honest actions, is the source of all injustice and violence" (T, 480). Next, Hume eliminates private or limited benevolence because just acts often conflict with private benevolence or what would benefit only our family and friends. Finally, Hume rejects public benevolence for two reasons. First, public benevolence is "a motive too remote and too sublime to affect the generality of mankind" (T, 481). Second, "there is no such passion in human minds, as the love of mankind, merely as such, independent of personal qualities, of services, or of relation to ourself" (T, 481). The point of this last remark is that love and hatred are indirect passions which require a "double relation of impressions and ideas" in order to be exerted (T, 482). In short, Hume is opting for the sympathy mechanism. Clearly, the sentiment of humanity in the second *Enquiry* is a kind of corrected public benevolence which Hume refuses to reduce via the sympathy mechanism. This is a rather crucial difference.

We can if we like see the rejection of sympathy as due to Hume's now more sophisticated understanding of the relation between selfishness and benevolence. But there is a more important and related answer. Hume's theory of moral judgment requires that all such judgments be socially objective and corrected by general rules. This is a requirement he carefully repeats in the second *Enquiry*. At the same time, being the consistent empiricist he is, Hume insists that the predicates of moral judgments must refer to a sentiment, a moral sentiment. The importance of the sympathy mechanism is that it permitted the inferred moral idea to be converted into the very impression or sentiment it represented. This is why sympathy could be the general principle of morals in the *Treatise*. However, toward the end of the *Treatise*, in considering objections to his theory, Hume recognized the possibility of moral judgments that could not be confirmed, that referred to no real moral sentiment. He concludes: "The intercourse of sentiments, therefore, in society and conversation, makes us form some general inalterable standard, by which we may approve or disapprove of characters and manners. And though the *heart* does not always take part with those general notions, or regulate its love and hatred by them, yet are they sufficient for discourse, and serve all our purposes in company, in the pulpit, on the theatre, and in the schools" (T, 603). I cannot resist the temptation to point out that Hume, the moral philosopher often represented as a subjectivist, as the man who argues for the lack of objectivity in moral judgments, and as the man who reduces such judgments to the expression of personal feelings, is here faced with a choice between objectivity and the existence of the sentiment. His choice is to go along with objectivity.

If we go back to Book II of the *Treatise*, to the original discussion of the sympathy mechanism as it appeared in the treatment of the passions, we can find the source of Hume's difficulty. Sympathy cannot operate to produce the double relation of impressions and ideas when the self is involved. In short, where a conflict of interest exists, the sympathy mechanism cannot work:

> In sympathy our own person is not the object of any passion, nor is there any thing, that fixes our attention on ourselves; as in the present case, where we are supposed to be actuated with pride and humility. Ourself, independent of the perception of every other object, is in reality nothing: For which reason we must turn our view to external objects; and it is natural for us to consider with most attention such as lie contiguous to us, or resemble us. But when self is the object of a passion, it is not natural to quit the consideration of it, till the passion be exhausted; in which case the double relations of impressions and ideas can no longer operate. (T, 340–41)

Such is the reason for the demise of sympathy. We must note one important distinction. It is not necessary in Hume's theory of moral judgment that every judgment we make immediately commit us to action. It is necessary only that the judgment refer to a sentiment which is capable on occasion of committing us to action. The crucial element is the presence of a sentiment under standard conditions. It is no use appealing to the disinterested spectator, since we can only assume his position by sympathy, and if the sympathy mechanism is rendered inoperative we cannot assume the designated perspective. When Hume returns to this theme in the second *Enquiry*, we find that the sentiment of humanity, or extended benevolence, allows for correction by general rules and provides us with a moral sentiment even if only a weak one. Compare the following quotation with the similar statement from the *Treatise* made above: "And though the heart takes not part entirely with those general notions, nor regulates *all* its love and hatred by the universal abstract differences of vice and virtue, without regard to self, or the person with whom we are more intimately connected; yet have these moral differences a considerable influence, and being sufficient, at least for discourse, serve all our purposes in company, in the pulpit, on the theatre, and in the schools" (EPM, 229, italics mine). Notice the recognition of the self as a source of conflict. Notice as well the use of the words "all" and the use of the phrase "considerable influence."

Before discussing how the rejection of sympathy helps to explain the restructuring of Hume's later thought, we should note that such a rejection is also explained by Hume with reference to the Newtonian rules. In the first section of the *Enquiry concerning the Principles of Morals*, Hume reasserts the rules of the experimental method. However, he mentions only the rules of finding "universal principles," the rejection of "hypotheses," and the appeal to "experience" (EPM, 174–75). He does not mention the rule of simplicity which seemed to be mentioned in the *Treatise* almost every time the rule of universality was mentioned. These other rules are referred to throughout the second *Enquiry*. The reason for not mentioning simplicity is that Hume now considers his own first theory of the *Treatise* as unduly simplistic. This rejection of a false simplicity he states in a mild form when discussing humanity as a general enough principle for his immediate purpose in moral theory: "It is not probable, that these principles can be resolved into principles more simple and universal, whatever attempts may have been made to that purpose. But if it were possible, it belongs not to the present subject; and we may here safely consider these principles as original:

happy, if we can render all the consequences sufficiently plain and perspicuous!" (EPM, 220n.). In the appendix on self-love, Hume is much more vehement: "to the most careless observer there appear to be such dispositions as benevolence and generosity. . . . plainly distinguished from those of the selfish passions. And as this is the obvious appearance of things, it must be admitted, till some hypothesis be discovered, which by penetrating deeper into human nature, may prove the former affections to be nothing but modifications of the latter. All attempts of this kind have hitherto proved fruitless, and seem to have proceeded entirely from that love of *simplicity* which has been the source of much false reasoning in philosophy. I shall not here enter into any detail on the present subject. Many able philosophers have shown the insufficiency of these systems" (EPM, 298). One cannot help but think of the *Treatise*.

What are the consequences of the rejection of sympathy for the restructuring of Hume's thought? To reject sympathy is to reject the importance of the communication of vivacity as the connecting link of the three books of the *Treatise*. Without denying the importance of association or the communication of vivacity, it remains that a major reason for presenting all of Hume's views as part of a single work has been lost. More specifically, the rejection of sympathy severs the important connection between Books II and III of the *Treatise*, between Hume's theory of the passions and Hume's moral theory. Aside from sympathy, the major connecting link between the passions and moral theory was the theory of motivation and the subordination of reason to sentiment. Hume has retained this theory, but it now fits into his moral theory as part of the discussion of the relationship between reason and sentiment. The passions are thus no longer needed for the exposition of Hume's moral theory. That is why the theory of the passions can be presented as a separate work, as one of the *Dissertations*. This also explains why the uselessness of vivacity to Hume's new moral theory dispenses with the necessity for employing the idea-impression distinction in the exposition of that theory.

Since the passions no longer serve as the connecting link between the theory of the understanding and the theory of morals, there is also little reason for connecting the treatment of the passions with the treatment of the philosophical issues of the understanding. Hume's ardor for the transfer of vivacity and the consequent importance of the association of ideas has cooled. If there is no important reason to connect the theory of the passions to the understanding, then we may ask if any part of the material in the passions is needed to explain the material in the treatment of the understanding. One such item is the relation between liberty and necessity. Hume found he could extract and integrate this with his treatment of causation. We have already noted this integration in discussing the first *Enquiry*. The second item is the nature of personal identity as it concerns the passions. The treatment of personal identity with regard to the understanding can only be understood, as I maintained earlier, by noting its connection with personal identity as it concerns the passions. To explain the self with regard to the passions would require an exposition of the double association of ideas and impressions, and therefore a large part of the material of the passions. Rather than do that and detract from the clarity of pointing out the implications of the Newtonian analysis of causality, it was easier simply to drop the topic altogether from the first *Enquiry*. Finally, I should note that Hume's discussion of the continued and distinct existence of perceptions, that is, the belief in an external physical world, utilized the now suspect notion of a communication of vivacity. There are other reasons, no doubt, but this use explains again in part why Hume did not include that material in the first *Enquiry*.

If my interpretation is correct, then Hume was perhaps aware of the difficulties by the time he completed the *Treatise* and certainly he must have been before he wrote the first *Enquiry*. There is, in fact, a passage in the very first and introductory section of the *Enquiry concerning Human Understanding* in which Hume seems to suggest that he recognizes the oversimplistic system he had developed in the *Treatise*. The passage is as follows:

> Moralists have hitherto been accustomed, when they considered the vast multitude and diversity of those actions that excite our approbation or dislike, to search for some common principle, on which

this variety of sentiments might depend. And though they have sometimes carried the matter too far, by their passion for some one general principle; it must, however, be confessed, that they are excusable in expecting to find some general principles, into which all the vices and virtues were justly to be resolved. . . . Nor have their attempts been wholly unsuccessful; though perhaps longer time, greater accuracy, and more ardent application may bring these sciences still nearer their perfection. (EHU, 15)

Hume himself later expressed a preference for the *Enquiries* over the *Treatise*, and it is true that either one of the *Enquiries* alone would be enough to guarantee Hume's place in the philosophical pantheon. But after all this, it remains that the *Treatise* is his greatest work and one of the greatest of modern philosophy. Like Kant's first *Critique* it did not have to be successful to become a landmark.

CHAPTER 9

Philosophy of Religion: God Without Ethics

HUME'S philosophy of religion is complicated by his personal life and beliefs and the consequent speculation to which this gives rise in his readers. Nevertheless, I believe there is a core position which can be objectively defended. As the saying goes, some of Hume's best friends were clergymen, but he certainly had an antipathy to most clergymen, an antipathy which was no doubt mutual. Hume was also opposed to the organized religion in his time, and he never left any doubt that he believed such religion had pernicious intellectual and moral consequences. It is also clear that Hume did not believe in the traditional personified view of God. Finally, Hume was unrelenting in his attack upon the pretentious intellectual foundations of religion. Still when all is said and done, there is much latitude in what Hume might still believe. I shall describe below what remains, but it might be suggested that what I describe as being left was all pretense and camouflage for a complete atheist. There is no way to really answer this suggestion, but I might say that if it is all pretense, then (a) that pretense remains a consistent position in all of Hume's works, (b) it is pretense which is consistent with Hume's general philosophical outlook, and (c) calling it a pretense does not seem to help in understanding Hume.

I shall begin by summarizing Hume's philosophy of religion in terms of six major theses. Each of these theses will then be discussed in detail, and by exemplifying them in all of Hume's writings from the *Treatise* to the *Dialogues*.

Thesis I. Hume believed in the existence of God.

Thesis II. He rejected the ontological argument.

Thesis III. He accepted in one form the argument from design.

Thesis IV. God exists, but his properties are unknown and unknowable by us.

Thesis V. Morality is independent of religion.

Thesis VI. All of the characters in the *Dialogues* speak for Hume, and the message of the *Dialogues* is that morality is independent of religion.

Thesis I. Hume never denied the existence of God. In none of his writings does Hume say or imply that he does not accept the existence of God. On the contrary, Hume says in several places that he accepts the existence of God. Of course, the God whom Hume accepts is not the traditional Judeo-Christian God, for Hume does not believe that we can know anything about the deity. This God is the God of the philosophers, a kind of principle of order, although we really do not, and probably will never, fully comprehend it. This definition does not say very much, and it is easy to see how one could come to believe that this attitude is just a pose, a polite form of atheism. Yet, it should be remembered that Hume believes in a real order to the universe, and he believes that the natural relation of causation is a built-in instinctual belief in causal relations. It is natural to believe and speculate about a cause of some kind for the universe. If Hume did not, then he would be disconfirming one of his most basic generalizations about the human mind.

Thesis II. Hume objected to the ontological argument. This objection can be found in the *Treatise* (T, 96n.), in a letter which I shall discuss below, and in the *Dialogues* (D, 189–90).

After the publication of his *Treatise*, Hume soon became aware of the fact that his position was being misrepresented. In the political maneuvering to deny Hume the chair of Moral Philosophy at the University of Edinburgh, the opposition accused him of atheism by referring to his alleged denial of causation (so necessary for the design argument) and to his rejection of the "ontological argument." Hume, in a letter of rebuttal,[1] admitted his rejection of the "ontological argument" ("*metaphysical* Argument *a priori*"), but he also reaffirmed his acceptance of causation. Moreover, he strongly reasserted his acceptance of the argument from design ("Arguments *a posteriori* from the Order and Course of Nature"). This brings us to Thesis III.

Thesis III. Hume accepts God's existence, and he accepts as legitimate the argument from design. This thesis brings such a shocked reaction, even from serious Hume scholars, that a prefatory note would seem to be in order. To begin with, there is no context in which Hume ever challenges the argument from design. None of his interpreters ever documents the claim that Hume rejects the argument from design. Second, and more important, there are many contexts in which Hume explicitly embraces the argument from design.

(a) "The order of the universe proves an omnipotent mind . . ." (T, 633n.).

(b) "Wherever I see order, I infer from experience that *there*, there hath been Design and Contrivance . . . the same principle obliges me to infer an infinitely perfect Architect from the infinite Art and Contrivance which is displayed in the whole fabric of the universe" (L, 25–26).

(c) In the *Enquiry concerning Human Understanding*, Hume's friend, and the spokesman for Epicurus, accepts the argument from "the order of nature" (EHU, 148).

(d) In *The Natural History of Religion*, Hume begins his introduction with the announcement that "the whole frame of nature bespeaks an intelligent author; and no rational enquirer can after serious reflection, suspend his belief a moment with regard to the primary principles of genuine Theism and Religion" (Hendel edition, p. 253).

(e) The *Dialogues* reaffirm the "truth so obvious, so certain, as the *being* of a God" and the acceptance by Philo and Cleanthes of the argument from design (D, 214).

What some readers take as a refutation of the argument from design is really not a refutation at all. Hume makes several points about the argument from design. First, it is a very weak argument by analogy, but a weak analogy is not a violation of the laws of logic. Second, insofar as there is a design argument it fails to accomplish what most proponents of the argument claim for it. The argument will not justify any assertion about the nature of this "cause." On the contrary, as Hume shows so relentlessly in the *Dialogues*, when we draw an analogy at all, the principle of order in the universe cannot be personified and, if it is anything, is more like an impersonal force or principle.

One recurrent issue originally raised by Hume himself is the extent to which we are justified in making any causal inference in a single case of a unique event. Let us recall first that as a natural relation causal inferences are made immediately as an instinctual reaction. That we make such inferences does not justify them, but then neither does it show that such inferences are false. Second, there are legitimate cases where we make causal inferences after one example and such inferences are justified. Such is not the case here, because, in the allowable instance, we see both the alleged cause and the alleged effect. In the design argument we are only aware of the alleged effect. We are naturally led to look for, or to speculate about, a cause, but we are not justified in inferring any specific cause. But once again, no rule is violated if we make no specific claims about the cause.

Thesis IV. Even though God exists, we cannot know any of his properties or characteristics. The argument from design suggests the existence of a cause but not the nature of the cause. It is the failure to note this distinction which leads some readers to misinterpret Hume and attribute to him a rejection of the argument from design.

The difficulties which engross our conception of God are especially noticeable when we deal with the question of God's power and the existence of evil. Hume makes these points in the *Treatise* (T, 159–60, 248, 249, 633 n.), in the *Enquiry concerning Human Understanding* (EHU, 72–73, 103), and throughout the *Dialogues*.

Recognition of this thesis helps to clarify the relation of faith to reason. Hume comes to grips with this problem at the very end of the *Enquiry concerning Human Understanding*.

> Divinity or Theology, as it proves the existence of a Deity, and the immortality of souls, is composed partly of reasonings concerning particular, partly concerning general facts. It has a foundation in *reason*, so far as it is supported by experience. But its best and most solid foundation is *faith* and divine revelation. (EHU, 165)

Hume's position is that reason (in the design argument) leads us to admit the existence of God, but reason can tell us nothing more. To accept a particular religion or religious belief (immortality, for example) beyond the mere belief in God is an act of faith.

Miracles, moreover, do not provide an independent rational basis for accepting any one particular religion. In fact, the belief in miracles is itself an act of faith (EHU, 131). In the *Treatise* (T, 474), Hume had asserted that the Christian religion was founded upon miracles. In the *Enquiry concerning Human Understanding*, he argued that one who accepts the miracles on which the Christian religion is founded does so as a matter of faith and not by an act of reason (EHU, 127, 130).

Thesis V. Hume denied that morality needs an explicit religious foundation. In the *Treatise*, he argued that morality can be explained in a completely naturalistic manner (T, 474). At the same time, he freely admits that the belief in an afterlife of rewards and punishment can reinforce moral behavior (T, 410–11). These very same points are made in the *Enquiry concerning Human Understanding* (EHU, 102–03, 147), where the original title of section XI was "Of the Practical Consequences of Natural Theology." There is a particularly crucial paragraph there which summarizes his entire philosophy of religion.

> The course of nature lies open to my contemplation as well as to theirs. The experienced train of events is the great standard, by which we all regulate our conduct. Nothing else can be appealed to in the field, or in the senate. Nothing else ought ever to be heard of in the school, or in the closet. In vain would our limited understanding break through those boundaries, which are too narrow for our fond imagination. While we argue from the course of nature, and infer a particular intelligent cause, which first bestowed, and still preserves order in the universe, we embrace a principle, which is both uncertain and useless. It is uncertain; because the subject lies entirely beyond the reach of human experience. It is useless; because our knowledge of this cause being derived entirely from the course of nature, we can never, according to the rules of just reasoning, return back from the cause with any new inference, or making additions to the common and experienced course of nature, establish any new principles of conduct and behaviour. (EHU, 142)

In the *Enquiry concerning the Principles of Morals*, Hume develops his entire moral theory with utter disregard for religion. He does make an important statement about God in order to show that his moral theory is compatible with the existence of the God one finds in the argument from design (EPM, 294). Since God is the "cause" of nature, including human nature, the naturalistic ethics to be found in man is also the "effect" of God. The important distinction to be kept in mind is that Hume's ethics is consistent with the existence of his God, but it is not derived from religion.

One interesting sidelight of the *Enquiry concerning the Principles of Morals* occurs in the conclusion. After summarizing his views on the natural basis of the virtues, Hume mentions a rhetorical Cleanthes who possesses all of these virtues. In the next paragraph, Hume notes that the monkish virtues are really vices. These are not idle comments nor is the juxtaposition a coincidence. The Cleanthes of the *Dialogues* also possesses the natural virtues without the monkish vices. Both of these works were largely completed in the same year (1751), although the latter was not published for some years thereafter. As I shall show below, this juxtaposition explains why Cleanthes is the hero of the *Dialogues*.

Hume argued that the attempt to draw practical moral conclusions from religion is dangerous. In the *Treatise*, he said that "the errors in religion are dangerous" (T, 272). In the *Enquiry concerning Human Understanding*, we find the ubiquitous Humean critique of superstition (EHU, 11). The entire work *The Natural History of Religion* is devoted to this point. It may be neatly summarized in the title of section XIV, "Bad Influence of Popular Religions on Morality." The concluding general corollary shows the contrast of the rational belief in a Supreme Being with the irrational practices of religion. With regard to actual religions (but not God), Hume maintains a skeptical posture.

Thesis VI. It is now time to examine the eighteenth century's most outstanding work on the philosophy of religion: Hume's *Dialogues concerning Natural Religion*. We have already seen how Hume upheld his position in this work, specifically, his acceptance of God's existence, his rejection of the "ontological argument," his acceptance through Philo and Cleanthes of the design argument, and his arguments against our ability to know God's personality.

The conclusion of the *Dialogues* is that religion is not the basis of morality. This point is not unique in that we have already seen it in Hume's other works. What is interesting is that all three characters accept this point, that religion is not an independent test of morals and that no practical moral implications can be drawn from religion as such. Philo points out the dangers of such a practice (D, 222–23), while Cleanthes notes the proper limits (reinforcement) of religion:

> The proper office of religion is to regulate the heart of men, humanize their conduct, infuse the spirit of temperance, order, and obedience; and as its operation is silent, and only enforces the motives of morality and justice, it is in danger of being overlooked, and confounded with these other motives. When it distinguishes itself, and acts as a separate principle over men, it has departed from its proper sphere, and has become only a cover to faction and ambition. (D, 220)

Thus, no matter how we come to know God, we cannot legitimately infer moral conclusions from theological premises, and such illegitimate inferences frequently have disastrous social consequences.

The natural question which a reader raises at this point is which character represents Hume. The answer is easy enough to determine. Since Hume has included all of his theses in the *Dialogues*, one need only find which of the characters articulates all of the theses. But a careful reading of the text reveals that no one character articulates all of the theses. Hence, we may conclude that no one character represents Hume's position.

That Hume's position is to be understood in terms of the entire work is evident from two other considerations. First, all of the characters agree that God exists. Second, all of the characters agree that no moral implications follow from the initial agreement.

Ingenious arguments have been devised to identify Hume with one or another of the characters.[2] There is no point in reviewing these arguments since each proponent is able to refute fully the other possibilities without establishing his own.

In any case, both Philo and Cleanthes, the major candidates, support some but not all of Hume's previous philosophical and religious positions. Cleanthes is willing to believe in immortality, and Philo is willing to accept revealed truth. Only by disregarding some of their respective statements can Cleanthes or Philo be identified with Hume. No one can be said to speak for Hume, and no case can be made to prove otherwise without employing question-begging assumptions and *ad hoc* considerations. Finally, these arguments may obscure, but they cannot diminish, the force of the conclusion that God's existence has no moral implications.

Granted that everyone yet no one speaks for Hume, why is Cleanthes the "hero"? Why does Hume go out of his way to present Cleanthes in so favorable a light? The Cleanthes of the *Dialogues* is not unlike the Cleanthes of the *Enquiry concerning the Principles of Morals* who possesses all of the natural virtues and none of the monkish vices. Cleanthes represents the position of the intelligent layman and liberal theologian of Hume's time. It is always to this audience, and to the vulgar, that Hume addresses himself. It was his lifelong ambition to draw their attention to the social danger of inferring moral implications from religious premises. He had failed to do this by emphasizing the skeptical point of view. This is why Philo is refuted. Why not try to show that the same conclusions followed from their own point of view? This is why Cleanthes is the hero.[3]

Hume's philosophy of religion is delineated most clearly in his mythical conversation with Charon (as reported by Adam Smith):[4]

> "Good Charon, I have been correcting my works for a new edition. Allow me a little time, that I may see how the Public receives the alterations." But Charon would answer, "When you have seen the effect of these, you will be for making other alterations. There will be no end of such excuses. . . . " But I might still urge, "Have a little patience, Good Charon, I have been endeavouring to open the eyes of the Public. If I live a few years longer, I may have the satisfaction of seeing the downfall of some of the prevailing systems of superstition." But Charon would then lose all temper and decency. "You loitering rogue, that will not happen these many hundred years. Do you fancy I will grant you a lease for so long a term?"

Hume's challenge may be put concisely. We cannot legitimately infer moral conclusions, that is, practical conclusions for guiding human behavior, from theological premisses. This challenge places in jeopardy one of the major institutions of Western civilization.

The philosophical significance of Hume's challenge is that it separates the question of God's existence from the question of the moral implications of religion. Prior to Hume it was common for philosophers first to "prove" God's existence and then to draw moral implications from that proof. Hume pointed out that these are two separate questions, and the positive answer to the first by no means implies a positive answer to the second. Even if philosophers could present an acceptable proof for God's existence, we could not draw any moral guidance from either the proof or a whole system of theology. In fact, no theological consequences can follow from such a proof. Many serious theologians have long complained of the sterility and inconsequential nature of the philosophical arguments designed to prove God's existence, no matter how ingenious those arguments might be. Hume showed why these complaints were justified.

The major reason for the failure to appreciate Hume's challenge is the traditional approach taken to Hume's writings on religion. Guided by basic misunderstandings of Hume's position on causality or at the very least the negative aspects of Hume's skepticism, most readers assume that the central question is one concerning God's existence. Inevitably, commentators ask whether Hume believed that God exists; hence the concern over which character in the *Dialogues* speaks for Hume. As I have shown, this approach ignores Hume's constant reiterated acceptance of God's existence and the design argument; it ignores the continuity of Hume's position in all of his works; it misrepresents what is important to him; and it overemphasizes the importance of the *Dialogues*. No doubt, the *Dialogues* is a philosophical and literary masterpiece, deserving a special study of its own, but it contains no novelties with respect to Hume's philosophy of religion.

Another reason for the failure to appreciate Hume's challenge is the widespread misconception that Hume argued against the possibility of deriving moral judgments from any nonmoral basis. On this view, Hume's challenge appears superfluous. However, as I have shown elsewhere, Hume did *not* argue for the autonomy of morality. Instead he sought to found morality on his conception of human psychology. It is precisely because he bases morality upon human nature that he divorces morality from the religion of his time.

CHAPTER 10

Skepticism and Hume's Legacy

I *The Myth*

TRADITION has it that David Hume was a disingenuous philosopher, perhaps inspired by the devil, who was motivated only by the desire to achieve notoriety through formulating shocking paradoxes, which had the effect of subverting the basic principles of Western civilization. The foregoing myth has by now been laid to rest, but it has been supplanted by others. To many, Hume is now to be regarded as a preromantic espouser of giving in to feeling in the face of skeptical triumphs. Such a view still maintains that Hume is a serious skeptic, except now we are to view his skepticism as sincere. Most recently, Hume has been viewed as a philosopher profoundly puzzled by serious skeptical arguments with respect to certain issues which he was the first to see clearly, but being unable to solve these logical puzzles Hume settled for explaining away skepticism through psychology.[1] There is an increasing amount of justice in these views, but it is not complete.

Perhaps if we list the skeptical topics in Hume, or those issues about which Hume raised or allegedly raised skeptical objections, we might arrive at a fairer evaluation. The following list constitutes all those areas wherein Hume is supposed to have created a skeptical problem:

1. the reliability of sensory experience
2. the rationality of causal inference (inductive arguments)
3. the meaning of mathematical statements
4. the existence of the self
5. the rationality of moral judgments
6. the existence of God
7. the existence of the external world

With regard to the first issue, the reliability of sensory experience, Hume refutes it in the traditional way: "These sceptical topics, indeed, are only sufficient to prove, that the senses alone are not implicitly to be depended on; but that we must correct their evidence by reason" (EHU, 151). The latter recommendation certainly does not fit the myth. With regard to the second issue, the rationality of causal inference, we have already seen that Hume is not raising the so-called problem of induction. In attacking the Aristotelian notion of a formal cause, Hume is denying that one can construe causal arguments as deductive arguments; and it is not Hume but his opponents who wish to construe all arguments as either deductive or defective. Hume maintains no such position. What Hume offers is a logical refutation of such a dichotomy based upon the assumed truth of Newtonian mechanics. *In addition*, he supplements his logical refutation with a psychological theory to show that we need not worry about men failing to act because men lack absolute logical certainty.

With regard to the third issue, the meaning of mathematical statements, Hume was never satisfied with his own treatment of the issues.[2] He once planned to publish a treatise on *Some Considerations previous to Geometry and Natural Philosophy* but was persuaded by his friend the eminent mathematician Lord Stanhope to withdraw it. The manuscript is apparently lost. The fact that Hume knew his own treatment was inadequate indicates that he saw the possibility of a theory but was unable to construct one to his own satisfaction. This is hardly skepticism. The one sense in which he does link mathematics with skepticism is in arguing against those people who had exploited the well-known paradoxes of infinity to serve as a justification for obscurantism.[3] Rather than subscribe to either skepticism or obscurantism, Hume suggests that "reason must remain restless and unquiet" precisely because "She sees a full light which illuminates certain places, but that light borders on the most profound darkness" (EHU, 157). This is hardly the recommendation of a skeptic, but of a man who knows that much remains to be accomplished.

As should be clear from our discussion of the passions, Hume maintains no skepticism with regard to the existence of a self, the fourth allegedly skeptical topic. The problem in Hume's theory of the self is that it raises the difficulties of dualism, the seventh problem noted above. As far as it goes, Hume is satisfied with his theory. He denies the existence of a simple self; he offers his own view of how we acquire the complex idea of a self. But he came to realize that the problem of substance was just thereby postponed to another level.

With regard to moral judgments, we have seen Hume deliberately maintain the objectivity of moral judgments in the face of serious difficulties which forced him to modify his moral theory. In this context, we should recall the remark made in the first section of the *Enquiry concerning the Principles of Morals:* "Those who have denied the reality of moral distinctions may be ranked among the disingenuous disputants; nor is it conceivable, that any human creature could ever seriously believe, that all characters and actions were alike entitled to the affection and regard of everyone. . . . The only way, therefore, of converting an antagonist of this kind, is to leave him to himself. . . . it is probable he will, at last, of himself, from mere weariness, come over to the side of common sense and reason" (EPM, 169–70). Finally, it should be clear from the previous chapter that Hume was not concerned with disproving the existence of God as he understood Him, but rather with showing the lack of a basis for inferring anything about God's attributes, especially his moral attributes.

The final skeptical topic, the existence of the external world, constitutes the major unresolved difficulty in Hume's philosophy, and I shall devote a special section to it below.

II *Skepticism as a Device*

It has always seemed to me that Hume's pretense at skepticism was a literary device in the *Treatise* with which to tease his opponents and to prepare the reader for a more favorable reception of his own theory of the passions. There is something irreverent about Hume's tone which some of his less sympathetic readers have taken for a lack of sincerity. Fortunately, we are now in possession of a long letter which confirms that Hume never intended to have some of his "sceptical" remarks taken seriously by his readers. He apparently overestimated their sense of humor. The *Letter from a Gentleman to his friend in Edinburgh* contains as clear a statement of the function of Hume's skepticism as we are likely to find:

As to the *scepticism* with which the Author is charged, I must observe that the doctrines of the *Pyrrhonians* or *Sceptics* have been regarded in all ages as principles of mere curiosity, or a kind of *jeux d' espirit*, without any influence on a man's steady principles or conduct in life. In reality, a philosopher who affects to doubt of the maxims of *common reason*, and even of his *senses*, declares sufficiently that he is not in earnest, and that he intends not to advance an opinion which he would recommend as standards of judgment and action. All he means by these scruples is to abate the pride of *mere human reasoners*, by showing them, that even with regard to principles which seem the clearest, and which they are necessitated from the strongest instincts of nature to embrace, they are not able to attain a full confidence and absolute certainty. *Modesty* then, and *humility*, with regard to the operations of our natural faculties, is the result of *scepticism*; not an universal doubt, which it is impossible for any man to support, and which the first and most trivial accident in life must immediately disconcert and destroy.... It is evident, that so extravagant a doubt as that which scepticism may seem to recommend, by destroying *everything*, really affects *nothing*, and was never intended to be understood *seriously*, but was meant as a *mere* philosophical amusement, or trial of *wit* and *subtlety*.... he has not been contented with that, but expressly declared it. And all those principles, cited in the *specimen* as proofs of his *scepticism*, are positively renounced in a few pages afterwards, and called the effects of *philosophical melancholy* and *delusion*. These are his very words; and his accuser's overlooking them may be thought very prudent, but is a degree of unfairness which appears to me altogether astonishing.[4]

By the time Hume wrote the first *Enquiry*, he went out of his way to be more explicit in showing that skepticism was a literary device employed to serve other purposes. "When he awakes from his dream, he will be the first to join in the laugh against himself, and to confess, that all his objections are mere amusement, and can have no other tendency than to show the whimsical condition of mankind, who must act and reason and believe; though they are not able, by their most diligent enquiry, to satisfy themselves concerning the foundation of these operations, or to remove the objections, which may be raised against them" (EHU, 160). The general purpose of Hume's skepticism is to serve as a stick with which to beat the rationalists. What better way was there to show the inadequacy of the rationalist model of explanation and the extravagant claims made on its behalf than to use such "reason" to subvert "reason" itself. Finally, one of the more specific uses of such skepticism is to protect Hume from theological critics angered by his refusal to admit more than the existence of the most ambiguous notion of God. There is no conflict between genuine modesty and a rejection of intellectual arrogance.

III *Hume's Refutation of Skepticism*

In an age when philosophers blithely discovered self-evident first principles in every intellectual field of endeavor, Hume denied such self-evidence, and this made of him a skeptic. In an age when philosophers believed in essences and thought that they could perceive formal causes, Hume cautioned them that even our most basic instincts might be "fallacious and deceitful" (EHU, 159). He did not say that the instincts were fallacious, only that they might be. Such a recognition of the possibility of error earned Hume the reputation of a skeptic. Consistent with his basic plan as constructed and expressed in the introduction to the *Treatise*, Hume advises us to concentrate on those things which are within the reach of human reason. This is the same message as that of his skepticism. What was provocative in his time would hardly raise an eyebrow now and that is because of his influence. At this point, it does not seem very helpful to talk about Hume's skepticism.

Hume gave his own very special refutation of skepticism, and it is a rather simple one. Nobody could consistently be a skeptic because his practice would contradict what he asserted. Nor could anyone advocate skepticism since this advocacy would be a piece of dogmatism inconsistent with skepticism itself.

Just as the academic variety of skepticism, which Hume advocates (be humble and careful), was consistent with the science-of-man program, so the refutation of the extreme form of skepticism called pyrrhonism is consistent with Hume's advocacy of common sense. Nobody, including philosophers, can take such skepticism seriously in practice, in our action, and since it is our action which Hume seeks to understand, no philosophy of action need pay attention to it.

It may be argued that Hume's refutation is not a logical one but a psychological one, and here the distinction between logic and psychology is not intended to denigrate the success of the psychological refutation but to call attention to Hume's unwillingness to deal with logical refutation. In answer it should be noted that there is a sense in which Hume did offer a logical refutation of skepticism. The success of the skeptical critique depends upon certain outrageous claims made on behalf of reason. Once we give up those pretensions, the skeptic's case is pointless. Second, there is a sense in which Hume believed that at least one skeptical argument could not be refuted, namely, the argument concerning the existence of the external world. It is not that Hume ignores logic, but only that he finds it inadequate to solve that problem or to provide a refutation in that one case.

Finally, I should like to call attention to the fact that in the framework of what Hume was trying to do, the psychological refutation was not only successful but the only relevant one. Recall that Hume's enemies the rationalists argued for the combat of passion and reason and the possibility of reason overcoming passion. In showing the utter inability of reason, in the rationalist sense, to control or even to influence human behavior, Hume was showing the impossibility of a rationalist system of ethics. Man's capacity to ignore the serious skeptical challenge was a tribute not only to the power of instinct and the providential bounty of nature, but an argument in favor of Hume's moral theory.

IV *The Existence of the External World*

In the early part of this book we indicated the extent to which Hume sought to bring his philosophy into alignment with the major developments in science up to his time. The account we gave began with the Copernican theory and its opposition to the Ptolemaic theory. The existence of two viable theories created a special problem for those intellectuals who believed in the power of reason, especially as mathematically conceived. How could reason be the key and yet provide two theories, both of which were mathematically reasonable and both of which fit the facts known at that time? Galileo's answer was to offer a compromise, a compromise which exalted his faith in mathematics and made it look as if no problem existed at all. Galileo was the first, or among the first, to distinguish between primary and secondary qualities, a distinction between the mathematical qualities of real objects and the subjective or secondary qualities, which existed only in the minds of men. There were thus postulated two worlds, a phenomenal world which we continued to describe in everyday (and, I might add, Aristotelian) terms and an intelligible world governed by mathematical forms. The two worlds were supposedly connected by the fact that the intelligible world caused the phenomenal world to come into being when men interacted with the physical world.

In Galileo the view is only sketchy. In Descartes it becomes the basis of all of modern philosophy. Encouraged by his work in the field of vision, Descartes developed the Galilean distinction into the modern dichotomy of mind and body. In the real world of intelligible objects, objects do not have color. Such objects merely reflect light waves of certain wave length, these light waves then strike the retina, and go through a physiological system including the brain until at last they reach the mind, at which point we have the sensation of color. The final step in this transmission is not clear, because we never really find that place in the brain where the color actually appears, even though everybody who is not blind reports the presence of this experience. Philosophers thought that they could solve this problem by postulating an unextended mind that is mysteriously connected with the brain.

Now the crucial fact to remember is that it was taken to be a scientific fact by everybody, including Newton and Hume, that external objects caused us to have internal impressions. I repeat, it was considered a fact of science. The causal relation between object and experience was the key issue. For Descartes, Locke, and Berkeley there was no serious philosophical problem, or so they thought, because all three of these philosophers, and most others, still conceived of the world in Aristotelian terms. Our experiences had to have causes. For Descartes, God guaranteed the veracity of the senses. For Locke, the primary qualities were self-certifying of the fact that they came from external physical objects. Even for Berkeley, the very existence of ideas required a causing mind.

When Hume developed his Newtonian analysis of causation in which he denied the possibility of formal causes and essential powers, he cut off any possibility of making an inference between an external body which causes the internal impression and the impression. Science said that we could not see the bodies directly, but we knew they were there as the causes of our experience. In short, all we had was the effect, from which we inferred the cause. By now it should be clear that Hume's analysis could permit no such inference from an observed effect to an unobserved and permanently unobservable cause. It is thus the Newtonian analysis of causation which is the key to understanding Hume's construction of the skeptical argument against the existence of the external world. No thinker, skeptical or otherwise, could have invented this argument prior to Hume. And Hume invented it, or formulated it, as a direct consequence of the analysis of causation.

Several points here are worth noting. Thomas Reid, Hume's contemporary and one of his antagonists, who had previously been a follower of Berkeley, recognized the nature of Hume's argument, at least the novelty of the claim that we really could not infer the object from the experience. But Reid attributes this to Hume's working out of the inner logic of the new way of ideas popularized in England by Locke. Locke, of course, was really following Descartes. It is thus Reid who established the apparently impregnable tradition of viewing Hume as the heir to the tradition of Locke and Berkeley and as the man who finally bankrupted the tradition. But it should now be clear that Hume's devastating analysis was not the working out of the inner logic of the theory of ideas but the application to that theory of the Newtonian analysis of causation.

In the 1770 edition of the first *Enquiry*, Hume added an advertisement in which he claimed that the *Treatise* was a juvenile work, against which his opponents had employed polemical devices and bigoted zeal "contrary to all rules of candor and fair-dealing." In a letter he wrote in 1775, Hume identified his opponents as Reid and Beattie. Again in the advertisement Hume wanted his *Enquiries* to be taken as "containing his philosophical sentiments," but the popular myth of his skepticism had already hardened.

There is undoubtedly some truth in every interpretation,

and it would certainly be absurd to deny the influence of Locke and Berkeley and others on Hume. But it is equally absurd to assume that philosophers read and are influenced only by other philosophers. Philosophers are influenced by general intellectual currents. It is also clear that even Locke and Berkeley were reacting to Newton, but it remains that Hume alone fully comprehended the philosophical implications of Newton's views.

In the *Treatise*, Hume asserted the common sense position which he was never to challenge that we must, and cannot do otherwise than, take for granted the existence of the external world. After all, where would the Newtonian program be without an external world? The only question is why we continue to believe in it despite the inability to prove the belief. Hume answered this question by providing a theory of the imagination in which he argued that the idea of a continued existence produces the idea of a distinct existence. We arrive at the idea of a continued existence by means of the principle of identity, or duration over time, as well as through the resemblance of our impressions created by means of the principles of constancy and coherence. The idea of a continued existence is one in which we believe because vivacity is communicated to it by the lively ideas of our memory. Once more we see the principle of the transfer of vivacity and its crucial role in the *Treatise*.

As we have already seen, Hume became less enthusiastic as time went on about the principle of vivacity. Besides, there is something very different about this particular dilemma. Where reason was supplemented in other parts of Hume's theory by the psychological mechanisms he attributes to the imagination, the supplement always involved a projection of items previously experienced. Thus, in an inductive or causal inference, our basic human nature forces us to project past conjunctions into the future. There is nothing strange about that because both cause and effect are known. But in the case of the account of our belief in the existence of the external world, we are told how a fiction is projected. Hume's account is noticeably artificial, and he himself must have recognized the fact, for he drops it altogether from the first *Enquiry*.

In the first *Enquiry*, he again raises the issue, although now he does not provide an explanation. Again he reassures us that the issue is irrelevant, and, in an important sense, he is correct. But he also says, after dismissing the silly skeptical issues, that "there are other more profound arguments against the senses which admit not of so easy a solution" (EHU, 151). In fact, Hume argues that belief in the existence of the external world cannot be justified because such a belief "exceeds the power of all human capacity" (EHU, 152). Hume believed that this problem could not be solved, because we are dealing with an alleged scientific fact that is impossible to explain:

> It is a question of fact, whether the perceptions of the senses be produced by external objects, resembling them: how shall this question be determined? By experience surely; as all other questions of a like nature. But here experience is, and must be entirely silent. The mind has never anything present to it but the perceptions, and cannot possibly reach any experience of their connection with objects. The supposition of such a connection is therefore, without any foundation in reasoning. (EHU, 153)

Hume does not say that a belief in the connection is unreasonable. What he is claiming is that the inference from a perception to an external world is unreasonable. It is a matter of fact that can never be substantiated. What are we to do? Can we give up our belief in the external world? No, because it is psychologically impossible. Can we give up the claim that objects cause experiences? No, because it is supposed to be a scientific fact. Can we change our view of causation? No, because Newton seems to be right. Surely, this is a profound problem.

Generations of philosophers have continued to offer variations on this theme. We had sense-data, possible sense-data, linguistic phenomenalism, etc. All of these theories were testaments to human ingenuity, but they all fell before Hume's Newtonian analysis of causation. Even Hume's alleged try at a solution in the *Treatise* was attacked by those who forgot that Hume invented the rebuttal. To this day there are those who think that the problem remains unsolved.

It is now generally accepted in academic philosophical circles that the problem is either insoluble or a pseudoproblem.

The most popular version of the latter has two parts. First, there is a more or less sophisticated restatement of the Humean point that no inference is justifiable. Second, there is an appeal to the obvious fact that the problem can only be formulated by doing violence to the ordinary rules of our language. Language was not invented to describe sense-data but to describe the external social world.

There is another even more radical way of declaring the problem to be a pseudoproblem. There is a philosophical position called scientific realism,[5] in which it is argued that science does not reveal, as was believed by Hume and others, that external objects cause us to have experiences. What science shows is that external physical objects, external to our respective nervous systems, cause us to have internal physical states. There are no experiences as traditionally conceived. In short, dualism is rejected in favor of a form of materialism. The only objection to materialism as stated by Hume himself is that it conflicts with our normal way of speaking. Hume condemned the materialists for attempting to "conjoin all thought with extension" (T, 239), and the reason he gave is that some objects do not occupy space. "A moral reflection cannot be placed on the right or on the left hand of a passion" (T, 236). But how do we know that this cannot be so? The only answer is that it sounds absurd. But I think that it can be argued against Hume at this point that ordinary language has no commitment to dualism or to materialism or to mentalism. It is neutral with respect to these philosophical difficulties, which arose later. But neutrality does not make for incompatibility, and certainly our ordinary language can accommodate itself to new scientific discoveries. No one ever spoke about the spatial location of a "moral reflection," because no one ever knew about its exact physiological nature. At least, this is what a scientific realist might argue.

Hume seems to have taken the philosophical speculations of scientists about dualism for scientific facts. He accepted what Descartes and Newton had said about primary and secondary qualities as if they were facts revealed in research. He was not alone in making this mistake. This criticism of Hume in no way detracts from his other achievements. Rather, it serves to underscore the validity of Hume's conception of philosophy and in ironic fashion confirms his contention that a better knowledge of man can help in the speculations of science. After all, scientists themselves operate within preexisting conceptual systems.

After all is said and done, it remains that Hume uncovered one of the major difficulties, if not the major difficulty, of all of modern philosophy, namely, the problem of how we are to account for the relation of the external world and our perceptions. To be sure, others had raised the issue, but they had remained content with the Aristotelian inference from effect to cause. Hume's Newtonian analysis showed the inadequacy of this type of solution. Moreover, Hume came to distinguish clearly between an account of how we acquired the belief in the external world and the genuine difficulty embedded in the assumptions made by most modern philosophers. This difficulty has nothing to do with the *via moderna*, and it is misleading to call this skepticism. There is a difference between the traditional skeptical arguments about perceptual relativity and corrigibility and the difficulty of modern philosophy which derives from the distinction between primary and secondary qualities. The latter is a result of trying to transcend outmoded categories and not skepticism.

V *The Legacy*

In his own lifetime, Hume achieved prominence for his views on specific political issues and notoriety as a man with the unlimited capacity to enrage theologians. We must recall that it was not God that Hume objected to but clergymen. Toward the end of his life, Hume achieved prominence and a deserved respect as a great historian, not only in Great Britian and the United States but on the continent as well. As far as his metaphysical and epistemological work was concerned, Hume was, with the exception of his alleged skepticism, either overlooked, ignored, or misunderstood.

There was one philosopher who vaguely saw the implications of Hume's thought, but drew the wrong conclusions about Hume's enterprise as a whole. That man was Thomas Reid. In the dedication to his own *Inquiry into the Human Mind* (1764), Reid established the tradition of viewing Hume as the great skeptic and "nay" sayer:

> I never thought of calling in question the principles commonly received with regard to the human understanding, until the "Treatise of Human Nature" was published in the year 1739. The ingenious author of that treatise upon the principles of Locke—who was no sceptic—has built a system of scepticism, which leaves no ground to believe any one thing rather than its contrary.... For my own satisfaction, I entered into a serious examination of the principles upon which this sceptical system is built; and was not a little surprised to find, that it leans with its whole weight upon a hypothesis, which is ancient indeed, and has been very generally received by philosophers, but of which I could find no solid proof. The hypothesis I mean, is, that nothing is perceived but what is in the mind which perceives it.... I thought it unreasonable ... to admit a hypothesis which, in my opinion, overturns all philosophy, all religion and virtue, and all common sense....

Reid has a point, but he ends by ignoring the problem, not solving it. Reid's estimation survives to our own day despite the heroic efforts of a number of commentators.

Reid's blindness was not shared by the great Prussian philosopher Immanuel Kant. Kant understood the implications of Hume's Copernican revolution, for he accepted the notion that the world consisted of experiences caused by external physical objects and structured by a human mind. That is, Kant shared the perspective of modern philosophy and learned from Hume that certain principles were supplied by the activities of the knowing mind and were not to be found in nature, that is, the assumption of a causal order. Kant differed from Hume in not accepting the latter's empirical assumptions about the deterministic and biological basis of the human mind. In his *Prolegomena* (1783) Kant offered the following tribute to Hume: "I honestly confess that my recollection of David Hume's teaching was the very thing which many years ago first interrupted my dogmatic slumber, and gave my investigations in the field of speculative philosophy a quite new direction." Kant was apparently directly acquainted only with Hume's first *Enquiry*, and in that work there is at least one statement which comes close to what Kant said about the noumena: "Bereave matter of all its intelligible qualities, both primary and secondary, you in a manner annihilate it, and leave only a certain unknown, inexplicable *something*, as the cause of our perceptions; a notion so imperfect, that no sceptic will think it worth while to contend against it" (EHU, 155). This passage may very well have inspired the Kantian remark that Hume "did not suspect such a formal science, but ran his ship ashore, for safety's sake, landing on scepticism, there to let it lie and rot; whereas my object is rather to give it a pilot, who by means of safe principles of navigation drawn from a knowledge of the globe, and provided with a complete chart and compass, may steer the ship safely whither he listeth."[6] Kant was not blind but he may have been myopic. Consider Hume's remark in the *Treatise*:

> Methinks I am like a man, who having struck on many shoals, and having narrowly escaped ship-wreck in passing a small frith, has yet the temerity to put out to sea in the same leaky weather-beaten vessel, and even carries his ambition so far as to think of compassing the globe under these disadvantageous circumstances. . . . Fain would I run into the crowd for shelter and warmth; but cannot prevail with myself to mix with such deformity. I call upon others to join me, in order to make a company apart; but no one will hearken to me. Every one keeps at a distance, and dreads that storm, which beats upon me from every side. I have exposed myself to the enmity of all metaphysicians, logicians, mathematicians, and even theologians; and can I wonder at the insults I must suffer? . . . Can I be sure, that in leaving all established opinions, I am following truth? (T, 263–65)

The nineteenth century preferred Kant's pilot, and this led to the triumph of idealism on the continent and its great influence even in Great Britain.[7] Hume continued to be known as an historian, and Thackeray in *Vanity Fair* (1848) could describe one of his characters as having read Hume's *Histories*. However, Hume did have an important influence in ethics by inspiring the utilitarian school of Bentham. You will recall, however, that Hume was not a complete utilitarian, and Bentham was to chide Hume for even bothering with the moral sentiments. But Bentham does pay tribute: "I well remember, no sooner had I read that part of the work [Book III of the *Treatise*] which touches on this subject than I felt as if scales had fallen from my eyes. I then, for the first time, learnt to call the cause of the people the cause of Virtue. . . . That the foundations of all *virtue* are laid in *utility*, is there demonstrated, after a few exceptions made, with the strongest evidence; but I see not, any more than Helvetius saw, what need there was for the exceptions."[8]

The real heir to Hume's Enlightenment program of the science of man is the great nineteenth-century philosopher John Stuart Mill. Hume's influence on Mill was indirect, coming through other philosophers such as Bentham; James Mill, his father; Hartley; Brown; etc. There are striking parallels between the work of Hume and the work of John Stuart Mill, and John Stuart Mill certainly had respect for the power of Hume's thought, although he shared the prevailing view of Hume as the skeptic: "France had Voltaire, and his school of negative thinkers, and England (or rather Scotland) had the profoundest negative thinker on record, David Hume: a man, the peculiarities of whose mind, qualified him to detect failure of proof, and want of logical consistency, at a depth which French sceptics, with their comparatively feeble powers of analysis and abstraction, *stopped* far short of, and which German subtlety alone could thoroughly appreciate or hope to rival."[9] In the same essay, J. S. Mill considers his father as the carrier of the positive program of the eighteenth century.

In order to explain the continuing perspective taken of Hume during the nineteenth and twentieth centuries, it is important to return to the world picture of modern philosophy.

Hume and Kant both continued to believe in the reality of the external physical world, even though they recognized the inadequacies of their own accounts of it. Nevertheless the problem of the existence of the external world continued to plague other philosophers. The answer to this problem given by nineteenth-century idealism was simply to deny the existence of an external world and to argue for some kind of more or less sophisticated version of modern philosophy wherein we speak only of the relation between the subject and the subject's experience. In romantic versions we might find someone advocating that the subject creates reality. We should recall the title of Schopenhauer's work *The World as Will and Representation.* There is also within this new framework the problem of the existence of other minds, for if we are each confined to our own experience, there is as little reason to believe in other minds as there is to believe in an external world. Together the problems of the existence of the external world and the existence of other minds are referred to as the problem of solipsism. Hegel's solution was to argue for some kind of group or social mind. This new perspective of explaining the world as the creation of the knowing subject, although foreshadowed by Hume and Kant is not what either Hume or Kant would have tolerated, although Kant suggested it much more than Hume. That is why both Hume and Kant continue to be interpreted as precursors of this new subjectivism.

Within the new subjectivism, all philosophical problems are treated in terms of the activities of the knowing subject. In Kant we had the categories as a development of Hume's notion of a habit of mind. In Hegel we find a kind of historical and evolutionary concept of the knowing subject in social terms. Modern phenomenology, not to be confused with phenomenalism, is a very obvious continuation of the Hegelian analysis of experience. Heidegger is very much of a piece with this tradition. American so-called pragmatism, especially in Dewey, is likewise an attempt to explain reality in terms of an active subject molding the world. Those who find parallels, once they get beyond the jargon, between pragmatists and phenomenologists should not be surprised. Finally, it should be noted that contemporary analytic philosophy both in its positivistic and linguistic branches is also of a piece with this Kantianism as developed by the idealists. The positivist emphasis on both a phenomenal analysis of experience in terms of sense-data and the interpretation of the mind in terms of logical distinctions is a clear development of a strain in Kant. The linguistic branch, in attempting to explicate the social preconceptions of our language system and to spell out the rules of our language, is a clear combination of Kantian categorial analysis and Hegelian notions of a community. Again, those who find parallels between Ryle and Heidegger should not be surprised.

Now let us return to specific views of Hume. When the logical positivist reads Hume, he is more likely than not to read the first *Enquiry* (perhaps under the influence of Kant), wherein he finds not only what he considers the forerunner of Kant's analytic-synthetic distinction but a motto to place on the lance of positivism: "When we run over libraries, persuaded of these principles, what havoc must we make? If we take in our hand any volume; of divinity or school metaphysics, for instance; let us ask, *Does it contain any abstract reasoning concerning quantity or number?* No. *Does it contain any experimental reasoning concerning matter of fact and existence?* No. Commit it then to the flames: for it can contain nothing but sophistry and illusion" (EHU, 165). The fact remains that Hume did not reject metaphysics as the positivists claim that they do, but specifically school and divinity-school metaphysics. Aside from this important misconception, positivists were responsible for perpetrating the myth that Hume was, like most of them, an ethical subjectivist. Schlick alone recognized that the belief in determinism led in the direction of Hume's making ethics a development of human psychology. Positivists simply failed to understand Hume's science of man, because they still adhered to a demonstrative conception of science.

In England, where the first book of the *Treatise* is more likely to be read and emphasized, the attention went to Hume's theory of perception and the theory of the external world. One of the prominent sense-data theorists, H. H. Price, wrote an influential book entitled *Hume's Theory of the External World* (1940), which confirmed the tendency to view Hume as a phenomenalist reconstructing reality out of impressions. This found a ready audience with the positivists, who shared this view of Hume. In even more bizarre fashion, the phenomenologists, as distinguished from the phenomenalists, picked up this part of Hume's philosophy. Witness the following remark by Husserl: "It is therefore not surprising that phenomenology is as it were the secret longing of the whole philosophy of modern times. The fundamental thought of Descartes in its wonderful profundity is already pressing towards it; Hume again, a psychological philosopher of the school of

Locke, almost enters its domain, but his eyes are dazzled. The first to perceive it truly is Kant. . . . but Kant misinterprets the same [the phenomenological ground] as psychological, and therefore eventually abandons it of his own accord."[10] Here phenomenology joins hands with positivism in viewing Hume and Kant as succumbing to psychology.

Flew has called attention to the similarity between Hume's notion of mental geography in the first *Enquiry* and Ryle's notion of logical geography. The connection is even closer. In the discussion of association in the *Treatise*, Hume comments that the imagination is "guided by some universal principles, which render it, in some measure, uniform with itself in all times and places. . . . and is the cause why, among other things, languages so nearly correspond to each other" (T, 10). Thus it is possible that the analysis of language itself might lead to the same conclusions. In the *Enquiry concerning the Principles of Morals* Hume makes linguistic distinctions his starting point.

The one thing which Hume did which would not have been appreciated until lately was to go beyond the linguistic or mental structure into the underlying causes. This was where other analytic philosophers would have stopped short for fear of discussing irrelevant psychological issues. Now, however, it appears that philosophers have recognized that they cannot leave the issue at such a superficial level. It is not enough to say that "those questions" are decided on pragmatic grounds. The development of action theory is a clear indication that philosophers recognize the need seen by Hume for going beyond the obvious level. Those contemporary "linguistic" philosophers who recognize the need for a broader scope are the true heirs of Hume's philosophical enterprise. Finally, we should note that in reviving the *via moderna* or the Copernican point of view in the twentieth century, such men as Kuhn and Toulmin are accepting the Humean legacy. The important difference is that they have substituted an evolutionary perspective for the Newtonian one.

List of Abbreviations for Hume's Works

T ...... *Treatise of Human Nature,* edited by Selby-Bigge.
EHU ... *An Enquiry concerning Human Understanding,* edited by Selby-Bigge.
EPM ... *An Enquiry concerning the Principles of Morals,* edtited by Selby-Bigge.
A ...... *An Abstract of A Treatise of Human Nature,* as appended to C. W. Hendel's edition of the first *Enquiry.*
D ...... *Dialogues Concerning Natural Religion,* edited by Norman Kemp Smith.
L ...... *A Letter from a Gentleman to his friend in Edinburgh.*

Note: Spelling and punctuation have occasionally been modified to conform to modern American usage.

Notes and References

Chapter Two

1. I. Kant, *Prolegomena to any Future Metaphysics*, ed. by Lewis White Beck (Indianapolis: Bobbs-Merrill, 1950), pp. 6–7.

2. Hume, *Abstract*, ed. Hendel, p. 196. In the preface to the *Abstract* (p. 182), Hume bemoans the fact that he is to be judged by the learned instead of by "*the people*, who in all matters of common reason and eloquence are found so infallible a tribunal." In *A Dialogue* which Selby-Bigge appended to the edition of the *Enquiries*, Hume concludes by saying: "When men depart from the maxims of common reason, and affect these *artificial* lives, as you call them, no one can answer for what will please or displease them. They are in a different element from the rest of mankind; and the natural principles of their mind play not with the same regularity, as if left to themselves, free from the illusions of religious superstition or philosophical enthusiasm" (p. 343).

3. See N. Capaldi, "The Copernican Revolution in Hume and Kant," in *Proceedings of the Third International Kant Congress*, ed. by Lewis White Beck (Dordrecht, Holland 1972), pp. 234–40. See also P. Duhem, *Essai sur la notion de théorie physique de Platon à Galilée*, (Paris: Marcel Riviere & Cic, Paris, 1908).

4. Much has been written about Newton's notion of a hypothesis. The best recent discussion is to be found in James Noxon, *Hume's Philosophical Development* (1973), Part II.

5. N. Capaldi, *The Enlightenment* (1967). See introduction.

6. See the *A Dialogue* mentioned above, pp. 324–43; see also the *Treatise*, p. 401.

7. J. H. Randall, Jr. *The Career of Philosophy* (1962), I, 23–43. As should be clear, my interpretation is somewhat different from Randall's. Specifically, I would argue that the skepticial problems of the *via moderna* are different in the eighteenth century from the problems of the fourteenth-century, and that the problems of the eighteenth century can only be explained by reference to the scientific presuppositions of the age including the distinction between primary and secondary qualities.

8. Among those who accuse Hume of confusing psychology and logic or substituting one for the other are Kemp Smith, *The Philosophy of David Hume* (1949), pp. 560–61; Passmore, *Hume's Intentions* (1952), pp. 18, 77, 155; Antony Flew, *Hume's Philosophy of Belief*

(1960), pp. 117ff. and 211; and F. Zabeeh, *Hume: Precursor of Modern Empiricism* (1960), p. 158.

9. *Abstract*, p. 189; *Treatise*, p. 103; first *Enquiry*, pp. 42–45.

10. In the modern philosophical period, I would make the following distinctions. We begin by distinguishing between science and metaphysics. There were three kinds of science: Classical or Aristotelian, Cartesian, and Newtonian. There were three kinds of metaphysics: Platonic, Aristotelian, and what I would call Copernican (i.e., Randall's *via moderna*). Descartes offered a Platonic metaphysics to his own or Cartesian science; Hobbes and Spinoza offered Aristotelian metaphysics as an interpretation of Cartesian science; Locke offered an Aristotelian metaphysics for Newtonian science; Leibniz, Berkeley, and Kant gave a Platonic metaphysical interpretation of Newtonian science; Hume, finally offered a Copernican metaphysics for Newtonian science.

There is this difference between Platonic and Aristotelian metaphysics. For the Platonist, first principles are a priori; for the Aristotelian, first principles are abstracted from experience. For both of these views, all explanation is deduction from permanent first principles. In this Chapter I have lumped together both Platonists and Aristotelians as rationalists in order to contrast them as a unit with Hume's views. In other contexts, one would have to distinguish more clearly between Platonic rationalists and Aristotelian rationalists.

See my paper "The Moral Limits of Scientific Research: An Envolutionary Approach," in Knorr, Strasser, and Zilian, eds., *Determinants and controls of Scientific development* (Dordrecht, Holland: Reidel, 1975.)

Chapter Three

1. One of the best treatments of Newton's influence on Hume, but with a different emphasis from mine, is to be found in James Noxon's *Hume's Philosophical Development* (1973).

2. See Henri Frankfort, *Before Philosophy* (Baltimore: Penguin; 1949), chapters 1 and 8.

3. Even before Aristotle's works were generally available, many of the same views were to be found during the medieval period in the *Timaeus* of Plato. It should also be noted that the Greeks did not believe in creation, which is a Judeo-Christian concept. It is important to emphasize that Hume is attacking the Aristotelian tradition, not Aristotle. In Hume's famous letter (1745) he singled out "The *Platonick* and *Peripatetick* Schools" as well as the "Schoolmen" (pp. 27–28). The fundamental importance and persistence of the Aristotelian position has been documented by J. H. Randall, Jr. in his *Career of Philosophy* (for example, Vol. I, p. 265).

An interesting example of the persistent influence of Aristotle can be found in Descartes. Although Descartes rejects Aristotelian physics for his own or Cartesian physics, Descartes retains Aristotle's notion of causal explanation only now as a self-evident metaphysical principle. It is important to distinguish Aristotelian physics from Aristotelian metaphysics. The context should make this clear. See note 10 of chapter two.

4. For an example of this error see A. E. Michottee, *Peception of Causality* (1962).

5. As I show in chapter 9, Hume never denied either the existence of God or the reasonableness of the cosmological argument; rather, what Hume attacks is the notion that we can infer anything with assurance from the existence of an alleged effect. What Hume does is to cripple the cosmological argument. Hume's crippling effect applies not only to the so-called naive cosmological argument in which "first" cause is taken in the temporal sense but applies as well to the sophisticated version in which "first" cause is taken in the logical sense. In the latter version, it is admitted that there may be an infinite series but God as first cause both decides that there shall be a series and chooses which series from among the alternatives to bring about. However, it is not clear just "when" this decision is made. But the real issue is why anyone should think that it is necessary to postulate a chooser. Is this not still an Aristotelian preconception being applied to a Newtonian universe? If motion needs no explanation, presumably it needs it neither in a temporal nor in a logical sense. Finally, it is not clear what "logical" means in this context.

6. "Mere chance, probability, and causation then are equally states of the imagination. The 'equal necessity of the connexion between all causes and effects' means not that any 'law of causation pervades the universe,' but that, unless the habit of transition between any feelings is 'full and perfect,' we do not speak of these feelings as related in the way of cause and effect." T. H. Green, Introduction to *Hume's Works*, p. 289.

7. *Abstract*, ed. Hendel, pp. 184–85.

8. Newton's third rule allows him to form universal propositions about natural properties of objects. Although Newton accepted the Galilean distinction between primary and secondary qualities because his own work in optics convinced him that colors do not reside in light rays but are produced in our minds, he still rejects the Cartesian notion that reason alone grasps the primary qualities and that the latter are purely mathematical. Newton still insists that the senses are indispensable sources of discovering real properties or primary properties. Hence Newton adds to the list of primary qualities such things as hardness, impenetrability, and inertial powers. Further, Newton believes that these qualities belong as well to those bodies

which we cannot sense. Finally, we note that for Newton gravity is a universal quality but not a primary one, because it varies with distance. Hume accepted much of this, including the idea that what we discover in our experience can be extended to those objects beyond the present range of our experience.

9. In the last two editions, Hume changed the word "power" to "matter."

10. EHU, p. 15. Hume's critique of simplicity will be important for interpreting changes in his ethical theory.

11. See preface to first edition of *Mathematical Principles of Natural Philosophy*, ed. Florian Cajon (Berkeley, Calif., 1946), pp. xvii–xvii. There is a great deal of nonsense in the charge that empiricist philosophies of science deny the role of prior hypotheses. The emphasis is always on the confirmability of hypotheses. See Noxon's book cited above for how this applies to Newton.

Chapter Four

1. There are several issues here which must be distinguished: (1) does Hume assume or take for granted that there are external physical objects which cause us to have experiences; (2) is this assumption justifiable; (3) does Hume attack the notion of the existence of powers in nature; (4) is this attack justifiable.

In the context in question I am only concerned with issue (1). It has been traditionally assumed that Hume does not believe in the existence of an external physical world and that he attacks such a belief. I have argued, on the contrary, that he does assume such an external physical world. Independent of every other issue, it is therefore important that this point be made.

With respect to issue (2) it may be plausibly argued that Hume is creating problems for himself. That is precisely what I point out in the last chapter. Nevertheless, the fact that Hume's assumption creates difficulties does not negate the existence of the assumption.

The answer to issue (3) is that Hume does attack the existence of powers. If it be asked if this attack is justified, issue (4), the answer depends on what position or argument is offered for the existence of powers. Hume's opponents argued that the existence of powers could be legitimately inferred as a causal inference. Hume clearly showed the folly of this approach. If, however, one merely asserts the existence of powers as an assumption, then the assertion is far weaker than Hume's opponents would have been willing to accept. Finally, such an assumption would be little more than an article of faith, and it was precisely this point which Hume made when he attacked the intellectual pretensions of those who allegedly "argued" for God's existence.

2. *Dissertation Of the Passions* (Green and Grose edition), p. 139.
3. *Ibid.*, p. 163.
4. EHU, p. 20; see also pp. 60, 77n.
5. N. Capaldi, "Copernican Revolution in Hume and Kant," *Proceedings of the Third Kant Congress* (1972), ed. Lewis W. Beck, pp. 234–40. Flew also recognized this anticipation (*Hume's Philosophy of Belief*, p. 213).
6. See *Treatise* pp. 60–61. We must distinguish between the problem of how a physical object interacts with a mental state (which is a problem for all dualists), and the problem or impossibility of inferring a physical object from a mental state.
7. For a discussion of this topic, see the appropriate chapters in the books by Kemp Smith, Flew, and Zabeeh.
8. *Abstract*, p. 186; see EHU, pp. 21–22.
9. EHU, pp. 19–20.
10. *Dissertation Of the Passions*, p. 166.

Chapter Five

1. *Natural History of Religion* (Green and Grose edition of *Works)* II, 316. See also *EHU*, pp. 77–78n; *L*, p. 27.
2. *Dissertation of the Passions*, pp. 160–61.
3. D. Livingston, "Hume on Ultimate Causation," *American Philosophical Quaterly* (1971). Vol. 8, pp. 63–70. Hume is specifically criticizing Locke. See Locke's *Essay* (Volume II, pp. 216,260 ed. Fraser).
4. This quotation and most of my discussion of the problem of counterfactuals is borrowed from Ernest Nagel, *The Structure of Science* (New York: Harcourt, Brace, 1961), chapter 4. I have previously defined "Aristotelian" in chapter two. In this chapter, "Aristotelian" as a metaphysical classification is applied to those who adhere to the following: (1) that all knowledge can be reconstructed in the form of demonstration; (2) that the first principles of demonstration are abstracted in some manner by reason from experience (this is what distinguishes it from Platonism); (3) that all adequate explanations must be entailments.
5. C. J. Ducasse, "Critique of Hume's Conception of Causality," *Journal of Philosophy* (1966). Vol. LXIII, No. 6: March 17, 1966; pp. 141–148.
6. *Treatise*, p. 75n. refers to Hume's later discussion at Part IV, section 5 of Book I.
7. Both Thomas Reid and later C. J. Ducasse mention this classic example. J. S. Mill offered a refutation of it in his Humean analysis of causation in the *System of Logic*.

8. The clock example is mentioned by Flew, *Hume's Philosophy of Belief*, p. 131.

9. What happens when we try to take induction as a serious problem can be seen in N. Capaldi, "Why There is No Problem of Induction," *Journal of Critical Analysis* (1971). Vol. III, No. 1, April 1971, pp. 9–12.

10. Letter to John Stuart, 1754 in Greig.

11. *EHU*, pp. 76–79.

12.Passmore, *Hume's Intentions*, p. 77; K. Popper, *Conjectures and Refutations* (London: Rontledge & Kegan Paul, 1963), pp. 42–59.

13. See also *EHU*, p. 108; *Treatise*, p. 179.

14. Flew, *op. cit.*, p. 98.

Chapter Six

1. See also the *Treatise*, p. 298; *Dissertation of the Passions*, p. 148.

2. Copleston, *A History of Philosophy*, (Garden City N.Y.: Doubleday, 1964) Vol. 5, Part II, pp. 172–73. T. Penelhum, "Hume on Personal Identity," *Philosophical Review* (1955), Vol. LXIV, p. 573.

3. Important discussions of Hume's theory of the self are to be found in Kemp Smith, Passmore, Laird, Penelhum, and in an article by Noxon. See annotated bibliography.

4. *Abstract*, p. 194. The *Abstract*, as far as we know, was written on the first two books. Hume divided ideas into simple and complex as well as those derived from sensation and those derived from reflection. He denied that there was a simple idea of the self. He asserted that the idea of the self was derived from reflection. This makes the idea of the self a complex idea of reflection. In order to explain a complex idea of sensation such as substance it was necessary to raise the difficulties of mind-body or mental-physical interaction. Hume had hoped to avoid these difficulties when discussing the self. However, by making it a complex idea, even one of reflection, he did not avoid the problem. This is the root of his dissatisfaction. However, the *Dissertation* we know was written long after the appendix.

5. Laird is incorrect in claiming that Hume makes the will a direct passion. See his *Hume's Philosophy of Human Nature*, p. 202.

6. See Ryle, *Concept of Mind* (1949), p. 85; R. D. Broiles, *The Moral Philosophy of David Hume*, pp. 63–64.

7. See Flew, *op. cit.*, chapter 5.

8. *Dissertation of the Passions*, p. 139.

9. *Ibid.*, p. 163.

10. N. Kemp Smith, *op. cit.*, p. 11; this interpretation has been attacked by Glathe and Broiles among others.

11. I owe this insight to an unpublished paper by David F. Norton entitled "Hume's Defense of Rational Metaphysics."

Chapter Seven

1. In his article, "Hume's Account of Obligation," Bernard Wand does not include a discussion of sympathy and its crucial importance to all aspects of Hume's moral theory. Wand's article appeared in *Philosophical Quarterly* (1956). Vol. VI, pp. 90–97.

2. For the importance of the distinction between judgment and sentiment see the articles by N. Capaldi, "Some Misconceptions About Hume's Moral Theory," *Ethics* (1966), and Ronald Glossop, as listed in the bibliography.

3. See N. Capaldi, *Judgment and Sentiment in Hume's Moral Theory* (Ph.D. diss., Columbia University, 1965).

4. I. Hedenius, *Studies in Hume's Ethics* (1937), p. 481.

5. "When I am fully cognisant of the non-ethical relations I cannot infer from them and them alone, the ethical relations." C. D. Broad, *Five Types of Ethical Theory* (Paterson, N.J.: Littlefield Adams, 1959), p. 112.

"Reason is concerned with positive knowledge or with relations of ideas and matters of fact; and it is impossible to derive from such knowledge the conception of good and bad or of obligation." B. M. Laing, *David Hume* (London: E. Benn, 1932), p. 188.

"... many British moralists of the present time would agree with Hume's short but pregnant criticism (469 sq.) that his opponents in this matter had illegitimately attempted to deduce *ought* from *is*." J. Laird, *Hume's Philosophy of Human Nature* (London: Methuen, 1932), p. 215.

"... insists that an 'ought' cannot be deduced from an 'is'." D. Daiches Raphael, *The Moral Sense* (New York: Oxford, 1947), p. 65.

"Hume's demand ... to show how ethical propositions may be deduced from non-ethical ones." A. N. Prior, *Logic and the Basis of Ethics* (New York: Oxford, 1949), p. 33.

"Hume's point is that ethical conclusions cannot be drawn validly from premises which are nonethical." W. K. Frankena, "The Naturalistic Fallacy," reprinted in W. Sellars and J. Hospers, eds., *Readings in Ethical Theory* (New York: Appleton-Century-Crofts, 1952), pp. 104–5.

"He is asserting that the question of how the factual basis of morality is related to morality is a crucial logical issue, reflection on which will enable one to realize how there are ways in which this transition can be made and ways in which it cannot." A. MacIntyre, "Hume on 'Is' and 'Ought'," *Philosophical Review* 68, no. 4 (October, 1959), 465.

"Hume makes ought-propositions a sub-class of is-propositions." G. Hunter, "Hume on 'Is' and 'Ought'," *Philosophy* 37, no. 140 (April, 1962), 149.

Also see R. F. Atkinson, "Hume on 'Is' and 'Ought': A Reply to Mr. MacIntyre," *Philosophical Review* 70, no. 2 (April 1961), 231–38; M. J. Scott-Taggart, "MacIntyre's Hume," *ibid.:* 239–44; A. H. Basson, *David Hume*, (Baltimore: Penguin, 1958), pp. 94–95; A. C. Ewing, *Ethics* (New York: Free Press, 1962), p. 92; R. M. Hare, *The Language of Morals* (New York: Oxford, 1952), pp. 29, 44; P. H. Nowell-Smith, *Ethics* (New York: Philosophical Library, 1959), pp. 36–37; W. Salmon, *Logic* (Englewood Cliffs, N.J.: Prentice-Hall, 1963), p. 17.

6. " . . . having found, in many instances, that any two kinds of objects—flame and heat, snow and cold—have always been conjoined together; if flame or snow be presented anew to the senses, the mind is carried by custom to expect heat or cold, and to *believe* that such a quality does exist, and will discover itself upon a nearer approach" *Enquiry*, p. 46.

Consequently, when Hume says, "Take any action . . . action" (T, 468–69), he is talking about a presently observed action. Hence, there is no possibility of matter-of-fact inference to an unobserved quality. This is a point on which V. C. Chappell, *The Philosophy of David Hume* (New York: Modern Library, 1963), p. li, seems confused.

7. Hume's statement "and . . . practice" (T, 469) is a reminder of the inevitable attitude of the vulgar. Moreover, since all perceptions are "in the mind," there is nothing exceptional in the fact that moral perceptions are in the mind.

8. MacIntyre, pp. 463–65, believes that "vulgar" refers to the religious systems of the eighteenth century. Atkinson, p. 236, believes that Hume is using the word "vulgar" in a pejorative sense. Neither MacIntyre nor Atkinson presents any contextual evidence for their respective interpretations. Scott-Taggart, "Hume's ontology is by no means that of common sense," p. 240, fails to see the sense in which Hume does accept the vulgar attitude.

My interpretation of the "vulgar systems of morality," namely, that they are systems in which moral distinctions are independent of human perception, *is supported by Hume's correspondence.* In a letter to Hutcheson (March 16, 1740; see Greig, *Letters of David Hume*, vol. I, pp. 39–40, letter no. 15), Hume refers to ["When you pronounce. . . . Influence on Practice"] the paragraph preceding the is-ought paragraph and says " . . . since Morality, according to your

Opinion as well as mine, is determined merely by Sentiment, it regards only human Nature and human Life. . . . If you make any Alterations on your Performances, I can assure you, there are many who desire you would more fully consider this Point; if you think that the Truth lies on the popular [*vulgar*] Side." Note that the two sentences Hume refers to are those which remind us of the vulgar attitude in perception.

9. See MacIntyre, above.

10. See N. Kemp Smith, *The Philosophy of David Hume* (London: Macmillan, 1949), p. 201.

11. Failure to distinguish judgment from sentiment in Hume's writings has led to all sorts of misinterpretations. See my article "Some Misconceptions about Hume's Moral Theory," *Ethics* 76, n. 3 (April, 1966).

12. The following authors quote the is-ought paragraph in incomplete form: Basson, p. 94; R. D. Broiles, *The Moral Philosophy of David Hume* (The Hague: Nijhoff, 1964), pp. 86–87; Chappell, p. 1; P. R. Foot, "Hume on Moral Judgment," in D. F. Pears, ed., *Hume, a Symposium* (New York: St. Martin's, 1963), p. 74; R. M. Kydd, *Reason and Conduct in Hume's Treatise* (London: Oxford, 1946), p. 53; Laing, pp. 188–89; Nowell-Smith, pp. 36–37; Salmon, p. 17; T. D. Weldon, *The Vocabulary of Politics* (Baltimore: Penguin Books, 1955), pp. 181–82.

13. Frankena, Prior, Ewing, and MacIntyre have recognized this problem.

Chapter Eight

1. Those who believe that the first *Enquiry* is a *mere* republication of the *Treatise* include: Reid, *Essays on the Active Powers* (1818), p. 130; Selby-Bigge, in the introduction of his edition to the *Enquiries*; Basson, pp. 15–16; Maund, pp. 28–30; Laing, p. 31; MacNabb, "David Hume," *Encyclopedia of Philosophy* (1967), IV, 74–75. Those who argue for serious revisions include: Flew, chapter 1; see also his "*On the Interpretation of Hume*," *Philosophy* (1963), vol. XXXVIII, pp. 178–182; Hendel, chapter 4; Passmore, chapter 1; Kemp Smith, p. 532.

2. See Hume's *New Letters*, edited by Klibansky and Mossner (Oxford: Clarendon Press, 1970), number 1, pages 2–3.

3. See Flew's brilliant chapter on miracles in his book *Hume's Philosophy of Belief*.

4. Those who deny that Hume rejects sympathy include: Laird, p. 239; Stewart, pp. 331–37.

Chapter Nine

1. David Hume, *A Letter From A Gentleman to his friend in Edinburgh*, pp. 22–26.
2. The popular view championed by Norman Kemp Smith among others is that Philo speaks for Hume. Smith has been conclusively refuted by James Noxon in "Hume's Agnosticism," *Philosophical Review* (1964), Vol. LXXIII, pp. 248–261.
3. In a letter to his publisher, William Strahan, in 1776, Hume explains that the *Dialogues* offer nothing new in content and a lot less in the way of provocative statements: "it be no more exceptionable than some things I had formerly published . . . I there introduce a Sceptic, who is indeed refuted, and at last gives up the Argument . . . after . . . you . . . have publickly avowed Your Publication of the *Enquiry concerning Human Understanding*, I know no reason why you should have the least Scruple with regard to these Dialogues. They will be much less obnoxious to the Law, and not more exposed to popular Clamour." *Letters*, ii, 323–24.
4. Letter from Adam Smith to William Strahan, Nov. 9, 1776 (reprinted in Kemp Smith's edition of the *Dialogues*, p. 245).

Chapter 10

1. The three stages I have in mind are best represented by Thomas Reid, Norman Kemp Smith, and Popkin and Flew in that order.
2. See Flew's discussion of Hume's mathematical views.
3. Flew, *op. cit.*, pp. 256–57.
4. *Letter from a Gentleman to his friend in Edinburgh*, pp. 19–20; this letter was not available either to Popkin or to Flew when they originally wrote on Hume's skepticism.
5. The best contemporary exposition of scientific realism is to be found in the works of Wilfrid Sellars. Hume's dissatisfaction with his analysis of the self reflects dissatisfaction with his dualism. See *Treatise*, p. 633; *EHU*, pp. 68–69, 153.
6. Kant, *Prolegomena to any Future Metaphysics*, ed. L. W. Beck, p. 10.
7. B.M. Laing, *David Hume* (1932), p. 232.
8. J. Bentham, *Fragment on Government* (1776), Chapter One, note. (Oxford: Blackwell, 1948) pp. 49–50.
9. J.S. Mill, Essay on *Bentham* (1838), originally published in the *London and Westminister Review*.
10. E. Husserl, *Ideas* (New York: Collier, 1962), p. 166. (Originally published in 1913.)

Annotated Bibliography

1. *Hume's Works*

The standard and absolutely indispensable edition of *A Treatise of Human Nature* is the edition first edited by Selby-Bigge in 1888 (Oxford: Clarendon Press) and now available in paperback. This edition contains a sixty-eight-page analytic index. But beware: there are some incorrect page numbers; some synoptic phrases are misleadingly interpretive; and the words chosen for the index are indicative both of Selby-Bigge's own interests and the prevailing interpretation of the time. Thus, there are no entries for "materialism" or "ought."

Equally standard as the common reference is Selby-Bigge's edition of Hume's *Enquiries*, second edition (Oxford: Clarendon Press, 1902), also available in paperback. This edition not only contains an analytic index but also tables comparing the *Enquiries* and the *Dissertation on the Passions* with the three books of the *Treatise*. However, the comparative tables are inaccurate in several places. In addition, please note that Selby-Bigge has reproduced the posthumous edition of 1777 without recording all of Hume's personal editorial changes from edition to edition. Finally, the analytic index is exasperating in referring to paragraph numbers instead of page numbers. The paragraph numbers are the creation of the editior and were not used by Hume.

Until a new edition is published, it is useful to employ C. W. Hendel's edition of *An Inquiry concerning Human Understanding*, which also contains the *Abstract* and a table comparing the *Abstract* with the first *Enquiry*. Hendel also has an edition of *An Inquiry concerning the Principles of Morals.* Both of his editions contain all of Hume's own editorial changes. Both are published in paperback by Bobbs-Merrill.

Prior to Selby-Bigge, the standard edition of Hume's works was *The Philosophical Works of David Hume*, edited by T. H. Green and T. H. Grose in four volumes. It contains all of Hume's works except the *History*, the *Bellman's Petition*, the account of *Stewart*, the *Abstract*, and *A Letter from a Gentleman to his friend in Edinburgh.* Green, an eminent philosopher in his own right, concluded his 371 page introduction to Hume with this statement: "Our business, however, has not been to moralize, but to show that the philosophy based on the abstraction of feeling, in regard to morals no less than to nature, was with Hume played out, and that the next step forward in speculation could only be an effort to re-think the process of nature and human action from its true beginning in thought. If this object has been in any way attained, so that the attention of Englishmen 'under five-and-twenty' may be directed from the anachronistic systems hitherto prevalent among us to the study of Kant and Hegel, an irksome labour will not have been in vain." Imagine poor Hume having as the editor of his collected works a man who finds his philosophy to be a dead end and the editing of it an irksome labor. It seems to have been Hume's fate that many of his major commentators were unsympathetic to his whole enterprise.

As is obvious, Green understands Hume to be the villain characterized by Reid, and he interprets Hume as a failed idealist and pre-Kantian. Nothing could be further from the truth. Kemp Smith among others has taken Green to task. In addition, consider the reaction of B. M. Laing, above (p. 232), who thinks that Kant's reaction to Hume was a step backward. Green's "study" of Hume is, in my estimation, one of the most disgraceful incidents in the whole history of philosophical exegesis. When Green finds a statement in Hume which conflicts with his interpretation of Hume, Green declares that Hume is inconsistent.

An Abstract of a Treatise of Human Nature (1740): *A Pamphlet hitherto unknown by David Hume.* Reprinted with introduction by J. M. Keynes and P. Sraffa. Cambridge: Cambridge University Press, 1938. The existence of the abstract was known and originally attributed to Adam Smith, even though no copy was known to exist. Keynes and Sraffa made their discovery and proved that Hume was the author.

A Letter from a Gentleman to his friend in Edinburgh (1745). Edited by E. C. Mossner and John V. Price. Edinburgh: Edinburgh University Press, 1967. Like the *Abstract*, Hume's authorship of this pamphlet was not known until 1954. This is a gold mine of commentary on the *Treatise*, with special reference to Newton, theology, and skepticism. Hume wrote it when he was applying for the chair at Edinburgh. It was not available to commentators prior to 1967.

Dialogues concerning Natural Religion. Edited by Norman Kemp Smith. London: Thomas Nelson & Sons Ltd., 1947). Contains valuable supplementary material, although Kemp Smith's own interpretation is now suspect.

The Letters of David Hume. Edited by J.Y.T. Greig. 2 vols. Oxford: Oxford University Press, Clarendon Press. 1932.

New Letters of David Hume. Edited by Raymond Klibansky and

E.C. Mossner. Oxford: Oxford University Press, Clarendon Press, 1954.

David Hume: Writings on Economics. Edited with lengthy commentary by Eugene Rotwein. Edinburgh: Nelson, 1955.

David Hume: Philosophical Historian. Edited by David F. Norton and R. H. Popkin. New York: Bobbs-Merrill, 1965. For Hume's views on history, which are quite important and which I regret not being able to include for discussion, there is no better introduction than Norton's essay "History and Philosophy in Hume's Thought."

2. *The Five Most Important Secondary Sources*

1. Norman Kemp Smith. *The Philosophy of David Hume.* London: Macmillan, 1949. This is by far the largest (566 pages) and most detailed treatment of Hume to date and for this reason alone is must reading. Developing an original article from 1905 on Hume's naturalism, Kemp Smith convincingly argues against the Reid-Beattie-Green interpretation that Hume is a scoundrel and an empiricist dead end. Unfortunately, Kemp Smith then suggests a theory about the primacy of feeling in Hume, a view which in some ways makes Hume even more irrationalist than in the Reid interpretation. Read for the details and not the overview.

The best part of the book is its linking of Hume with Hutcheson (p. 43), but even here differences are overlooked. Kemp Smith argues that Hume was extending Hutcheson's doctrine of the primacy of feeling to every theoretical domain. This argument obscures the real connection of logic and psychology in Hume. The worst example of it is a misquotation and misinterpretation wherein Kemp Smith says that for Hume "reason is and ought to be the slave of the passions" (omitting the "only"). He has been soundly taken to task for this by Glathe, Laird, and Popkin among others. Ironically the first person to make this same error was Thomas Reid: "Mr. Hume gives the name of passion to every principle of action in the human mind; and, in consequence of this, maintains, that every man is and ought to be led by his passions . . . " (*Active Powers*, III, part iii, 6). Kemp Smith has perpetuated the Reid misinterpretation.

Kemp Smith attempts to buttress his view by arguing that the "new scene of thought" letter proves the Hutcheson influence. Then he speculates that Hume wrote Book II of the *Treatise* before writing Book I, so the epistemology must follow from the ethics. The evidence for this is the alleged difficulties with the notion of the self. As I have shown, there are no difficulties in Hume's treatment when properly understood. See my chapter on the structure of the *Treatise.* Laird has also interpreted the letter as signifying the influence of Newton, and in this I think Laird is correct.

2. Antony Flew. *Hume's Philosophy of Belief.* London: Routledge

and Kegan Paul, 1961. Best and most authoritative study of Hume's first *Inquiry*. Flew makes a convincing case for treating it as a serious work in its own right. The discussion of miracles in chapter 8 is the best thing ever done on the subject.

3. Páll Ardál. *Passion and Value in Hume's Treatise.* Edinburgh: Edinburgh University Press, 1966. This is the first serious effort to relate the theory of the passions in Book II to the moral theory in Book III.

4. Robert F. Anderson. *Hume's First Principles.* Lincoln: University of Nebraska Press, 1966. A truly outstanding, careful, and scholarly analysis of the material foundations of Hume's philosophy. An excellent antidote for traditional misconceptions about Hume.

5. James Noxon. *Hume's Philosophical Development.* Oxford: Clarendon Press, 1973. Three excellent elements: a careful analysis of the Newtonian influence on Hume; a convincing developmental thesis in which Noxon shows the methodological and metaphysical problems of the *Treatise* leading Hume away from introspective psychology and toward history; a spirited defense of the use of psychology in Hume's philosophy.

3. *Other Books*

BASSON, A. H. *David Hume.* London: Penguin, 1958. This has since been republished under the author's new name, Cavendish. No improvement.

BROILES, R. DAVID. *The Moral Philosophy of David Hume.* Hague: Nijhoff, 1964. Good critique of Kemp Smith, and Broiles does see Hume's position on motivation, although he is unsympathetic to Hume's conception of moral philosophy.

CHURCH, R. W. *Hume's Theory of the Understanding.* Ithaca: Cornell, 1935. Good discussion of relations and the distinction between natural and philosophical. He sees that the causal analysis is independent of the psychological distinction between ideas and impressions.

GLATHE, A. B. *Hume's Theory of the Passions and of Morals.* Berkeley: U. of California Press, 1950. A pioneering effort now superseded by Ardál. Still, Glathe was the first to emphasize the importance of vivacity transfer.

HEDENIUS, I. *Studies in Hume's Ethics.* Stockholm, 1937. This must qualify as the worst book ever written on Hume's ethics.

HENDEL, C. W. *Studies in the Philosophy of David Hume.* 1925; reprinted, New York Bobbs-Merrill, 1963. Contains a strong emphasis on Hume's concern with religion. Rambles, but contains many useful insights unencumbered by preconceptions.

HURLBUTT, R. H. III. *Hume, Newton, and the Design Argument.* Lincoln: University of Nebraska Press, 1965. Excellent scholarly study of the background.

KUYPERS, M. S. *Studies in the Eighteenth Century Background of Hume's Empiricism.* Minneapolis: University of Minnesota Press, 1930. Good background study of the Newtonians with special stress on the importance of Clarke for Hume (pp. 88–94). Kuypers also sees that "it is not causation which Hume reduces to custom or habit, but the reasoning based upon it" (p. 75). This book is far superior to either Willey's or Becker's for understanding the period.

KYDD, R. M. *Reason and Conduct in Hume's Treatise.* New York: Oxford, 1946. Takes second place to Hedenius. She does not discuss sympathy. Kydd cannot substantiate her distinction between judgments of virtue and judgments of obligation in Hume's moral theory.

LAING, B. M. *David Hume*. London: Benn, 1932. Laing recognized that Reid misinterpreted Hume (pp. 228–29). Marred by the assumption that Hume is dealing with sense-data (p. 89) and the interpretation of the is-ought paragraph as an anticipation of Kant.

LAIRD, JOHN. *Hume's Philosophy of Human Nature.* London: Methuen, 1932. A valuable and much underrated book. It contains the best presentation of the historical sources of Hume's views; rightly interprets Hume's "new scene of thought" as the influence of Newton (p. 20); gives a good criticism of Kemp Smith on the subordination of reason to instinct (pp. 185–86); interprets Hume's ethics as a combination of the moral sense and utilitarianism (p. 236); lengthy discussion of causation. Marred only by an emphasis on the principles of sensory phenomenalism (p. 25) and the failure to see Hume's rejection of sympathy (p. 239).

MACNABB, D.I.C. *David Hume: His Theory of Knowledge and Morality.* London: Hutchinson, 1951. Good introductory level summary of Hume.

MOSSNER, E. C. *The Life of David Hume.* Austin: University of Texas Press, 1954. Excellent authoritative biography. Mossner's numerous articles are always worth consulting.

MAUND, C. *Hume's Theory of Knowledge.* London: Macmillan 1937. Maund attempts to interpret Hume from a purely epistemological point of view even though she admits that in her view "Hume confused psychological, metaphysical, and epistemological statements." This would seem to indicate that such a purely epistemological interpretation cannot be made. Further, her view of epistemology is totally post-Kantian, "process of knowing in relation to what is known."

PASSMORE, J. A. *Hume's Intentions.* Cambridge: University Press, 1952. Widely respected, Passmore interprets Hume as a phenomenalist, positivist, and one who confused logic and psychology—all sins in my view. Passmore has a real antipathy to Hume's notion of philosophy. See Passmore's later book *Philosophical Reasoning* (1961). New York: Scribner's Sons.

PEARS, D. F. ed. *David Hume: A Symposium.* London: 1963. The articles are too short to be of much value.

PRICE, H. H. *Hume's Theory of the External World.* Oxford: University Press, 1940. Interprets Hume as a neutral monist (p. 105).

PRICE, J. V. *The Ironic Hume.* Austin: University of Texas Press, 1965. A study of Hume's languages. And *David Hume.* New York: Twayne Press, 1968. A study of Hume as a man of letters and historian as well as a philosopher. Both are very useful in presenting a side of Hume often missed.

RAPHAEL, D. D. *Moral Sense.* London: Oxford U. Press, 1947. Studies of Hutcheson, Hume, Price, and Reid. Best chapters are the ones on Price and Reid with whom he is sympathetic. Does not discuss the influence of Locke and the importance of Clarke.

SALMON, C. V. *The Central Problem of David Hume's Philosophy: An Essay towards a phenomenological interpretation of the First Book of the "Treatise of Human Nature."* London: Halle, 1929. Just what it says. Naturally, Hume fails to measure up.

STERN, GEORGE. *A Faculty Theory of Knowledge: The Aim and Scope of Hume's First "Enquiry."* Lewisburg: Bucknell University Press, 1971. Interprets Hume as dissenting from the principle of methodological simplicity. Does not really make a convincing case, but some of the individual points are well taken.

STEWART, J. B. *The Moral and Political Philosophy of David Hume.* New York: Columbia University Press, 1963. The emphasis here should be on the political. The moral part is thin.

WILBANKS, J. *Hume's Theory of Imagination.* Hague: Nijhoff, 1968. Interprets the imagination from the point of view of Hume being a moderate skeptic.

ZABEEH, F. *Hume, Precursor of Modern Empiricism: An Analysis of his Opinions on Meaning, Metaphysics, Logic and Mathematics.* Hague: Nijhoff, 1960. I think it is misleading to interpret Hume in this light, but Zabeeh does make some illuminating remarks.

4. *Articles and Chapters By Topic*

Much too often writers seem to take one of three views toward Hume. First, some treat him as the denouement of the empiricist tradition. Second, some consider Hume as a pre-Kantian on the assumption that some form of idealism is correct. Third, some treat Hume as seen in the light of post-Kantianism on the assumption that Kant is the way but idealism is not. The interpretation of Hume as a pre-positivist or forerunner of phenomenology is a example of the third view. The reader should also beware of the fact that analytically trained philosophers in the US and Great Britain have a habit of taking Humean arguments out of context and making them grist for their own mill. All this is very interesting and sometimes philosophically illuminating but does little to help in the understanding of Hume.

A. *General*: Robert Paul Wolff, "Hume's Theory of Mental Activity, "*Philosophical Review* (1960), Vol. LXIX, pp. 289–310. Interprets Hume as a clumsy pre-Kantian and then fabricates an interpretation. He completely ignores the transfer of vivacity and the physical basis of mental activity. T. E. Jessop. "Some Misunderstandings of Hume," *Revue Internationale de Philosophie* (1952). Provides food for thought. Those who still interpret Hume as a phenomenalist include, besides the books mentioned above, W. S. Haymond, "Hume's Phenomenalism" *Modern Schoolman* (1963–64), and D. M. Armstrong, *Perception and the Physical World* (1961), chapter 4. Those who accuse Hume of confusing logic and psychology include Church, Flew, Price, Zabeeh, Passmore, Stern, and George Santayana, *Scepticism and Animal Faith* (1923), p. 295. See also A. J. Ayer, *Language, Truth, and Logic* (1964), p. 137f.

B. *Influence of Newton*: J. H. Randall, Jr. attributes to Hume a view of science called observationalism in *The Career of Philosophy*, vol. I (1962), Book IV, chapters 1 and 5, and *Nature and Historical Experience* (1958), pp. 173–76 and 185–86. Randall has been attacked by Mossner (Chappell volume), by Noxon (p. 79), and by Robison in a forthcoming article in the *Journal of Critical Analysis*. A very good article by T. E. Jessop again, "Hume: Philosopher or Psychologist? A Problem of Exegesis" in the 1968 collection published in Italy, not only throws light on the Newtonian influence but represents quite a change from Jessop's article cited above. *Studi su Hume* (Firenze: La Nuova Italici, 1968).

C. *Mathematics*: Hume's views on mathematics still seem in need of some exegesis. For a start consult Flew, Zabeeh, and the article by R. F. Atkinson entitled, "Hume on Mathematics," *Philosophical*

Quarterly (1960), and Zabeeh, "Hume on Pure and Applied Geometry," *Ratio* (1964).

D. *Causation*: Three excellent articles worth noting are J. A. Robinson, "Hume's Two Definitions of 'Cause,'" *Philosophical Quarterly* (1962); Donald Gotterbarn, "Hume's Two Lights on Cause," *ibid.*, (1971) and; Donald Livingston, "Hume on Ultimate Causation," *American Philosophical Quarterly* (1971).

E. *Self and Personal Identity:* The classic article is by T. Penelhum, "Hume on Personal Identity," *Philosophical Review*, (1955). Penelhum has been criticized by J. Noxon. "Senses of Identity in Hume's Treatise," *Dialogue* (1970), although the reader of this book will see wherein I disagree with Noxon. P. Butchvarov, "The Self and Perceptions: A Study in Humean Philosophy," *Philosophical Quarterly* (1959) has a good critique of Kemp Smith.

F. *Ethics*: The following articles are in my opinion all excellent and very useful: F. C. Sharp, "Hume's Ethical Theory and Its Critics," *Mind* (1921); John Sweigart, "The Distance between Hume and Emotivism," *Philosophical Quarterly* (1964); Ronald J. Glossop, "The Nature of Hume's Ethics," *Philosophy and Phenomenological Research* (1967); J.T. King, Jr., *The Development of Hume's Moral Philosophy from 1740–1751: the relationship of the 'Treatise' and the second 'Inquiry'* (Ph.D. University of Notre Dame, 1967); T. K. Hearn, "General Rules in Hume's *Treatise*," *Journal of the History of Philosophy* (1970).

G. *Is-Ought:* From my point of view there is a regrettably large literature on this topic by ethical theorists who are not Hume scholars and by Hume scholars who should know better. Some of these articles are reproduced in V. C. Chappell's useful collection of essays *Hume* (Garden City: Doubleday, 1966) and W.D. Hudson, *The Is-Ought Question* (London: 1969).

H. *Religion:* The difficulties here are to try to separate Hume's personal views from his published views. Four excellent articles which should form the starting point are: J. Noxon, "Hume's Agnosticism," *Philosophical Review* (1964); William H. Capitan, "Part X of Hume's Dialogues," *American Philosophical Quarterly* (1966); George J. Nathan, "Hume's Immanent God," in V.C. Chappell's collection along with the first two articles above: Peter Jones, "Hume's Two Concepts of God," *Philosophy* (1972). A. E. Taylor's book *David Hume and the Miraculous* (1927) has been largely demolished by Flew. The Aiken and Pike editions of the *Dialogues* contain long introductions. For those who read French there is the monumental study by A. Leroy, *La Critique et la Religion chez David Hume* (1930). For laughs, one should not fail to read Archbishop Richard Whatley's essay "Historic Doubts relative to Napoleon Bonaparte"

(1819) reprinted in H. Peterson and J. Bailey, *Essays in Philosophy*.

I. *Skepticism*: On whether or not Hume was a skeptic about induction see the excellent article by D. Stove, "Hume, Probability, and Induction," *Philosophical Review* (1965). The classic article is Richard Popkin, "David Hume: His Pyrrhonism and his Critique of Pyrrhonism," in *Philosophica Quarterly* (1951). Both Popkin and Flew wrote on this topic before the publication of Hume's *A Letter ...*, published by Mossner and Price in 1967. For a critique of Green and Kemp Smith see Wade L. Robison, "Hume's Scepticism," *Dialogue* (1973).

J. *History*: See Norton article cited above. See also, E. C. Mossner, "Was Hume a Tory Historian," *Journal of the History of Ideas* (1941); Donald W. Livingston, "Hume on the Problem of Historical and Scientific Explanation," *The New Scholasticism* (1973); C.N. Stockton, "David Hume Among the Historiographers," *Studies in History and Society* (1971).

K. *Aesthetics*: Ralph Cohen, "David Hume's Experimental Method and the Theory of Taste," *Journal of English Literary History* (1958); J. Noxon, "Hume's Opinion of Critics," *Journal of Aesthetics and Art Criticism* (1961); Peter Jones, "Another Look at Hume's Views of Aesthetic and Moral Judgments," *Philosophical Quarterly* (1970).

V. *Further Bibliography*

T. E. Jessop, *A Bibliography of David Hume and of Scottish Philosophy from Francis Hutcheson to Lord Balfour* (London: Brown, 1938). Roland Hall, *A Hume Bibliography from 1930* (Published by Roland Hall, Department of Philosophy, University of York, Heslington, York, England, 1971).

Index